THE SOCIAL THEORY
of
GEORG SIMMEL

THE
SOCIAL THEORY OF
GEORG SIMMEL

By

NICHOLAS J. SPYKMAN, M.A., PH.D.

NEW YORK

RUSSELL & RUSSELL · INC

1964

FIRST PUBLISHED IN 1925
REISSUED, 1964, BY RUSSELL & RUSSELL, INC.
L. C. CATALOG CARD NO: 64-20674

PRINTED IN THE UNITED STATES OF AMERICA

PREFACE

WESTERN civilization has reached a crisis. It cannot survive in its present form. But if it is to survive at all, man must find a solution for the urgent problems of internal and external relations. If the social forces which at present are spending themselves in ruthless conflict remain unchecked, there is nothing ahead but utter destruction.

Society, the great superindividual structure of man's own making, has become so large, so intricate, so complex, so independent of its maker that it threatens to overwhelm him and to make him the victim of his own creation. Forces beyond his control drive man to national and civil wars. Powers that he only vaguely comprehends draw him into conflicts that must end in self-destruction.

Man cannot continue to trust blindly in social progress as he once trusted in a benevolent Providence. He has to control these forces or become further enslaved by them. He has to obtain a mastery over his social structure comparable to his mastery over nature, or his civilization will perish in suffering and bloodshed.

The eighteenth century gave us an ideal, namely, individual liberty. The nineteenth century brought political liberation, democracy. But democracy did not bring individual liberty. It gave us the possibility of opposing personal oppression, but it did not free us from the impersonal social forces. We are still the slaves of the great leviathan. Our knowledge and control of social life has never kept pace with its growing complexity, and we are farther behind than ever before. The liberation of the individual is still to be obtained. It will be the great task of the twentieth century.

But that liberation of the individual from the clutches of the great leviathan implies a mastery over that leviathan. The liberation of the individual from those impersonal forces means a mastery over those impersonal forces. It means the substitution of a rational social structure for the uncontrolled and uncontrollable social world in which we live.

That liberation and mastery can be obtained. What is needed is an earnest desire to do so on the part of the individuals composing society, a consensus of opinion among the majority with regard to the ends to be obtained, and an adequate knowledge with regard to the means to these ends.

The first two points do not immediately concern us here. Our problem is the problem of the adequacy of our knowledge about social life and the means of obtaining it. It concerns the methodology of the social sciences.

It is undoubtedly true that there is an approximately adequate knowledge available for certain problems which are left unsolved on account of prejudice and selfishness; but let us not overstate the case. Our knowledge and fundamental understanding of social life is hardly sufficient to guarantee the desired results from its application to the handling of the great social problems. A few enthusiastic social reformers have sufficient religious faith in their own doctrines to promise us a happier and better world if we will only follow their suggestions, but it is perhaps just as well for the world and for their own reputation that they are not too hard pressed to make good. The Russian experiment has not been completely convincing.

Among the more earnest students of social life there is a growing realization of the inadequacy of our knowledge and a growing feeling that all is not well with the social sciences. While our electrical, mechanical, and civil engineering technique apparently conquer all obstacles, our social engineering technique is in its infancy and largely guesswork. While progress in the natural sciences leads immediately to improved technique, progress in the social sciences seems to lead merely to an increased output of books. It will therefore be worth while to make a comparison between the procedures followed to obtain a control over nature and the procedures from which we are to expect a control over our social environment. That comparison will yield some valuable methodological suggestions, which are not impaired by the fact that the subject-matter of the social sciences is different in nature from the subject-matter of the natural sciences.

Man's increasing success in his control over nature is due to a clear understanding of the different problems involved, to a distinction between ends and means, between applied science and fields of theoretic inquiry, and between scientific method and philosophic method. *The work is done on the principle of differentiation and specialization in the field of theoretic inquiry and integration and co-ordination in the field of practical application.*

Nobody, for instance, confuses the problem of how to build a bridge with the very different issue whether the building of the bridge is desirable.

The problem of how to build a bridge is a problem of applied science. It involves the integration and the co-ordination of the knowledge obtained from a great many different fields of scientific inquiry, but nobody confuses a problem of bridge-building with a problem of theoretical mechanics.

Within the fields of theoretic inquiry there is a sharp distinction between philosophic and scientific method. No-

body confuses the problem regarding the ultimate reality
of matter with the problem regarding the relative tensile
strength of steel and iron. The different natural sciences
which supply the knowledge to be applied to the practical
problem are all based on a common method, the scientific
method, and that is why their results can be co-ordinated.
Within each field of inquiry there is a far-going specialization and division of labor, but because all results are obtained by a common method, they naturally integrate in a
homogeneous body of knowledge.

With regard to man's control over his social environment, on the other hand, the situation is one of utter confusion. There is a confusion between means and ends, between practical problems and problems of theoretic inquiry. There is in the social sciences no common agreement as to method and no distinction between scientific
and philosophic inquiry. There is very little specialization within each field; and a lack of uniformity in method,
making co-ordination impossible, reduces its value to zero.

With regard to social problems, there is a constant confusion between means and ends. All the solutions suggested imply a value judgment of what society ought to be.
The problem whether the society which is thus to be improved actually desires the results which would follow from
the change advocated is never considered separately. The
problem regarding the result to be obtained is never kept
clear and distinct from the problem regarding the ways to
obtain that result.

The problem regarding the means is a problem of applied science. It involves the integration and co-ordination of the knowledge made available by a great many different social sciences. But in the world of social phenomena, engineering problems are confused with problems of
theoretic inquiry. They are dealt with as if they were prob-

lems of a special and limited science instead of problems
requiring a co-ordination of the knowledge available from
all social sciences.

Within the fields of theoretic inquiry there is no sharp
distinction between the philosophic and the scientific method. Philosophy is still rampant in the so-called social sciences. Economics has been dominated for a century by
speculations about values and by mental gymnastics with
the concepts of land, labor, and capital which are comparable only to the scholastic antics with the true, the good, and
the beautiful. Political science is still trying to emerge
from its wrappings, is still trying to free itself from the
metaphysical doctrines which have carefully protected it
from crude contacts with the harsh world of actuality.
Jurisprudence is only beginning to discover that there is
something more to law than a logically coherent system of
legal "ought" concepts.

The light is dawning, and the social sciences are beginning to make some progress toward a scientific methodology, but the goal is yet far off. Psychological obstacles prevent a speedy journey.

There is still in every social scientist an irresistible urge
to become a social philosopher and to interpret the whole
of social life in terms of his own specific interest as its ultimate category. This tendency to interpret society in terms
of a single category is induced by the laudable motive to
see life whole. But it leads to trouble if the philosophic results are taken for science. Every time a new science comes
into being or an existing inquiry makes rapid progress,
there follows an effort to interpret society in terms of the
fundamental category of that special inquiry. After the
first development of jurisprudence, society was discovered
to be a contract. After the growth of the new metaphysics,
society was discovered to be an idea. After the develop-

ment of biology, society was discovered to be an organism. After the growth of economics, society was discovered to be a system of production and distribution. After new developments in psychology, society was discovered to be imitation. These philosophical and semiphilosophical interpretations have a value in and for themselves, but they do not provide the type of knowledge on which any rebuilding of the social structure can be based.

There is also in most social scientists a suppressed desire to become social reformers and saviors of their fellowmen. A deep-felt sympathy with suffering humanity, a chivalrous tendency to take the side of the "under dog," and an impatient desire to improve conditions quickly apparently give them a "will to believe" in remedies which resemble too much our patent medicines to inspire complete confidence.

According to the physical anthropologist, we must save Western civilization by keeping the race pure. The specialist in eugenics tells us to save society by scientific breeding. The psychologist who specializes in mental tests urges us to put the high "I.Q.'s" in the high places. The economist advocates a new system of production and distribution. The political scientist tells us that the fundamental trouble lies in our political system, that we need more democracy or less democracy. The lawyers tell us that we need more and better laws, and the students of religion inform us that we need more religion. These men are earnest, well-meaning human beings, scholars offering us suggestions which are based on years of learning and devoted study. The results would be humorous beyond all measure were it not that they throw a light on the very sad conditions existing in the social sciences.

This tendency to philosophic interpretation and this will to believe in simple remedies spring from our funda-

mental desire for unity and simplicity. Humanity has always been in search of the mystic simple formula which
would explain the whole universe, and that search will be
continued as long as man shall live. It springs from a fundamental motive operative in all of us, but it will never produce scientific knowledge. There is a beauty of form, an
aesthetic value, in a well-constructed metaphysical system
which no mere science can ever possess. There is something
esoteric about an interpretation of society in terms of a
single category as its essence and symbol. It has an emotional appeal with which no scientific analysis can compete. But, whatever the beauty and the value of these
products of the human mind, they do not give us a type of
knowledge on which an applied science can be built.

The same motives mentioned above have been the fundamental motives in the development of sociology. Sociology was born partly of a dissatisfaction with the fragmentary character of the knowledge obtained in the social
sciences, of a desire, that is, to see social life whole, and
partly of a desire to find a technique of social improvement.
But neither of these two needs can be satisfied by a science.
The first can only be satisfied by a social philosophy, the
second by an integration and co-ordination of the knowledge obtained in all the social sciences. When there also
arose a science of sociology, the confusion was complete.
The term came to be applied indiscriminately to three distinct types of knowledge: to social philosophy, to a specific
social science, and to a body of knowledge that purported
to be social engineering. Sociology was anything that had
to do with social life, from a social metaphysics to public
sanitation.

This confusion with regard to sociology is indicative
of the lack of a clear understanding of the fundamental
presuppositions and of the mutual relations of the social

sciences. We need not expect any real progress in theoretic
inquiry or any real advancement toward a practical solution of problems until the situation is cleared up and the
relation between sociology and the other social sciences
definitely determined.

In the United States the so-called science of sociology
has made the greatest strides. The number of books published as sociology runs second only to fiction. It has risen
to the rank of an academic discipline, it is being taught in
colleges and high schools, and it expresses its self-assurance
in the form of innumerable textbooks. The result of this
formidable advancement is not clarity, but a formidable
confusion. Some of these textbooks actually resemble an
organized body of theoretic scientific knowledge. A great
many others contain a combination of social philosophy
and social ethics. The rest consist of anthologies of the
masterpieces of literature pertaining to social affairs and
of handbooks for social reformers. These latter are related
to the first as a country carpenter's manual to a text on
theoretical mechanics.

This confusion is not due solely to the psychological
motives already mentioned, but the difficulties are also the
result of the conflicting demands which are made upon the
man whose fate it is to bear the title of sociologist. He
is supposed to be a scientist, a teacher, and an engineer.
These demands conflict, and the result has been that research has been sacrificed to teaching. That this is not en-
couraging for the prospects of a rapid advance in social
engineering is evident.

As a teacher, the American sociologist has been required to give his students an understanding of the com-
plexities of social life. His subject has been a sort of glori-
fied high-school civics. As a college course, his subject is
extremely valuable, and it should be included in all cur-

ricula, but it is not a science. It is not even a synthetic
science. It is a more or less systematic presentation of the
knowledge made available by different social sciences.

As a consulting engineer for public or private enterprises of social reform, the sociologist is supposed to design policies and to advise on problems of technique. But
the different fields of theoretic social science on which that
advice must ultimately rest follow at present a method of
their own, and their results cannot as yet be satisfactorily
co-ordinated.

As a scholar and "scientist," he is supposed to advance
his "science" of sociology, and he will therefore have to
specialize on a small part of the general field.

These demands are conflicting, and if anything is accomplished at all, it is due to the caliber of the men, not to
the conditions under which they work or the methods they
apply.

This confusion in the social sciences in general, and in
sociology in particular, must be cleared up if a mastery over
our social environment is ever to be obtained. *Here also
the work will have to be done on the basis of a differentiation
and specialization in the field of theoretic inquiry and integration and co-ordination in the field of practical application. To make that possible, the first prerequisites are a common method and a consensus of opinion regarding the relation of the "science" of sociology to the other social sciences.*
Neither exists, and the discussion about method, which
was dropped at the beginning of the century, must therefore be resumed. The social scientist must become fully
conscious of the presuppositions of his inquiries and investigations before he can hope for real progress in his
work. The distinction between social philosophy and
social science and between the social sciences and social
engineering must be fully appreciated before the investi-

gation of social phenomena can be placed on a really scientific basis. Only when this is accomplished can we undertake the liberation of the individual from the clutches of the great leviathan. Only then will a knowledge become available which will make possible a mastery over the social environment comparable to the mastery over nature obtained through progress in the natural sciences.

It is for the purpose of reopening the discussion of methodological problems that this study on Simmel has been written. Georg Simmel more than any other philosopher occupied himself with the methodology of the social sciences. During the first part of his career he set himself the task of doing for the social sciences what Kant had done for science in general, of giving, that is, a critical exposition of their presuppositions. He fiercely attacked in the critical writings of his first period the conceptual realism that is still rampant in the social sciences, and thereby rendered a service which can hardly be overestimated. His critical work reached completion, however, only after the interest in methodological problems had waned in this country, and for that reason it has not had the attention which it deserves. A number of his articles have been translated in the *American Journal of Sociology*, but his larger works have not been read as widely by English and American sociologists as his contributions justify.

If the discussion of methodological problems is to be resumed, as the writer thinks necessary, Simmel's work is the best starting-point. In the original it cannot serve that purpose, and it is for that reason that this exposition of his work has been written. If a more or less general agreement can be reached regarding Simmel's fundamental propositions, this study may eventually serve as a methodological orientation for the social sciences. Whether it can fulfil that function can only be judged from the study as a whole, not from any single chapter. The different social sciences may develop a special technique, but they must follow a common method and be conscious of their mutual relations. An understanding of these relations can only be obtained by viewing them in their totality, not by merely inquiring into the method and presuppositions of a single social science. It is for that reason that the material of this study, although primarily orientated toward the methodological problems of sociology, has been so organized as to afford a bird's-eye view of these relations and thereby to throw light on the central problem of all social methodology.

This study deals only with a restricted field of Simmel's work. His publications cover a wide range of subjects, many of which are not immediately related to our problem. He was primarily a philosopher, not in the sense of a builder of metaphysical systems, but in the sense of an interpreter of life. The works of his second period are an interpretation of Western civilization and modern culture. In that capacity he also deserves a wider attention in English-speaking countries than has been accorded him. But the scope of this study does not permit an attempt at a comprehensive view of Simmel's interpretation of our modern world. It is orientated toward his philosophical contributions in the more narrow sense of the term, not toward his metaphysical contributions. Its aim is to give his fundamental contributions to the methodology of the different fields of theoretic inquiry regarding socio-historical phenomena.

In his sociological works, as in his other contributions, Simmel's analytic tendency has hardly been counterbalanced by a corresponding synthetic tendency. This characteristic, together with the fact that most of it was first published in the form of articles, gives his work a

fragmentary character which puts great obstacles in the
way of a comprehensive treatment. To overcome these difficulties, his differentiated analytical contributions have
been integrated on the basis of his central idea regarding the
relation of philosophic inquiry to exact science. According
to Simmel, each exact science is flanked by two fields of
philosophic inquiry, an epistemology and a metaphysics.
This idea has been made the guiding principle for the
organization of the material of this study, and it is for
that reason that it is divided into three books. It is hoped
that in this form it will be a unified and comprehensive
totality, while yet giving Simmel's own thought with the
least amount of distortion and interpolation.

The social sciences have not reached as yet that cosmopolitan nature which is characteristic of the natural
sciences. Physics and chemistry are international, but the
social sciences carry a distinct mark of nationality. American, English, French, German, and Russian sociology,
each has characteristics of its own. It is therein that they
show most clearly their limitation and announce to the
world how far they are removed as yet from that absolute
scientific objectivity which is the aim of every scientist.
Only an intensive cross-fertilization of thought can coun-
teract the dangerous tendency toward national self-sufficiency and keep open the road toward advancement and
success. Only an international discussion of fundamental
presuppositions can give us a common method.

Should the following study contribute in that direction,
the labors involved will not have been in vain.

                                                    N. J. S.

ACKNOWLEDGMENTS

THIS study could not have been written without the valuable and stimulating suggestions of Professor G. P. Adams and Professor F. J. Teggart. Especially to the latter I owe a debt which I have not been able to acknowledge in direct reference or in quotation marks. His books and the personal contact of years have been an inspiration for which I take this opportunity to express my gratitude.

In the revision of the manuscript I have received the valuable advice and criticism of a number of friends; in particular, Miss Lola Jean Simpson and Miss Leona Fassett.

CONTENTS

BOOK III. SOCIAL PHILOSOPHY

METAPHYSICS

LIST OF ABBREVIATIONS

The titles of the books and periodicals most frequently referred to have been abbreviated as follows:

Soziologie	*Soz.*
Soziale Differenzierung	*Soz. Diff.*
Grundfragen der Soziologie	*Grundfr. der Soz.*
Probleme der Geschichtsphilosophie	*Probl. der Gesch.*
Philosophie des Geldes	*Phil. des Geldes*
Hauptprobleme der Philosophie	*Hptprobl. der Phil.*
American Journal of Sociology	*A.J.S.*

THE LIFE OF GEORG SIMMEL
(March 1, 1858—September 26, 1918)

GEORG SIMMEL was born in Berlin. His cradle stood in a house on the corner of the Friedrich and Leipziger Strasse in the very heart of the city. As a metropolitan he was born, as a world-citizen he lived and died. He grew up a man with great breadth of vision and a consuming interest in all phases of human life.

Although later professing the evangelical faith, Simmel was of Jewish descent. There are certain elements in his thinking which are characteristically Jewish. His gift for analysis and abstraction, the subtleness of his dialectic, and his use of analogy and symbols may well be attributed to his Semitic stock. Apart from his rich intellectual endowments, he was gifted with a keen appreciation of beauty and a fine intuitive understanding of human nature.

At the age of twelve young Georg entered the gymnasium, and after six years was admitted to the University of Berlin. Here he followed a regular course of four years of study, devoting most of his time to philosophy, psychology, and history. In 1881 Simmel obtained the degree of Doctor of Philosophy on a dissertation on Kant's theory of matter (*Das Wesen der Materie nach Kants physischer Monadologie*) and three theses.

Simmel had great teachers. He studied history under Droysen, Mommsen, von Sybel, von Treitschke, Grimm, and Jordan, psychology under Lazarus and Bastian, and philosophy under Harms and Zeller. It cannot be said that Simmel became an immediate adherent of any of these great men, however. He had too much individuality, too

xxiii

much that was specifically his own, to be a mere follower. He was original in the sense that he combined in his own characteristic way elements which were borrowed from the most divergent sources. Yet his college studies as a whole had a profound influence on his thought and greatly strengthened his natural inclinations. A great deal of purely historical study reinforced his predisposition to a historical point of view. And his work with Bastian, Lazarus, and Zeller, all of whom had a historical approach toward their subject, fortified this tendency still more. The general character of his university studies may then perhaps be a partial explanation of his characteristic philosophy, which has a genetic, functional relativism as its main theme. It may perhaps partly account for a viewpoint from which all existence is seen as a phase in a process of becoming and all phenomena in relation to an ever changing environment, as functions of numerous variables. His philosophy is the philosophy of a man who sees the present as the product of the past. It is the philosophical expression of a historical point of view. For that reason it approaches in one important aspect the philosophy of Hegel. It is genetic and dialectic, but while for Hegel the absolute was the self-unfolding Idea, for Simmel the absolute was Life itself.

Apart from his immediate teachers, the other formative influences were Kant, Cohen, Goethe, Schopenhauer, Nietzsche, Hegel, and Heracleitus. To Cohen's interpretation of Kant he owed a great deal, even if he did not fully accept it. Goethe, Schopenhauer, and Nietzsche, and the whole of the anti-intellectualistic movement of the nineteenth century, strongly affected his thinking. Heracleitus, for whom he had the most profound admiration, undoubtedly had a great influence on the formulation of his relativism, and there is too much similarity in Simmel's and Hegel's dialectic to attribute it to a mere coincidence.

In 1885 Simmel became private lecturer (*Privat Dozent*) at the University of Berlin. During his long career as university teacher he lectured on a great many different subjects, such as logic, principles of philosophy, history of philosophy, modern philosophy, Kant, Lotze, Schopenhauer, Darwin, pessimism, ethics, philosophy of religion, philosophy of art, psychology, social psychology, political psychology, and sociology.

Nor were Simmel's activities limited to academic discourses and public lectures. His prolific pen has turned out more than a hundred essays and a number of volumes of considerable size. His most important books are: *Einleitung in die Moralwissenschaft, Philosophie des Geldes, Soziologie, Kant, Goethe, Schopenhauer, Rembrandt,* and *Lebensanschauung (Vier metaphysische Kapitel),* the latter published shortly after his death.

It was on the lecture platform, however, that he showed his real greatness. As a lecturer he realized to the fullest his manifold talents. His lectures were not only learned, they were an inspiration. He combined a clear, logical analysis with an artistic, impressionistic approach. A beautiful voice, an excellent diction, an appealing personality, all contributed to the charm of his address. A vivid gesticulation would bring suggestions of life and growth and give real expression to the dynamic quality of his thought. It would vitalize his discourse just where a mere conceptual abstraction seemed cold and rigid and even the best available word weak and inadequate. Form and subject-matter of his lectures were so perfectly adapted that the logical sequences seemed inevitable stages in a natural unfoldment. He gave his audience more than knowledge. He gave himself, and in so doing he gave of the best of his

time. He helped his hearers to live, to find an adaptation
to that vast cultural environment which is the European
social heritage.

Simmel was not only the philosopher of European culture, he was a bearer of that culture, a lover of the best it
had to offer. Not only did he know it, he lived it. He had
an understanding and a warm appreciation of music and
a profound love for the best of sculpture and painting.
His journeys to Italy and the periods there of intimate contact with the treasures of the Italian Renaissance became
an absolute necessity to his artistic soul. He had enough
artistic intuition to understand the great masters. He had
enough analytical power to translate that intuitive understanding into suggestive concepts. To this remarkable
combination we owe the peculiar charm of his works on
Goethe and Rembrandt and of his essays on Rodin and
Michelangelo.

Yet, although as a teacher and lecturer he was a great
success, beloved by his students and admired by all who
heard him, his academic promotion was slow and tedious.
He remained a private lecturer in Berlin until the day of
his departure for Strassburg in 1914. The Berlin University gave him in 1900 the title of Extraordinary Professor
(*Ausserordentlicher Professor*), but that meant merely an
honorable distinction, not a definite position with an adequate remuneration.

The causes of this slow promotion can only be sur-
mised. Certain difficulties with Dilthey are supposed to
have had something to do with it. But what was probably
largely responsible was the fact of his Jewish ancestry.
The Berlin University was Prussian in its atmosphere, and
the Prussian view of things was not likely to lead to a
speedy promotion and official encouragement of Jewish
teachers.

Yet at least some recognition of his work was forth-coming. The University of Heidelberg conferred upon him the degree of *Dr. rer. pol. honoris causa* in 1911.

In 1914 Simmel was called to Strassburg to take the position of professor of philosophy (*Ordinarius*). He dis-liked to leave Berlin, which, in spite of many disappoint-ments, had become very dear to him. His lectures at the university had been attended by large and interested audi-ences, and there had been no lack of appreciation on the part of his hearers. But financial reasons forced him to leave the place where he had worked and taught for nearly thirty years for a more lucrative position in a less con-genial environment.

A short time after he arrived in Strassburg the war broke out, and with it came the complete demoralization of academic life. The youth of the country was called to the front, and the faculty no less than the students con-tributed to the gruesome total of dead and wounded. From the academic point of view the Strassburg period was a great disappointment. The university had dwindled in size, the classes were small, and the selective process of military conscription had left a student body of a pecu-liar composition. Under these conditions Simmel lectured until shortly before his death, on September 28, 1918.

Simmel had a great influence on the numerous students who passed beneath his touch during his thirty years of teaching. But he made no school in the narrow sense of the term. He aided his students in finding themselves rather than encouraged them to continue his own work. This was due also to the peculiar characteristics of his philosophy. Containing practically no structure, being a method rather than a system, it was not likely to suggest any substantial additions. The only field in which he has obtained a more or less definite following is the field of sociology. Wiese and Scheler in Cologne and the *Viertel-jahresheft für Sozialwissenschaften* have definitely accepted Simmel's views regarding the study of sociology.

The immediate cause of Simmel's death was a mortal illness, but the great indirect cause was the world-war. The underfeeding which resulted from it for all classes in Germany undermined his powers of resistance to the fatal disease. But even stronger than this physiological factor was the mental shock which his sensitive nature received through the war hatred and its results. He was a European in the best sense of the term, incapable of narrow chauvinism, a lover of that European culture which was for him an indivisible unity.

The war threatened the very foundations of European culture. The burst of frenzied patriotism had divided the scientists and philosophers into fighting, squabbling national factions. Co-operation for the sake of truth had been succeeded by mutual destruction for the sake of hatred. The search for truth had been abandoned, and the rationalization and justification of national prejudices had taken its place. Scientists and philosophers had given up their eternal calling and become political propagandists.

All this grieved Simmel deeply. His faith in European culture was shaken. And added to his disappointment in the scientific world in general was his disappointment in some of his personal friends. Above all else he was disappointed in Bergson. Simmel had a profound admiration for his work and had done a great deal to introduce it to the German public. That Bergson should have been swayed by the national feeling in his country and should have turned chauvinist instead of keeping himself aloof from the political turmoil and intrigue hurt him deeply.

Simmel himself remained objective and analytical in the midst of the debacle which befell Europe, and that aloofness left him a lonely figure. He saw from his objective standpoint better than others what was happening to Europe, and he suffered more deeply than those who had been carried away by the rampant chauvinism of the time.

Simmel died like an ancient philosopher. Fully conscious of the fact that his days were limited, resigned to his fate, he occupied himself with the corrections of his last work. It has been felt as the final tragedy of his career that he should begin the synthetic period of his thinking when his bodily existence had begun its decay, that he should formulate a metaphysics of life when death had already called him. Perhaps it was his greatest triumph. He at any rate did not feel that tragedy. In the utterances of his last days there was complete resignation. According to himself, he had given the world all he had to give. New applications, new formulations of his ideas he might have given, had he continued to live, but nothing fundamentally new could have been expected of him. In that feeling of having given his best he found the strength to die a beautiful death amid great physical suffering and grave doubts regarding the future of European culture.

GENERAL INTRODUCTION

GENERAL INTRODUCTION
Synopsis of Simmel's Philosophy

THIS study has been written for a specific purpose, namely, to indicate Simmel's conception of the relations between the different fields of theoretic inquiry into the socio-historical actuality, to give his contributions to the methodology of the social sciences, and to illustrate his conception of sociology as a science. To obtain that end, different passages from his numerous works have been lifted out of their immediate setting and integrated in a more or less unified structure on the basis of his fundamental conception regarding the relation of philosophy to science.

It is hoped that this form of presentation will serve the particular aim in view, even if it does not do full justice to Simmel's work. He was one of the most interesting representatives of the philosophy of the early twentieth century and, as such, deserves attention from a point of view quite different from the one from which ·this study has been written. It is not our task to give an interpretation and evaluation of his work with reference to metaphysical problems, but before we proceed with our specific study, we must briefly sketch an outline of his general philosophy. This will indicate the main characteristics of his thought and serve as a background for an understanding of his specific contributions to our field.

Georg Simmel was primarily a social philosopher. His problems were not problems of conceptual abstractions. They arose out of an effort to reach an understanding of the socio-historical actualities, of art and economic values,

3

of morals and aesthetics, of religion and the function of money. He has treated the most varied subjects, the most divergent aspects of social life, has thrown new light on old problems, and given a new approach to the interpretation of modern culture in all its phases. Yet Simmel has not given nor even attempted a system of social philosophy. His period was not a period of systematic philosophy. He was primarily a fine and subtle analyst rather than a synthetic builder.

This, however, does not mean that there is no unity in his work, but it is a functional rather than a structural unity. What binds together his essays on the most diverse subjects is his treatment, his mode of approach, his own characteristic philosophy. There is no immediate relation between the contents of his works, but there is a decisive unity in the form of his thinking, although one can distinguish a gradual development and clarification.

It is possible to distinguish three phases in the development of Simmel's thought. During the first period of his life he was primarily occupied with the methodology and the presuppositions of the social sciences. During the second period he contributed a number of valuable essays containing philosophic interpretations of modern civilization. This period culminated in his metaphysics of culture. During his last period his interest was centered in a metaphysics of life.

What Kant had done for knowledge in general, Simmel undertook for our specific knowledge of the socio-historical reality. Kant had criticized the claim of rationalism that clearness and distinctness of thought is a criterion for objective validity, and had pointed out that there are non-empirical conditions of experience. Simmel denounced the claims of rationalism to give an adequate account of the socio-historical objectivity, and defended the social sci-

ences against metaphysical encroachments. On the other
hand, he pointed out that no social science is purely empirical, that it differentiates its subject-matter from the
actuality on the basis of a specific category of cognition
and shapes its data in forms which are themselves not empirically obtained from investigations within that science.

It was out of these critical inquiries into the presuppositions of the social sciences that he developed his formulation of the task and the scope of a study of sociology and
its legitimation as an empirical science.

If it may be said that Kant's critical philosophy is a
conciliation between rationalism and empiricism, then
Simmel's critical philosophy is a similar conciliation between two divergent tendencies in his own special field.
The divergent tendencies existing in Simmel's time in the
field of the social sciences were the tendency to claim exclusive validity for the historical method and the tendency
to claim exclusive validity for the naturalistic method.
Simmel's philosophy is a conciliation. He points out that
a complete understanding of the socio-historical actuality
requires both methods of approach, that they are mutually supporting and presuppose each other.

Simmel started from Kant. Like Kant's, his philosophy
is relativistic. Like Kant, he distinguishes sharply between subject and object, between knowing mind and
known world, between the organizing functions of the
mind and the data of experience, between form and matter. But Simmel's relativism is much less rigid than the
Kantian formalism. It is less purely intellectualistic, is
more elastic and flexible, and therefore wider in scope and
more comprehensive. It is a functional, a dynamic, a genetic relativism. His epistemological relativism is not primarily in terms of form and content, but in terms of process and raw material. The product, knowledge, is a func-

tion, not of a variable and a constant, but of two variables. The organizing thought forms themselves have become variables subject to change and development.

Not only his epistemology, however, but also his theory of values and his metaphysics of life are relativistic in essence, and this relativism has given his fine analytic and dialectic mind the widest possible scope.

Simmel's relativism has become a dialectic, something dynamic and functional. It is not primarily a formal structure, a doctrine; it has become a mode of thinking, a thought form, a method of approach. He is a relativist, not only in the more restricted sense of the term, but in the widest possible sense. He views unity as a reciprocity of parts, he resolves the fixed, the permanent, the substantial into function, force, and movement, and recognizes in all existence the historical process of growth. With his emphasis on process and function rather than on product and content, he approaches Nietzsche and Bergson in their conception of life itself as the ultimate value. With his emphasis on the significance of the external world for the judgment and valuation of scientific knowledge, he approaches modern pragmatism.

A full explanation of his relativistic philosophy would take more space than can here be devoted to that purpose. Therefore a short summary of its particular application to the problem of knowledge and a brief indication of the metaphysics of his pluralistic universe must suffice as an illustration of his thought and as a background and basis for comparison with his treatment of society.[1]

[1] For the complete development of Simmel's theory of knowledge, the reader is referred to the following works and essays: *Einleitung in die Moralwissenschaft*, Vol. I; *Philosophie des Geldes*, Intr. and pp. 62–86; *Philosophische Kultur*, Intr.; *Kant;* "Über eine Beziehung der Selectionslehre zur Erkenntnisstheorie," *Archiv für Syst. Phil.*, I (1895), 34–35; "Sur quelques relations de la pensée théorique avec les intérêts pratiques," *Revue de Mét. et de Mor.*, IV (1896), 160–78.

The truth for Simmel is relative, not absolute. A single idea is true, is valid, only in relation to another idea, and a whole body of knowledge is true only in a definite relation to the external world. The peculiar tendency of our mind to accept the truth of a proposition only on the basis of a proof leads to an infinite regression, which means the impossibility of finding the final truth which shall support the whole structure. If we do not want to accept dogmatically once and for all a proposition which shall need no further proof, we are forced to accept a reciprocity of proving between propositions as the basic form of cognition (*Erkennen*). Although in case of a special deduction this process of circular reasoning can be shown to be faulty, it may none the less be valid for the totality of our theoretic knowledge. Knowing (*Erkennen*) would then be a free-floating process in which the elements mutually determine each other's place—just as the masses of matter determine each other's place in space. Truth would then be a concept of relationship, like weight, and our picture of the world would float in space like the world itself. The necessity for proof either postpones the recognition of the truth till infinity, along a line of infinite regression, or it bends this line round to a circle. Then one proposition is true only in relation to another, this latter, however, in the last instance only in relation to the former.

The totality of our theoretic knowledge would then be no more true than that the totality of matter is heavy. Only in the relation of the elements to each other do they have this quality, a quality which the whole cannot be said to possess. The totality can only possess this quality in relation to something outside of itself. In the same way the laws of geometry build themselves on each other according to an internal autonomy, while the axioms and methodological norms, according to which this building and the whole structure is possible at all, cannot be proved geometrically. The whole of geometry is therefore not valid in the same sense as its single propositions are valid. While the latter can be proved within the system one by another, the whole is valid only in relation to something external, in relation to the nature of space and our categories of thought and perception.

This mutual determination which gives the elements within a body of theoretic knowledge the significance of truth seems as a totality to be born of a new relativity, a relativity between the practical and the theoretical interests of our lives. Our ideas of existential actuality are functions of a specific psycho-physiological character and are by no means merely mechanical reproductions. As different biological species equipped with different sense organs must have different ideas of the universe, it follows that none of these can be a pure reproduction of external nature. Each of these species, however, is able to survive and to adapt itself to its environment. The truth, therefore, can in essence mean nothing else but that idea or representation which guides a particular organism in the application of its forces toward useful results. An idea is not useful because it is true, but it is true because it is useful. It is true because it leads to a useful relation toward actuality, because it permits adaptation.

There are therefore in principle just as many kinds of truth as there are different organisms and life-conditions. What is true for the eagle may not be true for the insect with facet-shaped eyes, and vice versa.

These kinds of truth, however, do not lack a normative fixity for the specific species. In so far as the organism and its constitution and needs are given on the one hand, and objective actuality on the other hand, the truth for that particular organism is ideally determined. There are those ideas which are useful, and, as the result of a process of natural selection among the psychological processes, the useful ones become fixed and form in their totality the true picture of actuality. We have in fact no other definite criterion for the truth of an idea than that an action based on it gives the desired result.

If through the process of selection mentioned above a certain number of ideas have become permanently fixed because they are permanently useful, they build a realm of theory. A new idea can then be judged according to internal criteria as belonging to it or as being contradictory to it. Since the norms and facts once fixed become the proofs of others, the single elements of knowledge can mutually support and carry each other. But the whole of a body of knowledge has a validity only in relation to definite psycho-physical structures, their conditions of life, and the requirements of their activities.

Relativism renounces all dogmatic pretension that the highest abstraction, simplification, or synthesis can close knowledge. There is no finite system of knowledge, there is only an infinite process of knowing. For the contention that things are thus and so related, it substitutes: It is for our reasoning a practical necessity to act as if things were thus and so related.[1]

From this relativistic character of our knowledge it follows that the objective validity of a hypothesis is not finally determined merely by its logical coherence within a system of thought (philosophy), but that a new determination is required through a relation with the external world (science), and vice versa. This mutual dependence of the two directions of thought is visible in the most general and in the most specific problems. Should each of the two methods become dogmatically fixed and claim for itself

[1] *Phil. des Geldes,* pp. 68–73.

objective truth, there would result an irreconcilable conflict and mutual negation; but in the form of alternation
an organic unity is possible. Each of them becomes then
merely a heuristic principle, that is, each will have to
search for a foundation and a justification at every point
of its application. In this way every exact science has to
submit to an investigation of its presuppositions, and
these presuppositions themselves will have to be submitted
to a psychological and historical investigation.

This mutual dependence of the two methods is also
manifest in the most general opposition within our knowledge, the opposition between what is a priori and what is
experience. All experience results from an active, formative functioning of the mind on the immediate sense impressions, and it is only through this transformation that
the immediate data of experience become knowedge. But
the certainty that there are such a priori thought forms
is not accompanied by the certainty of what they are.
What has been accepted as an a priori form at one time
has been proven to be an empirical and historical structure at a later time. Not only are the a priori categories
not permanently fixed and static, but what is empirically
obtained in one field of inquiry may function as a priori
for another field of inquiry. A complete understanding of
experience involves, therefore, the double task of finding
the aprioristic norms which shape it and of tracing for each
single a priori its genetic growth out of former experience.
Each of these two methods still contains something subjective, but in the form of a mutual determination they
can picture that which we call objectivity.

The great advantage of this relativistic over other
epistemological doctrines is that it does not need to ask
for exemption from application to itself. The doctrine is
not destroyed by the fact that it is itself relativistic.

This idea of the relativity of truth should not be understood as an approximation to an otherwise independent concept of absolute truth, but as the essence of truth itself, as the way in which ideas become true. It does not mean a knowledge of the truth from which more might have been expected, but rather, on the contrary, the positive fulfilment and validity of its concept. The truth is not valid in spite of its relativity, but because of its relativity.[1]

Not only does empirical knowledge result from specific normative functions on the data of experience, but each field of mental activity constructs a picture of the world according to categories of its own. Art, religion, metaphysics, and science result from specific attitudes toward the world, from specific ways of dealing with things. The specific functional, formal activity of the mind is for Simmel the essence and significance of these fields. Their true value lies, not in their content, not in the religious dogma or in the metaphysical system, but in their function for life. They have value as functions of life.

In the case of metaphysics, this differentiation between the function and the content enables Simmel to give to the metaphysical tendency, or to the process or mental attitude which results from it, a value and significance which remain untouched by all the contradictions and untenable points in its content. Philosophy as a thought form is unprejudiced against all contents and obtains a flexibility and a possibility of extension which is unthinkable as long as one searches for the essence of philosophy in the factual content of its problems.

This differentiation therefore means more than a mere differentiation; it means also an accentuation. It means emphasizing the functional over the substantial aspect. It means a change in conception from metaphysics as dog-

[1] *Phil. des Geldes*, pp. 78–82.

ma to metaphysics as function. It means a stress, not on the content and the difference in dogma, but on the form and the unity of the thought movement.[1]

The formal principle of metaphysics is to obtain an inclusive view of the world, to create out of the discrete elements of the universe, their oppositions and manifoldness, a synthetic unity. Metaphysics has the formal value of striving for a complete picture of the world, of aiming at fundamental principles. It tries to reach that goal by taking out of the manifoldness one appearance which it sees often repeated and making this the measure of all things. This metaphysical explanation of the world stands beyond the truth and error which decide about the actual and exact world. Its value is independent of the material errors of its content and remains even when other than philosophic thought gives satisfaction to our thirst for knowledge. The axiom that the world is a unitary and coherent totality and, as such, intelligible is the vital concept of all metaphysics. It is a presupposition and will remain a presupposition as long as the larger part of the world's phenomena remain unknown. But this thought would never have arisen, could never have functioned as a guiding principle, had it been necessary to wait for a faultless knowledge of the world's factual content.[2]

Metaphysics is directed toward the totality of existence, and even if it deals with elements, they are of interest only in their relation to that totality. For that reason the philosophic truth is different from the scientific truth. Metaphysics does not picture the objectivity of things; that is the task of the sciences. It pictures a type of mental activity as it shows itself in a specific conception of things. Not correspondence in one way or another with

[1] *Philosophische Kultur*, pp. i–iii.

[2] *Probl. der Gesch.*, p. 93.

an object, but correspondence with the totality of its
world-conception, is the aim of the philosophic truth.
The essence of philosophic thought is its self-sufficiency.
It is unrelated to anything external and is directed above
the momentary singularity to the totality of knowledge
and to the totality of life.

Not only is there no immediate relation between the
metaphysical statement and the external world, but even
within the sphere of metaphysics that which holds good in
the height of its abstractions cannot be applied to the
single elements of existence. The specific concept of a
philosophic truth is peculiarly detached from the factual
content of its propositions. This is due to the fact that its
picture of the world results from the unification of the
totality of existence on the basis of a one-sided selection of
elements. The paradox of all great philosophic world-
conceptions lies in the fact that they pronounce absolute,
general statements which do not even fit the single cases
that are logically included. The reason for this is that the
general character of these statements is not a formulation
of the universal aspect of particulars, but of the universal
aspect of the mental reaction toward them.[1]

Metaphysics constructs a picture of the world according to categories which have little or nothing to do with the
categories of empirical knowledge. When for metaphysics
existence is the appearance of the absolute spirit or the
absolute will, moral action the expression of our noume-
non, when matter and spirit are two sides of one substance,
then all this lies in a plane which bears the criteria of its
significance and validity within itself. Within this thought
mirror the world forms a self-sufficient picture which
satisfies only metaphysical requirements, not requirements
springing from different needs. One may reject philosophic

[1] *Hptprobl. der Phil.*, pp. 27–42.

speculation on principle in certain cases, but one cannot do this on the basis of standards which decide for empirical, scientific knowledge about validity and significance. These standards do not apply to metaphysics because its problems and aims are different. It creates a world-picture according to its own laws, with its own methods, and by its own technique.[1]

But apart from the value and significance which philosophic thought possesses in and for itself, as a special function, as a special attitude toward the world, it has a meaning and significance as a forerunner of exact science.

Philosophy was the mother of all sciences, and only gradually have they obtained their independence. As the forerunner of science, it takes in a tentative grasp what is as yet unprovable and combines in inclusive concepts what is as yet unobservable as single facts. With these it draws pictures of the world which will be partially confirmed, partially refuted by methodological empiricism, but which are none the less the first approaches to knowledge.

Scientific thought begins with wide concepts and general reflections. It becomes more narrow in proportion as it becomes more exact. With a few ideas it will try to grasp the totality of existence, and only after innumerable trials and errors in the highest abstractions does it begin with analysis of complex concepts. It then follows the single threads of the weaving, which it formerly thought to understand without knowledge of its structure.

The form of some occurrence which has often been observed on the surface of appearances is postulated as a general law until the incidental character of the coexistence of its composing factors is discovered. Then the forms of the latter are postulated as the real general laws until the process repeats itself. From a tracing of the

1 *Probl. der Gesch.*, pp. 92–93.

complex phenomena to one of them as their substance and law, on the basis of superficial and unequally emphasized similarities, a gradual differentiation leads to the recognition of the primary forces which interact between their elements. That is the road from philosophy to exact science along a series of intermediate stations. The cosmic appearances are so manifold, complex, and interwoven that a first orientation cannot occur otherwise than by postulating an often observed fact as the center and source of the world and by tracing the other phenomena back to it. Although this may be possible only with many strains and breakings, it will none the less provide a first guiding line.

But metaphysics has made the mistake of considering this first unitary synthesis of the appearance of things as their last source. It has projected behind the actuality the distance which separates the actuality from the superficial appearance, and has considered the latter as the absolute source of the former, instead of a first approach toward it. The thought movement has tended to become rigid at the beginning of its journey, and this has placed great obstacles in the way of a further differentiation and a better knowledge of the actuality. But it has none the less produced a unification of and a mastery over the manifoldness of appearances which is not without value just because it is merely the beginning and not the end. The right to a philosophic treatment remains therefore unchallenged until the problems are finally solved within the field of exact science. And this historical development of our knowledge of the totality of the world is similar to the development of our knowledge of special fields. The metaphysics of the cosmos continues in a metaphysics of part of the cosmos. But there also it has a value only as a first anticipation, and must be followed by an exact inquiry.[1]

[1] *Ibid.*, pp. 93–94.

The philosophic thought form may serve as a first orientation in the manifoldness of the phenomenal world, but if it serves only as forerunner of and preliminary to science, it is to be succeeded by a further analysis which will bring recognition of the actual elements and the actually effective forces. The goal of the inquiry is then science and not metaphysics. The aim is then a scientific picture of the world, not a metaphysical picture. Science also creates a picture of the world according to its own laws, with its own methods, and by its own technique; but these are different from those of metaphysics. Metaphysics is a thought form which aims at an inclusive view of the totality of existence. Science is a thought form which aims at an understanding of the individual elements of the external world in their primary interrelations and interactions. It aims to construct an objective world-picture that shall have the form of empirical actuality, that shall make possible practical, purposeful activity.

But the metaphysical truth and the so-called empirical actuality are not the only forms in which the mental life shapes the contents of the world. They can also be formed artistically and religiously.

Art also is a category or a world which cannot be deduced from any other category. Art also works with the elementary contents of reality, but it becomes art only by giving them forms which derive from its own artistic needs of perception and feeling. These forms are separate and distinct from the categories which shape the world of actuality, and even the space of a picture is different from the space which the world of actuality manifests. Art has its own logic, its own concept of truth, its own causality, and with these it builds out of the same contents as metaphysics and science a new world which is equivalent to both.

It is the same with religion. From contents which are also perceived and conceived on the planes of science and metaphysics, the religious function creates a new world by means of special emotional attitudes and special syntheses. It transforms these contents through special evaluations and constructs a new world-picture with dimensions and perspective different from the empirical, the philosophic, or the artistic form. That world is a law unto itself; it has an immanent logic and a value and significance entirely independent of its correspondence to objective actuality.[1]

And science, philosophy, art, and religion are not the only fundamental categories, not the only independent forms in which the human mind shapes the contents of reality. The world of values and the world of norms (*Sollen*) are also specific pictures of the universe which result from special ways of dealing with its contents. They are fundamental in the sense that they cannot be derived from each other or from simpler elements.[2]

In this distinction between the different fields of mental activity and, within these fields, between the form and the content, Simmel's relativism reaches its widest scope. But the functional, dynamic character of his relativism enables him to reach, through and beyond these forms, a final unity in life itself. With the same relativistic dialectic with which he has first dissected the universe, he now co-ordinates those discrete worlds into a final synthesis which, although it can be formulated only in terms of two opposing relativities, is yet more than either because it embraces and transcends both.

[1] *Religion*, pp. 8–13.

[2] *Phil. des Geldes*, pp. 1–7; *Einleitung in die Moralwissenschaft*, pp. 1–12, 30–32; *Hptprobl. der Phil.*, p. 16.

The different metaphysical systems are contradictory in content and relative in value, but metaphysics as function has a value and significance independent of and beyond any contradictions in material content. The different exact sciences treat only a relatively small aspect of the actuality, but science as function has a value which lies beyond the fragmentary character of its special fields. The different types of art seem unrelated and mutually exclusive, but art as function has a meaning which lies beyond all discrepancies in style and technique. The different religions may be fundamentally diverse, but religion as function has a value beyond all the contradictions in dogma.

As function these forms of the mind have a fixity and universality in relation to their contents, but in relation to each other they have only a relative value. No single field of mental activity takes a position of superiority in relation to any other field. Neither religion, nor metaphysics, nor science, nor art is the one and absolute form to which the others must eventually be converted. They are autonomous worlds in which the totality of existence is expressed in a fully adequate language.

What is universal in relation to each of these worlds, because it co-ordinates and transcends all of them, is life itself. Life on the intellectual plane, as mind, is the creator of these worlds. They are adaptational products, instruments of adaptation, produced in the contact of life's processes with an environment. Mind lives in these forms and categories, *is* these forms and categories, just as the vital force lives in the forms and structures of individual organisms. But, although the product of life's processes, they cannot be defined in terms of processes alone. They are objective systems possessing an independent existence and confronting life's processes as external structures.

The structures of independent reality outside of life's processes were originally mere functions of life. At first life produced these forms and categories for the sake of life. Their task was to serve life. But, once they have obtained their self-sufficient status, it becomes the task of life to serve them for their sake. Life must then shape its contents according to their norms and fit them within their forms. Meaning and significance pertain at first only to the fitting and shaping of these forms to the demands of life. But later the fitting and shaping of life's contents according to these norms obtains a meaning and significance of its own.

These forms and categories help to build life even when they are still wholly submerged in life's processes. But up to that point they are merely passive. They must submit to the demands of life and modify themselves accordingly. But, once objectified, they become really productive. Then their own factual forms become the true determinants. Life's contents are then shaped according to their norms. Then the logical and methodological norms create in full autonomy the worlds of art, philosophy, and religion. The emphasis is then no longer on the contents of these worlds and their meaning for life, but on their forms and categories. They have become independent systems possessing an objective structure of their own.

Certain occurrences of the temporal and subjective life are the embryonic forms, the precursory formations of these worlds. Later, however, art, science, and religion obtain a superpsychological ideality and thus become nontemporal and objective. The formation of these independent systems is a historical process. Out of a mere knowing for practical purposes there grow science and philosophy, out of mere vital-teleological elements there grow art and religion. At first the search for truth is for the sake of life.

Later, when these independent structures have taken form, the search for truth is for the sake of truth in science, for the sake of beauty in art, and for the sake of God in religion. An objective cultural world now exists whose structure confronts life as a fixed station on its onward march.[1]

Life as process, continuous and essentially dynamic, creates the non-temporal forms, discrete and essentially static. These forms, once created, confront life, obstruct its free, unhampered flow, and try to shape it according to their norms. Out of this tension life's eternal dialectic is born. The processes of life create forms and embody themselves in structures. The forms of life, although the product of its processes, yet limit and define them. But life eternally transcends its self-created forms in order to find embodiment in new and better forms. These successive discrete forms direct and modify the ceaseless flow of life until, no longer capable of giving it adequate expression, they are superseded in turn by other forms. This is the eternal dialectic inherent in life itself. For life is not only a continuous process and, as such, relative in relation to these forms and structures; it is also, as process, at the same time creator of these forms and therefore more than either. It is that which is more than continuity and form, that which continually transcends itself and its creations. Its unitary function is its self-transcendence. Life is the final unitary synthesis which is the absolute of its own relativities.[2]

---

[1] *Lebensanschauung*, pp. 38–39, 50–56, 58–61.

[2] For a more complete development of Simmel's metaphysics of life, see his *Lebensanschauung* (*Vier metaphysische Kapitel*).

In the above paragraphs Simmel's relativistic philosophy has been briefly outlined. His philosophy is a method, not a system. Yet, even so, it is not wholly unsystematic. It has a fundamental principle and a method, or rather its fundamental principle is its method. The functional relativism is systematically carried through and pervades all fields.

Simmel's philosophy is one of the latest expressions of that relativistic tendency which began with the romantic movement and became increasingly prominent during the latter part of the nineteenth century. It belongs to that general school of thought which has been classified by its opponents as psychologism and historicism. And, like the metaphysics of many of his contemporaries in the same group, such as Nietzsche, Dilthey, Troeltsch, and Bergson, it places the emphasis on life as the ultimate category.

In how far his metaphysics is acceptable and satisfactory is largely a question of individual taste. To the type of mind which is content to live in an experimental and essentially dynamic universe, his formulation will be acceptable. That type of mind will not be disturbed by the thought that the forms and norms of life are born out of the interplay of its processes with an environment. To the type of mind which needs a form and norm outside of life fixed for all eternity and by means of which life may be shaped and ordered, Simmel's relativism will not be acceptable. Under the chaotic conditions of post-war Europe there is a tendency to return to systems of absolutism, and it may very well be that the extreme relativism of Simmel will close a period in European thought. If this is going to be the case, it will be due not so much to its fundamental inadequacy as to a failure to understand the implications of modern relativism.

Simmel has been accused of dissolving all forms and categories, an accusation which will seem hardly justified in the light of the foregoing analysis. Simmel's philosophy is a theory of functions, and although he was not a mathematician, his thought is very similar to that underlying modern mathematics. To see a form or a category in its relation to life is not to dissolve it, but to see it as a function relative to a system of reference. A function of one or more variables is not something inferior to a constant because, as quantity, it is variable. That would be to misunderstand its essence, which is not quantity, but relationship. The essential characteristic of a function is not variability of quantity, but constancy of relationship. This constancy of relationship between variables has therefore an element of absoluteness in relation to these variables. A function is itself a form. To see a category or a form as a function is therefore not to dissolve them, but to see them in the only possible way in which an absolute can appear in a changing dynamic system. It is only in the form of a function that such an absolute can adequately be expressed. It is only through such a relativation that true universality can be reached.

BOOK I

SOCIAL PHILOSOPHY
METHODOLOGY—EPISTEMOLOGY

INTRODUCTION

THIS first book has to deal with the field of inquiry which flanks on one side the field of the exact sciences of the socio-historical actuality. It is the field in which the thought movement has changed from the exact scientific to the philosophical, in which the method of empirical science, with its main emphasis on a correspondence theory of truth, searches for a support and a justification in the method of philosophy, with its main emphasis on a coherence theory of truth.

The inquiries of this field deal with the basic concepts, the fundamental presuppositions, and the a priori categories of the social sciences. They are inquiries into problems which cannot be settled within the field of inductive empirical investigation, since they form the basis on which that investigation rests. They deal with the problems of the philosophy and the methodology of these sciences, and with the problems of that field which Simmel, in harmony with his wider and more flexible concept of the a priori, calls the epistemology (*Erkenntnisstheorie*) of society.

CHAPTER I

THE CONCEPT OF SOCIETY

Society as Form and Society as Content

THE fact that society has an existence apparently independent of the single individuals gives it the appearance of a structure of independent reality. It seems to lead a life according to specific laws, by virtue of special forces, independent of its individual components. These laws and forces appear as products and functions of an impersonal structure. The social group appears as something objective over and above the individual and absolved from the limitation of personal life.[1]

On the other hand, it is certain that in the last analysis only individuals really exist. The group is not a unity of independent reality, is not the unitary subject of the group spirit or of the group mind. Apart from material objects, there are no human products except within human beings themselves, except within personal minds. Every attempt to think of psychic entities outside of personal minds, outside of the mental life of individuals, is a form of mysticism similar to the conceptual realism which makes independent substantial entities of human ideas.[2]

But if society were nothing more than an aggregate of individuals who were the actual realities, then only these individuals and their relationships could be the subject-matter of a social science. The concept of society would then dissolve. Society would be merely a subjective mental synthesis, not an objective unity. It might be an

[1] "Persistence of Social Groups," *A. J. S.*, III, 665.　　[2] *Ibid.*

object for speculation, but not for scientific thought, which aims to investigate actuality. Society or the group could then be the subject-matter of a social science only in the same sense as the firmament is the subject-matter of astronomy. The concept of society has significance only when it stands in some kind of contrast to that of the sum of the individuals.[1]

This is no doubt the case. The group is more than a merely subjective synthesis. It is an objective unity, judged by the one valid objective criterion of unity, namely, reciprocal activity of parts. Unity in the empirical sense is nothing but reciprocity of elements. It is a functional, a dynamic, and a gradual concept. An organic body is a unity because its organs are in a more intimate interchange of energies with one another than with any outside agent. In the last analysis, even the unity of the individual mind is nothing but the dynamic functional reciprocity of its energies.

The group possesses a unity of the same nature. A social group consists, in the last analysis, in mental attitudes or psychological occurrences within the minds of the individuals; but the fact that these attitudes and occurrences are the product of mutual determinations and reciprocal influences creates a dynamic functional relationship between the individuals, and that dynamic functional relationship creates and is the unity of the group. The group is a unity because of this process or these processes of reciprocal influencing between the individuals. The state is a unity because between its citizens there is a more intimate exchange of reciprocal influences than between these citizens and those of other states.[2]

[1] *Soz. Diff.*, pp. 10–11.

[2] *Soz.*, pp. 6–7; *Soz. Diff.*, pp. 13–14. The group therefore does not consist of individuals, but only of so much of them as enters into the functional relationship. See also Book I, chapter vii, pp. 82–83, 103, and Book II, chapter vi.

The superindividual character of social structures and the objectivity and independence of social forces and organizations are therefore only apparent. A further analysis resolves that appearance which seems to announce a new independent unity above the individuals into a reciprocity which plays between them. The latter view corresponds to the facts, the former is the result of a limited analysis; the latter is the ideal of complete understanding, the former the stage of understanding actually reached.

In many cases this complete understanding cannot be reached. The relations of human beings are so complex, so ramified, and so compact that it is often a hopeless task to try to resolve them into the constituent elements. We are consequently compelled in certain instances to treat these reciprocal relationships as unities. But it remains a mere methodological device to speak of the essence and the development of the state, of law, and of institutions as if they were unified entities. It is a mere scientific interim to treat them as if they had an independent existence.

This provisional convenience resembles the treatment of the life-process as though it were a proper entity instead of merely the synthesis of endlessly complicated reciprocities between the minutest parts of the organic body. In our knowledge of physical organisms we have succeeded in thinking beyond the idea of a vital power that seemed to hold sway over the separate organs and to compose a new entity in addition to them. We have in part at least substituted the reciprocal activities of the organs. In like manner we must attempt in the social sciences to approach nearer and nearer to the individual operations which produce the social structure, even if we have to stop short of complete analysis in many instances.[1]

[1] *Soz.*, pp. 495–96; "Persistence of Social Groups," *A. J. S.*, III, 665–66.

The essence of group unity, then, consists in the reciprocal relations of its elements, and a group or a society may be said to exist where individuals are in reciprocal relations.

The reciprocity arises always from specific impulses or by virtue of specific purposes. Erotic, religious, or merely associative impulses, purposes of defense or of attack, of play or of gain, bring human beings into relationships in which they act for, with, and against one another. They bring them into situations and conditions in which they mutually influence one another. These mutual reactions signify that out of the individual bearers of those impulses and purposes a unity, that is, a society, has come into existence.[1]

That social unity is not the result merely of harmonious tendencies and integrating forces, but the differentiating tendencies play also a positive rôle. Just as the cosmos needs love and hatred, attractive and repulsive forces, to obtain form, so also society needs a certain quantitative relation of harmony and disharmony, association and competition, friendship and jealousy, to obtain a definite structure. And these dissociations are by no means to be viewed merely as negative factors, so that the actual society results only from the positive social forces in so far as the former do not prevent it. It is a superficial way of thinking which concludes that the one factor tears down what the other builds up and that what at last remains is a subtraction. Society as it exists is the result of the two categories of interaction, which are both positive in their effect.

The above-mentioned misconception is partly due to a false conclusion drawn from the observation of a simple opposition between two individuals. It by no means fol-

[1] *Soz.*, p. 5.

lows, however, that a factor which is negative and diminutive in the relationship between certain individuals if considered in a given direction and by itself has the same effect throughout the totality of relationships. In the larger circle the perspective may be wholly different. The simplest illustration of such an instance is the competition of individuals within the economic system. Competition, which is a special form of conflict, is a relationship which, if viewed in the totality of social interactions, may be seen to play a positive rôle and to contribute to the unity of the group.[1]

The social unities which result from these processes of mutual influencing, these processes of socialization (*Vergesellschaftung*), may therefore be of different duration and of different gradation. They may range from the ephemeral association for a promenade to the permanence of the family group, from the temporary aggregation of guests in a hotel to the intimate bond of a medieval guild.[2]

It follows, further, that a given group of individuals may be socialized to a greater or less degree. With each new growth of synthetic formations, with each new party organization, with each association for common work or association on the basis of common feeling and thinking, the same group becomes more socialized than it was before. Socialization between persons incessantly takes place and ceases. Society is not a simple, fixed concept; there can be more or less of it. There is never in existence "society" in an absolute sense, as a condition necessary to enable these interactions to take place, for there is no reciprocal influencing in an absolute sense, there are merely particular species. With the occurrence of these socializations, society puts in an appearance. They are

[1] *Soz.*, pp. 249–50.
[2] *Ibid.*, p. 6.

neither the cause nor the result of society; they are themselves immediately society. There is not an internally self-contained, closed national or social unit which produces law, morals, religion, and language, but the social elements induced by purpose, need, or force build these social products, and this causes or rather means their unification.[1]

The more important the interests which bring men into mutual relationships, the more readily will they become fixed and objectified in institutions. But society does not obtain its unity merely from these institutions any more than the human organism consists merely of the larger organs. There are innumerable varieties of reciprocal relations which never become institutionalized. Not only the state and the labor union, the family and the political party, but all the thousand minor relationships playing from person to person, momentary or permanent, conscious or unconscious, create the social unity out of the individual elements. "That people gaze at one another and are jealous of one another; that they exchange letters and dine together; that, apart from all tangible interests, they affect one another sympathetically or antipathetically; that gratitude gives to the altruistic act an after-effect which is an inseparable bond of union between people; that one asks another to point out the way, and that people dress and adorn themselves for one another's benefit: all these relationships are incessantly binding men together."[2]

That which constitutes society in the real sense of the term is evidently the type of reciprocal influencing thus indicated. A collection of human beings does not become a society because specific impulses actuate the individuals

[1] *Soz. Diff.*, p. 14; *Soz.*, p. 11.

[2] *Soz.*, p. 19.

as such, but they grow into a unity only when these impulses lead to reciprocal influencing. Only when an influence is exerted by one upon another, whether immediately or through a third, has society come into existence out of the mere spatial proximity or the temporal contemporaneousness or succession of individuals.[1]

The term "society" is, however, also used in a broader sense. In that case it stands for the sum of all individuals concurring in reciprocal relations, together with all the interests which unite them. In the more narrow sense, the term designates the process of socialization or association as such, the interaction itself in abstraction from these interests. These two meanings of the term can be distinguished on the basis of a differentiation between the form and the content of socialization.

Everything which is present in the individuals, the immediate bearers of the socialization, in the form of impulse, interest, or purpose, and which brings about the socialization, may be designated as its content. This content is economic or religious, domestic or political, intellectual or volitional; but these materials with which the socialization is filled, these motives which impel it, are in and for themselves not sociological in nature. Neither hunger nor love, neither labor nor religiosity, as they are given immediately and in their strict sense, signify socialization. They constitute socialization only if they shape the spatial proximity of individuals into some definite form of interaction which belongs under the general concept of reciprocity.

These socializations, these processes of association,

[1] *Soz.*, p. 7. Simmel would therefore not consider an instinct of gregariousness a sufficient explanation of group unity. It could at best explain that a group of individuals aggregate. But it does not account for the fact that out of that group of individuals there arises a unitary society, the essence of which is reciprocal action of elements.

may take various forms. In these forms the individuals grow into a unity on the basis of various interests; and these interests, sensuous or ideal, momentary or permanent, functioning as causes or as purposes, are satisfied and find their realization within the framework of these socializations.

In every social phenomenon, content and social form constitute a unitary actuality. A social form can no more attain existence detached from all content than a spatial form can exist without substance. In actuality they are together the inseparable elements of which every social fact and occurrence is made up. They consist of an interest, a purpose, or a motive on the one side, and, on the other side, of a form or manner of reciprocity between the individuals through which this content attains social actuality.[1]

That these purposes and interests, however, attain to realization in the form of a society, in the form of a reciprocity between individuals, is the subject-matter of special scientific consideration. That men build a society means that they live for the attainment of those purposes in definite forms of interaction. If there is to be a science of society as such, it must therefore abstract these forms from the complex phenomena of social life, and it must make them the subject of determination and explanation.[2]

Such a science, therefore, can only apply the term "society" either to the abstract general concept of the social forms, to the genus of which they are the species, or to the aggregate of these forms in operation at a given time.[3]

---

[1] *Ibid.*, pp. 5–7.

[2] "The Number of the Members as Determining the Sociological Form of the Group," *A. J. S.*, VIII, 1.

[3] *Soz.*, p. 11.

The concept of society as applied in the scientific study of society is a formal concept. It stands for something quantitative and essentially dynamic. Society is not something concrete, but something functional. There can be more or less society. It is not a thing, but a process, or rather a number of interacting processes; and, on account of this fundamental characteristic, it is better to speak, not of society, but of *socialization*.

CHAPTER II

SOCIOLOGY

THE STUDY OF THE FORMS OF SOCIALIZATION

IN THE nineteenth century men came to realize that all human activity ran its course within society and that nothing could withdraw itself from its influence. It was consequently deduced that everything which was not science of external nature must be science of society. Since the subject-matter of ethics and of the history of civilization, of aesthetics and demography, of politics and ethnology, was to be found within the framework of society, society appeared as the inclusive territory in which all these sciences congregated. In other words, the study of man became the study of society.

This realization that man in his whole nature and in all its expressions is determined by the fact that he lives in reciprocal relations with other men, led to a new way of thinking in the field of the humanities. Historical facts in the broadest sense of the word, the contents of culture, the systems of production, the norms of morality, could no longer be explained solely in terms of the individual and his interests. But there was also no longer any necessity for having recourse to metaphysical or magical origins where this explanation failed. Historical phenomena could now be explained by the interactions and co-operations of individuals, by the aggregation and sublimation of countless separate contributions, and by the materialization of social energies in structures which exist and develop outside of the individuals.

But this did not create a new science. Neither did it mean that the existing social sciences had to renounce their independence and become subdivisions of one inclusive, synthetic social science which was to be called sociology. In so far as sociology, as a science, rested its claims on the ground that man must be understood as a social being and that society is the vehicle of all social experience, it contained no object which was not already treated in one of the existing social sciences. The actual situation was that sociology merely proposed a new way of dealing with the subject-matter of all these sciences, a method of science which, for the very reason that it was applicable to the totality of their problems, was not a special science in and for itself. In the same way induction, when it invaded all possible sciences as a method, was not for that reason a special science, let alone an all-comprehensive science.

One may call this method of investigating the sociohistorical actuality the sociological method; but that does not supply the justification and legitimation of a sociology which shall be a special and independent science. For that purpose it is necessary to define the particular subject-matter which it shall investigate.[1]

The term "sociology" has also been used in connection with certain problems regarding society and the social sciences which are in the last analysis problems of a philosophical nature. Such are the problems regarding the presuppositions of the social sciences which belong to the field of social methodology. Others are problems regarding interpretations of historical developments, and fall under the philosophy of history. Others, again, are problems regarding the relative value of individual and collective accomplishments, and belong to the field of social philosophy.

[1] *Soz.*, pp. 2–4; *Grundfr. der Soz.*, pp. 18–20.

In these cases there is a more or less clearly defined subject-matter, but the character of the problems precludes the application of the method of science. Neither the existence of these problems nor the fact that man is a social animal is therefore a sufficient legitimation of a sociology which shall be a science and not a philosophy. To be a science, sociology must not only have a well-defined subject-matter, but its specific problems must be capable of treatment according to scientific methodology.[1]

This does not mean that sociology has to discover an object which has previously been unknown. What is characterized as an object in the most general sense is a complex of definitions and relationships. Each of these complexes, if discovered among a plurality of objects, may become the subject-matter of a special science. Each science rests upon an abstraction. It regards the actual totality of any given thing from the viewpoint of some specific concept. The totality as such cannot be grasped as a unity by any science. Each science results, therefore, from a decomposition of the unity of things and a corresponding division of labor; and, by virtue of this decomposition, the object is resolved into specific qualities and functions. This differentiation and division of labor occur according to a centralizing concept which makes possible the methodological co-ordination into one subject-matter of the similar factors and functions abstracted from different objects. In the presence of the highly complex facts of historical society, which cannot be interpreted from a single scientific viewpoint, the concepts "politics," "economics," and "culture" are indicative of such categories of cognition. They may combine certain parts of the facts, with elimination of or merely accidental co-operation with the other

[1] For the distinction between sociology and social philosophy, see Book I, chapter iv.

parts, into a unique historical sequence; or they may combine different parts into groupings of elements which contain a timeless correlation.

Sociology as a special science might find its subject-matter in a similar fashion by drawing a new line through facts which, as such, are quite well known. It would need only the unifying concept which should co-ordinate into a new synthesis the similar aspects lying along that line. The new concept would therefore have to subject the socio-historical data to an abstraction and a co-ordination which should enable the recognition of the fact that certain peculiarities already observed in other relations can be grouped together. That new grouping will then be the subject-matter of the new science. The concept of society as the external aggregate of social phenomena cannot fulfil that function. *For that purpose it becomes necessary to distinguish between the content and the form of society and to use the latter as the unifying viewpoint.* This concept of *society as form,* or rather of the form of the socialization, makes possible the formation and the delimitation of the new science and is therefore the category of cognition and the central concept of sociology.[1]

Society in the wider and larger sense consists of both form and content. But if the subject-matter of sociology is to be society and nothing else, it can investigate only the processes of association, the kinds and the forms of socialization. Everything else found within society and realized by means of it and within its framework is not socialization itself, but merely content. A special science of society as such can be founded only when these two elements, inseparably united in actuality, are separated in scientific abstraction. The socio-historical actuality can be really projected on the plane of the purely social only if the forms of

[1] *Soz.,* pp. 4–7; *Grundfr. der Soz.,* pp. 22–33.

socialization are brought together under one unifying scientific concept in mental detachment from their content.

In order to differentiate the various fields of scientific inquiry from the unitary and complex actuality, it is necessary to abstract from that actuality the similar and related phenomena by means of such synthesizing concepts. But the mere subjective needs of cognition are not a sufficient legitimation of the use of such concepts. There must also be a justification in the structure of the objectivity for the specific concepts selected. If there does not exist a functional relationship of some sort between these integral concepts and the outside world, there is no protection against unfruitful inquiries and against the use of purely fortuitous and arbitrary concepts.

The concept of *society as form* can therefore be used as the integral concept of sociology only if there exists such a functional relation between that concept and the social actuality. The differentiation between the form and the content of social phenomena and the synthesis of the latter into a field of special scientific inquiry are legitimate only if that differentiation can be justified by the actual structure of society. That justification exists if two conditions are fulfilled. Similar forms of socialization must occur with quite dissimilar content, and similar social interests must be found in quite dissimilar forms of socialization.

That this is the case cannot be denied. There are similar forms of relationship between individuals in groups which are wholly dissimilar in aim and purpose. Superiority and subordination, competition, imitation, division of labor, formation of parties, and countless other forms of relationship are found both in civic groups and in religious communities, in bands of conspirators and in industrial organizations, in art schools and in families. However diverse the interests from which the socializations arise, the forms in which they occur may nevertheless be similar. On the other hand, the same content can be realized in very different forms of socialization. The economic interest may be realized both through competition and through deliberate organization of producers; it may be satisfied through detachment from other economic groups or through combination with those groups. The religious contents of life, while remaining identical in substance, demand now a free, now a centralized community form. The interests which lie at the foundation of the relation between the sexes are satisfied in a greater variety of family formations than can be enumerated. On the one hand, the forms in which the most divergent contents are realized may be identical. On the other hand, the substance may remain while the socialization that carries it may change into a variety of forms.

These facts furnish the legitimation of the sociological problem, although in their objective concreteness substance and form constitute an indissoluble unity. *That problem is the identification, systematic arrangement, psychological explanation, and historical development of the pure forms of socialization.*[1]

The aim is to discover in the countless historical groupings the principles of group formation as such. The object is to approximate the laws governing the influences which human beings exert upon one another in their reciprocal contacts. These laws are in themselves not affected by the material causes or purposes of these contacts, although the different contents of socialization will lead to various combinations, different degrees of strength, and different tendencies of development.

We reach a science of religion by turning our attention away from all other interests of life except religion, or

[1] *Soz.*, pp. 7–9.

at least by treating them as merely accidental. We gain a science of language by abstracting language and its immediate psychological conditions from everything that lies beyond, although, as a matter of fact, there would never have been any utterance without concrete motives.

In the same manner we shall obtain a sociology by an inquiry into the laws, forms, and developments of socializations. In reality they determine life only together with other functions and forces, but they can nevertheless constitute the subject-matter of a special science only in abstraction from these factors.[1]

Sociology, then, is the study of the forms of socialization. It is to investigate all forms of socialization: not merely those which have become objectified in social institutions, but also the minor and more ephemeral socializations which do not take objective form in permanent social structures. Society does not consist merely of the objective social structures which have obtained a certain independence of the individual bearers; it also consists of the thousand minor processes of socialization between individuals which contribute to the functional unity of the group.

It seems at first as if economic, political, and military organizations, castes, classes, and families, guilds, parishes, and similar great institutions actually constitute the whole of society. If that were the case, a sociological treatment of those institutions would cover the whole field of the science of society. It is obvious that the greater, the more significant a range of social interests and activities is, the more readily will the immediate interindividual life and the direct reciprocities crystallize in objective structures. But besides these prominent phenomena, imposing through their size and significance, there are innu-

[1] "Superordination and Subordination," *A. J. S.*, II, 415.

merable minor forms of relationship and types of reciprocal action between persons. Although these are perhaps
trivial if viewed separately, in reality they constitute in
aggregate that network of relationships which surrounds
the larger formations and creates the actual unity of society. The actual life of society cannot be construed from
the structures which constitute the traditional subject-
matter of the social sciences. It would be a mere aggregate
of discontinuous systems if it were not for the intermediate operations of the innumerable smaller synthetic processes. Sociology therefore has to concern itself also with
the thin threads of those minor relationships. It is the
continuous repetition of these minor interactions which
builds and supports the great objectified structures; and
these primary processes which build society out of the immediate individual elements must therefore be investigated in a manner similar to that in which we investigate
the more complex processes and their objectified forms.

From this extension of the investigation to the minute
processes of socialization we may expect an advance in
our knowledge and understanding of the social life similar
to that made in physiology since the beginning of micros-
copy. Investigation before that time had been confined
to the large and separated organs. Since then the life-
process has appeared in its relation to its minute bearers,
the cells, and has been identified with the innumerable
and incessant reciprocities between them. The major organs, in which the life-bearers and their reciprocities have
assembled in special tissues and functions, would never
have made the unity of life intelligible if those countless
processes which play between the minutest elements had
not unmasked themselves as the real, the fundamental
life.[1]

[1] *Soz.*, pp. 18–21; *Soz. Diff.*, p. 16.

Sociology, then, will have to investigate the whole range of socializations from the most simple to the most complex, from the most fleeting to the most permanent. It will have to deal with all the relationships and interactions which constitute human association: with imitation, representation, the creation of parties, the formation of classes and secondary subdivisions, and the incorporation of social reciprocities in special structures. It will have to investigate specialized problems, such as the social relations of the non-partisan and the poor, the effects of numerical limitation on the form of the group, and the sociological significance of the *primus inter pares* and the *tertius gaudens*. It will have to examine the more complex phenomena, such as the intersection of social circles, and study the more intricate modifications of social forms due to local concentration or spatial dispersion of elements.

The task of sociology is to investigate the pure forms of socialization in abstraction from their material content, to give their psychological explanation, and to trace their historical development. Sociology is to determine what is really socialization in society, just as geometry determines what is really spatial extension in material objects. Both geometry and sociology resign to other sciences the investigation of the contents which manifest themselves in their respective forms and the examination of the totality of phenomena whose mere formal aspect they observe.[1]

The historical development of the forms of socialization does not, of course, occur in actuality in that clear-cut form nor in strict accordance with the sociological scheme of explanation, but always in devious courses and obscured by all sorts of collateral phenomena. The sociological type is always an abstraction, even if not different from that at the basis of every other science. The object

[1] *Soz.*, pp. 12–14.

of a special science seldom occurs in the purity and isolation in which it is scientifically treated. In reality it is always mixed and entangled with phenomena to which other sciences are devoted. Each special science treats an abstraction, and the case of sociology is not different.[1] That abstraction is the form of socialization. To describe the different types of social forms and to find the laws according to which the members of a group and the groups themselves interact, sociology may draw its material from other sciences. In so far it is an eclectic science, but it is not a synthetic science.[2]

Sociology is a special and a limited science. It is a special science, not because its object belongs with other objects under a higher general concept, as is the case for classical philology, but because it approaches an entire field of objects from a special point of view. It is differentiated from other social sciences, not by its object, but by the special viewpoint which guides the abstraction of its subject-matter from the social actuality.[3] It is neither a social philosophy, a philosophy of history, nor a synthesis of the social sciences. It is a special science with a well-defined field of investigation and a clearly formulated task: *the study of the forms of socialization.*

[1] "Superordination and Subordination," *A. J. S.*, II, 176–77, note.

[2] *Soz. Diff.*, pp. 2, 4.

[3] *Soz.*, p. 10.

CHAPTER III

SOCIOLOGY AS DISTINCT FROM THE SOCIAL SCIENCES AND SOCIAL PSYCHOLOGY

THE term "sociology" has sometimes been used for certain scientific inquiries which, although closely related to sociology, are none the less not identical with sociology. One of these is social psychology, the others are certain social sciences. In the latter case the confusion arose only if these social sciences, such as economics or political science, made use of the so-called sociological method. It is therefore necessary to define once more the study of sociology, but this time in relation to and in contrast with the social sciences on the one hand and social psychology on the other. The distinction will then be seen to lie in the fundamental category of cognition by means of which these sciences abstract their specific subject-matter from the socio-historical actuality.

The socio-historical actuality, society in the broader sense of the term, consists of the sum of all individuals concurring in reciprocal relations, together with all the interests which unite them. In other words, it consists of individuals who are socialized on the basis of certain interests or for specific purposes, together with these interests and purposes. The socio-historical actuality may therefore be regarded from three distinct points of view:

1. It may be viewed with reference to the individual existences which are the bearers of the social situation. The social situation is then viewed as the result of specific psychological contents in the composing individual elements.

2. It may be viewed with reference to the forms of the reciprocal relations between the individuals. The social situation is then viewed in its purely formal aspect as the result of specific forms of socialization.

3. It may be viewed with reference to the factual content. The social situation is then viewed in its purely factual aspect, that is, with reference to its economic, political, and legal aspect, or with reference to the state of the industrial arts, of science, and of art proper.

These three viewpoints get constantly entangled in the actual investigation of social situations, but they should be kept separate and distinct in a methodological inquiry. The function of these viewpoints is twofold. In the first place, they fulfil a methodological function. They indicate the three modes of approach to an understanding of the socio-historical actuality. But they also fulfil an epistemological function. The last two viewpoints function as categories of cognition by means of which sociology and the social sciences abstract their subject-matter from the socio-historical actuality. They are therefore immediately indicative of the difference between sociology and the social sciences. The first viewpoint does not function immediately as a category of cognition for any science. But a comparison between this viewpoint and the second is the starting-point for a further consideration which will yield the distinction between sociology and psychology.[1]

Society in the wider and larger sense, as content, is the subject-matter of the social sciences. Their object is everything which occurs with and in society, and its laws and history are their aim. Society as such, however, is not open to scientific inquiry, and there has therefore occurred a division of labor among different social sciences on the

---

[1] *Soz.*, p. 16. For the methodological function of the three viewpoints, see Book I, chapter v.

basis of a difference in factual content. Economics and church polity, the history of education and of morals, politics and theories of sexual relations, have divided the realm of the social phenomena into separate regions of research.

Sociology as a special science, however, rests on an entirely different abstraction from the social phenomena and results from viewing the socio-historical actuality from a quite different standpoint. While economics is distinguished from politics merely by the difference in content of the social phenomena which it investigates, sociology is distinguished from both by the fact that it treats the form of socialization and not its content. The social sciences find their subject-matter by drawing lines through the historical actuality which encircle similar interest contents. Sociology comes into existence by drawing a line which, by intersecting all those already drawn, detaches the pure fact of socialization from its connections with the various contents. It may be that the periphery of this range of problems temporarily or permanently comes into contact with other circles and that boundary lines are vague; but the center remains none the less fixed and determined. Social facts and psychological knowledge may both play a rôle in the explanation of the form of socialization. This does not prevent the sociological problem from being distinct from both the psychological and the social problem. Sociology is interested in society as form, while the social sciences are interested in society as content.[1]

The distinction between sociology and psychology is also based ultimately on a difference in the category of cognition by means of which phenomena are viewed. But the category of cognition for psychology is not the first viewpoint already mentioned. The subject-matter of psychology is not the content of consciousness, but the form

[1] *Soz.*, p. 9.

of the psychological occurrences, the laws of the psychological processes. Psychology and sociology are both sciences dealing with psychical phenomena, but the one deals with the form of the psychological process, the other with the form of the sociological process. The first deals with the process by means of which a psychological content arises, the second deals with the process by means of which this content creates a form of interaction. Psychology is interested in processes within individuals, sociology is interested in interactions and relations between individuals.

It would seem at first that the investigation of reciprocal relations between individuals, and especially of those which have not yet taken superindividual form, lies in the field of psychology, or at least in the field of social psychology. All social occurrences have their seat in the individual souls, and socialization is a psychological phenomenon. A causal understanding of any social occurrence would therefore be obtained if it could be deduced from psychological data according to psychological laws.

That part of the socio-historical occurrence which is within our means of comprehension is a psychical concatenation which we reconstruct by means of either intuitive or methodical psychology. Only by these means can we bring it to subjective plausibility, can we obtain a feeling of the psychical necessity of the occurrence. The occurrence would not be more intelligible than the merging of clouds or the entangling of the branches of trees if we did not recognize psychic motivations, feelings, thoughts, and needs, not merely as the bearers of these externalities, but as their essence. To that extent every history, every depicting of a social condition, is an application of psychological knowledge.

But it is of great methodological importance and immediately significant for the epistemological principle on which the humanistic studies rest that the scientific treatment of psychical facts is not necessarily psychology. Psychological processes have a definite content, but this content may be the subject-matter of a great many different sciences. The sciences of language, art, morals, and religion treat such content of psychological processes in abstraction from those processes.

There is only a difference in degree between the humanistic studies and the sciences of external nature. Even the latter deal in the last analysis with facts of the mental life, with occurrences within the mind. The discovery of an astronomical or chemical truth, or the mental reproduction of this truth, is an event of consciousness which a complete psychology might deduce from purely psychological conditions and developments. These sciences of external nature come into existence by choosing as their subject-matter, not the psychic processes, but the relations between their contents.

No actuality can be scientifically comprehended in its immediate totality. It must be viewed from a series of different standpoints and regarded as a multiplicity of mutually independent scientific contents. The fact that in the psychical occurrence process and content are a unitary totality does not abolish the methodological and epistemological requirement of differentiating between the form of the process on the one hand and the content of the process on the other hand. And this differentiation is not only required for those psychical occurrences whose contents synthesize in an independent, objective spatial world, but also for those occurrences whose contents do not build an independent spatial world. In the first case the differentiation would yield psychology and the sciences of external nature. In the second instance the differentiation yields psychology and the humanistic sciences.

Sociology is the result of a similar differentiation. The socialization of individuals is the result of psychological processes within these individuals. But sociology is not interested in these processes as such. It is interested in the content of these processes, but from a special point of view, namely, with reference to the resulting relations between the individuals. It views the psychological occurrences within the individuals in their synopsis, that is, as a unity; and its interest is in the resulting association. Its subject-matter is not those processes, but the forms of socialization which are the result of those processes.

With regard to the fact that the relation of *primus inter pares* tends to become a relation of superiority and subordination, the sociologist is interested, not in the primary psychological processes, but in questions such as the following: How do the various stages of "superordination and subordination" succeed one another? To what degree is subordination in one relationship compatible with equality in others? Beginning with what degree of superordination does the superiority wholly destroy the equality?

Sociology abstracts the sociological form from the psychological actualities which are its bearers in the same way as geometry abstracts the spatial form from the material substance. Just as the study of geometry remains separate from physics or chemistry, just so the study of sociology remains separate from psychology. The data of sociology are psychological occurrences whose immediate actuality presents itself first to the psychological categories. The latter, however, although indispensable for a rendering of the facts, remain outside the purpose of sociological investigation.[1]

This difference between sociology and psychology is the identical difference which exists between sociology and

[1] *Soz.*, pp. 21–24.

social psychology. The latter is nothing but a special branch of general psychology. It deals with the same subject-matter, namely, the forms of the psychological processes, and it is therefore not an independent science.

The idea of a special social psychology and the efforts to justify its existence as an independent science are mainly due to an insufficient analysis of certain complex problems. The result has been the postulation of an independent superindividual mind whose manifestations were to be investigated by social psychology. The objective psychical structures like law, religion, and morals, the unitary aspect of the results of collective activity, and the phenomena of crowd psychology have suggested the existence of a social consciousness, a spirit of the times, a group mind, or a national conscience as actually creative forces and independent entities. A further analysis will show, however, that the question regarding a psychical bearer of these psychical phenomena of a superindividual nature is wrongly formulated.

Laws, morals, and religion are products of mind, but their development extends far beyond anything contained in the individual mind, and in their entirety they are relatively independent of the individual's participation. The language forms, the legal and moral norms, the dogmatic content of religions have a validity and dignity independent of the individual applications. This validity, however, still differs from the superhistorical validity of the laws of nature or of logic. But this validity of their content is not a psychological occurrence which requires an empirical bearer. They are valid just as the Pythagorean theorem is valid, quite independently of the fact whether they are thought or conceived in the individual mind.

As an objective mental content, language, law, and morals are not of a psychological nature. Neither is the logical significance of a judgment something psychological, although only within and through a psychological process can it obtain reality in consciousness. As unities, therefore, they are conceptual unities, and, as such, they may be content for the individual consciousness, but they have no actual historical origin as unities. The psychological actuality creates only parts of them or carries them on or thinks of these contents as concepts. There is a psychological bearer of the totality only when they are conceived as content in the individual mind. The empirical origin of the single elements and forms of language and their practical application in individual cases is a problem of individual psychology. In this same field belongs the problem of the transmission of cultural elements or the effectiveness of law as a psychological element in the merchant, the criminal, and the judge.

In actuality, therefore, the origin is of an individual psychological nature, not of a superindividual psychological nature. But there is not merely a single origin. The formation and development result from the contributions of a plurality of individual minds interacting with one another. As entities they have no origin at all, but are merely a conceptual content.

Another similar suggestion about the existence of a superindividual mind arises from the fact that, in case of collective activity, not only the activity itself but also the result appears as a unity. When a crowd destroys a house or passes judgment, the sum of the individual actions appears as a single unitary occurrence, as the realization of a single concept. The unitary external occurrence resulting from manifold subjective mental occurrences is conceived as the result of a single mental process, that of the collective mind. The unity of the objective appearance is reflected in the assumed unity of its psychic cause, but in actuality the psychic motivation may have been a different one in each individual.

A third factor which seems to justify the existence of a separate social psychology over and against the individual psychology consists in the qualitative differences which exist between the feelings, actions, and ideas of individuals when in a crowd and when by themselves. The individual in a crowd seems to become a new entity, which differs qualitatively from the solitary person. But, in the last instance, one still deals with the behavior of individuals, simply in this case with the behavior of individuals who have become influenced by the fact that they are surrounded by others and who undergo modifications in their nervous, intellectual, and moral responses. If these modifications, mutually interacting, change all members of the group in a similar way, then the collective behavior will be different from the behavior of the single individual.

But that which is of a psychological nature in this behavior remains none the less of an individual psychological nature. The collective behavior is merely the synthesis of the individual actions. What are compared are two things under different conditions: on the one hand, that which is uninfluenced by others, and, on the other hand, that which is influenced by others. Both things, however, occur in the individual mind and take place in the individual consciousness. There is therefore no necessity for postulating for the one side of the comparison a superindividual mental entity.

As a problem of social psychology there remains then only the following: What modifications does the mental process of an individual undergo when it occurs under definite influences from the social environment? But this problem is a problem of general psychology and therefore of individual psychology. As a branch of general psychology, social psychology is related to it in the same way as physiological psychology. The latter investigates the way in which the psychic process is determined by its relation to the body, the former the way in which it is determined by its relations to other minds.[1]

Social psychology deals in the last instance with the same problem as psychology, namely, the form and the laws of the psychological processes in the individual mind. The distinction originally pointed out between sociology and psychology therefore also holds good for sociology and social psychology.

Thus the difference between psychology, sociology, and the social sciences rests on the distinction between three categories of cognition and results from the different standpoints from which the socio-historical actuality may be viewed. Sociology is a different science, separate and distinct from psychology and its branch, social psychology, on the one hand, and from the social sciences on the other.

[1] *Soz.*, pp. 557–61.

CHAPTER IV

SOCIOLOGY AS DISTINCT FROM
SOCIAL PHILOSOPHY

THE term "sociology" has often been used for inquiries regarding the socio-historical actuality which are in the last analysis of a philosophical nature. It becomes necessary, therefore, to distinguish between the science of sociology on the one hand and social philosophy on the other. The word "sociology" does not stand for a special science but simply for a branch of philosophy as long as it is merely used for this latter discipline, and its legitimation as a science demands, therefore, a clear differentiation.

Social philosophy is in essence the same as and belongs to philosophy. It is the product of the application of the specific philosophic thought form to the subject-matter of society. It results from a specific functional relationship between the subject and the socio-historical actuality which differs from that functional relationship which produces scientific knowledge. It is the outcome of a way of dealing with the phenomenological world which is different from the way in which science deals with that same world. It results from the application of the philosophic method, and for that reason it should be classed with philosophy rather than with the social sciences or sociology. The latter forms of inquiry, although dealing with the same subject-matter, employ a wholly different method. The distinction between science and philosophy is therefore also the criterion for distinguishing between the social sciences and sociology on the one hand and social philosophy on the other.[1]

Science results from a definite mental attitude toward the world, from specific needs and demands. What these needs and demands are for each particular science is a subject of special investigation. Again, scientific knowledge, because it is based on immediate relations between the subject and the external world, must of necessity be limited in scope. For that reason every exact science which aims at immediate comprehension of experience becomes flanked by two fields of inquiry of a philosophic nature. In those fields the thought form changes from the exact scientific to the philosophical. Each science is thus embraced by two philosophic regions, an epistemology and a metaphysics. The one is interested in the science as function, as mental process; the other is interested in its content. The first is interested in the elementary concepts and the basic assumptions and presuppositions of the particular investigation. It deals with problems which cannot be settled within the science, since they refer to the foundation on which the actual investigation rests. In the second region the particular investigation is brought to completion and related to questions and concepts which have no place within the field of immediate experience and scientific knowledge. The science of sociology and the other social sciences are therefore flanked in a similar manner by two regions of philosophic thought. The first investigates the presuppositions of these inquiries, and the second carries them to completion.[2]

The epistemology of sociology or of any other social science is the inquiry into the basic presuppositions of the

---

[1] For the difference between science and philosophy, see General Introduction.

[2] *Soz.*, pp. 25–26; *Phil. des Geldes*, p. v.

scientific investigation which cannot be dealt with within the actual science itself. It deals with the a priori elements, not of knowledge in general, that being the task of general epistemology, but of social or sociological knowledge. Sociology, like other social sciences, could not proceed to actual investigation and could not state its findings in an intelligible manner if certain concepts, axioms, and procedures were not accepted without further discussion. As a science it is uncritical about these presuppositions and leaves their investigation to philosophy.

In the case of sociology, the main epistemological problem is the problem of the prerequisites of socialization. This is not in a historical sense, but in a logical and a psychological sense. The problem is not to describe the actual formation of a special society or to indicate the physical and anthropological conditions which would enable a society to be formed; nor is it a question of indicating the specific impulses which move individuals to reciprocal action. The question is rather: If such individuals exist, what are the conditioning qualities of their consciousness which enable them to be social beings? In the elements in and for themselves, society does not yet exist. In the forms of the interrelations between them, society has already become actual. What, then, are these subjective and basic prerequisites which enable individuals to become socialized and thereby to create society? What are the a priori factors which form and make possible the empirical structure of the individual in so far as he is a social being? Apart from the empirical forms of socialization which fall under the general concept "society," how is society as such possible, as an objective form of subjective minds?[1]

The metaphysics of sociology and the social sciences does not inquire into the prerequisites of society, but takes

[1] *Soz.*, pp. 26–27. See Book I, chapter v.

society for granted. In this field two different kinds of problems are dealt with, although in actual treatment they are usually not kept separate and distinct.

Dissatisfaction with the fragmentary character of scientific knowledge and the early exhaustion of the actually demonstrable data and the series of provable facts lead to an attempt at completion by means of speculation. Speculation is also the means by which the disconnected and incoherent fields of empirical knowledge are combined into a unitary synthesis. In this field the results of the different social sciences are correlated with the results of other sciences. In this field the metaphysical need for a unitary picture of the social manifoldness is satisfied by synthesizing the fragmentary results of the empirical inquiries or by interpreting a whole range of phenomena in terms of a selected phenomenon as its symbol and essence.[1]

Apart from this metaphysical inquiry which is directed toward the degree of knowledge, there is a second metaphysical inquiry which deals with existence in a different dimension. It deals with problems and questions regarding the meaning, the purpose, the absolute substance, and the religious significance of social life. It results from a spiritual attitude which asks questions like the following: Is society the goal and the purpose of individual existence or a means for the enrichment of individual life? Is it, perhaps, instead of being a means, an obstruction to the realization of individual perfection? Is the value of society to be found in its functional life, in the formation of an objective spirit, or in the ethical qualities which it calls forth in the individual?

These questions cannot be answered by means of ascertaining facts. They aim at a valuation of observed facts and at the construction of an inclusive view out of the un-

[1] For an interpretation of modern society in terms of money as its symbol and essential category, see Book III.

related fragments of scientific knowledge of the social actuality. They involve interpretations of a philosophical nature and may therefore be answered in many different ways. They may be based on either idealistic or realistic, intellectualistic or volitional, absolutistic or relativistic systems of philosophy, and this will largely determine their form.

The treatment of these problems has sometimes been called sociology. But it does not possess that categorical independence, that unique relationship between subject-matter and method, which would justify a conception of that treatment as a special science. All these questions are merely philosophical questions. That they have society for their object signifies only the extension of an already existing type of inquiry to a further territory. Whether philosophy be called a science or not, the philosophy of society has no right to withdraw itself from the advantages and disadvantages which result from its intimate relation to general philosophy.

The philosophic treatment of social phenomena may be regarded as a preliminary to an exact scientific treatment, as a means of obtaining a first bird's-eye view of the socio-historical actuality. In that case it is bound to be succeeded by an exact treatment on the part of the different social sciences and sociology. But the philosophic treatment of social phenomena may also be regarded as an independent and self-sufficient form of inquiry, as a metaphysics proper. In that case it will have a value in and for itself which is entirely independent of its relations to exact knowledge. As metaphysics proper, aiming at the completion of knowledge and a valuation of the data of experience, it does in no way compete with empiricism, because it then results from a different viewpoint and serves an entirely different purpose. In neither case is it identical with the social sciences or with sociology.[1]

[1] *Soz.*, pp. 25–26; *Grundfr. der Soz.*, p. 33; *Phil. des Geldes*, Introd.

CHAPTER V

SOCIOLOGY AS DISTINCT FROM THE PHILOSOPHY OF HISTORY AND THE SEARCH FOR HISTORICAL LAWS

THE general remarks made in the preceding chapter regarding the difference between sociology and social philosophy also apply to the difference between sociology and the philosophy of history.[1] The philosophy of history also embraces two fields of philosophic inquiry which flank the field of exact historical inquiry. The first is the epistemology of history, the second the metaphysics of history.

The epistemology of history is the inquiry into the thought forms which create "history" out of the available data of the historical actuality. It investigates the axioms, the presuppositions, and the procedures of historiography. It asks about the a priori elements of historical knowledge, about the categories that create the theoretic structure called history out of the data of the immediate historical actuality.

Whether the historical account is formulated in terms of a narrative or in terms of so-called historical laws, in neither case does it give a pure reproduction of the actual historical development as it really occurred. The historical account of a social development is always an interpretation.

---

[1] As the term "sociology" has been applied to certain types of philosophies of history ever since Comte, it is necessary to treat the methodological differences somewhat more extensively than those of sociology and social philosophy.

If it is formulated in terms of a narrative, it is usually an interpretation of occurrences in terms of volition and motives, either personal or collective. In that case the epistemological inquiry will be mainly an inquiry into the psychological presuppositions. If it is formulated in terms of historical laws, it is usually an interpretation in terms of an inherent dialectic of social institutions and sociological structures. In that case these structures and institutions are conceived as purely factual potencies. They are supposed to change their forms independently of the conscious volition of their actual bearers. These may stimulate or retard the movement, but they cannot prevent it or bring it about. The explanatory causes are then assumed to lie, not in the volition of individuals, but in the inherent logic of these forms and institutions, which expresses itself with mechanical necessity. Here motive and volition, either personal or collective, are left outside of the interpretation, and the epistemological inquiry will therefore be mainly concerned with the a priori categories which make possible a reading of historical laws into successive historical phenomena. Most histories use both forms of interpretation, and the epistemological inquiry into their underlying assumptions will therefore deal with both types of presuppositions.[1]

The metaphysics of history is directed, on the one hand, toward the completion of knowledge and, on the other hand, toward the valuation of its content. It asks whether the stages of social evolution are analogous to the stages of cosmic evolution in a way which suggests a single formula. But, apart from existential judgments, it also asks for value judgments. It questions whether each single historical fact and occurrence has a value in and for itself or only in relation to the whole historical movement. It asks

[1] *Probl. der Gesch.*, chap. i, pp. 1–74.

whether the historical movement is a self-sufficient unity or of value and significance only in relation to cosmic movements. It deals with the transcendental purpose and the transcendental reality which lie behind the historical actuality as the noumena behind the phenomena.

These and similar questions may leave the historical investigation itself largely untouched. They can be answered differently for the same historical facts. The acceptance of a personal God who guides the historical development for a purpose unknown or revealed would only change the causal into a teleological series without changing its content or the relations between its elements. The metaphysics of history takes the theoretic historical knowledge for granted. In so far as it deals with value judgments it is a non-theoretic accentuation of the historical series crystallized into a special structure.[1]

Historical Inquiry and the Search for Historical Laws

The essential characteristic of the exact historical inquiry is an interest in the historical actuality as such directed toward the factualness of its content and free from all metaphysical sublimation.

But the distinction between the exact and the metaphysical thought form, which are conceived as separate and distinct concepts in a methodological inquiry, is not maintained in the actual historical investigation. Historical interpretations, especially those which are formulated in terms of historical laws, are the result of both forms of inquiry. The reason for this is that an inquiry into the existence of historical laws is guided by a thought form which bears a much closer resemblance to philosophic speculation than to the method of exact science.

[1] *Probl. der Gesch.*, pp. 126–32.

The historical account is not only the result of the functioning of certain a priori categories which make history as such, as a theoretical structure, possible, but also of the functioning of certain a priori judgments about the significance and importance of the elements of history. The presuppositions of historical investigation are not only certain a priori categories of an epistemological character, but also certain existential judgments and value judgments of a metaphysical nature. These reflections which the non-theoretic and speculative interest projects into the historical data are elements of the metaphysics of history. The latter is orientated in a direction different from that of the exact historical inquiry, which aims at a purely theoretic picture of the historical actuality free from all metaphysical sublimation. But speculation about history, the metaphysics of history, is in practice usually not much more than a combination and co-ordination into one unitary system of the assumptions and presuppositions already at work within the historical inquiry. Therefore, while speculation about nature remains entirely outside of the field of the natural sciences, speculation about history becomes interwoven with historical inquiry. It is manifest both in the historical narrative and in the interpretation in terms of historical laws.

This analogy between the historical inquiry directed toward the finding of historical laws and philosophical speculation does not signify that history has become a part of philosophy. It merely shows that similar requirements and categories of cognition bring the material of both fields of inquiry into similar form. The conceptual forms which history creates, the historical laws, are similar to those of philosophic speculation, but they are not philosophic concepts.[1]

[1] *Ibid.*, pp. 135–55, 121–24.

That the term "historical law" has a very different meaning from that of natural law is evident. It is merely a formulation for the relation between conceptual unities treated as a single phenomenon without any regard for the actually effective forces within the composing elements. Historical laws are special laws, laws for occurrences within special fields which are conceived as separate from and independent of the single elements on the one hand and the wider cosmic circle on the other. They result from an extreme simplification of very complex material on the basis of presuppositions which imply a social and historical realism, a conception of certain phases of social and historical life as unities of independent reality.

Appearances of considerable internal difference are compared and treated as if they were identical. The state, religion, culture, the forms of production, the position of women, and innumerable other concepts of identical logical content are observed in certain relations which, because they are repeated, are considered inevitable. But no two of these cases are actually identical. The law which is deduced from the observation of one situation and its results is in reality valid for only that one case. Without an investigation into the single elements, we can never be sure that the actual forces do not lie just in those factors in which the cases differ, and we can never be certain that the differences are not more fundamental than the similarities.

The observed correlation between conceptual unities which result from a synthetic view of pluralities of coexistent phenomena does not yield any information regarding the actually effective elements and gives no guaranty of repetition. The historical law does not go down to primary forces; and this is even more evident in those laws which profess to explain the historical development of social in-

stitutions and of specific aspects of social life in terms of
the immediate factors only, such as the historical laws
which explain the development of the state and the forms
of production solely in terms of political and economic
factors.

It has been formulated as a law that the history of
every political unit commences with the political and civil
liberty of a few, spreads from these to the many and finally
to all, and then reverts back to the few and finally to a
single despot. But the fact that the few have liberty cannot be the cause of the fact that the many obtain it. This
conceptual formulation of the historical sequence is therefore not concerned with the inner causal connection of the
successive phenomena. The same holds good for the so-
called law of economic development. It explains nothing
to say that the forces of production in each period outgrow
the forms of production and finally break through them
and create new ones. The actual forces, which according
to this formulation change slavery into serfdom and serfdom into a wage system, are not referred to. It would be
impossible to picture with the help of this law the production form of the next stage. A real natural law would make
it possible to do this. That one succeeds the other is the result of a great many laws, but is not a law in itself.

Historical laws of this kind merely give the relation in
time of complex appearances on the surface of life, not the
relation between primary elements and their actual forces.
Each element within the complex is undoubtedly fully determined by and causally related to some preceding element, but the complex as a whole is not causally determined by the preceding complex in the same sense.

What the concept of a law of historical growth actually
stands for may be indicated by a comparison with botan-
ical growth. The laws of plant physiology which are effec-

tive in palm trees build these palm trees into characteristic forms which are different from those of other trees, yet one does not speak of the specific laws of palm growth. Historical material develops into specific forms in a similar fashion, but there are no specific laws of historical growth.

There is not a second law of a higher order above the laws of the first order which regulate the movements of the primary elements. The only realities in the development of a historical complex are the movements of the primary elements and the laws that regulate these movements. If the sum of these movements is viewed as a synthetic unity, we cannot claim a new law for that unity as an independent complex, because every composing movement is already determined by and related to its cause.[1]

Historical laws, therefore, are related to the actually effective laws as philosophic knowledge is related to exact knowledge. They are formulations for occurrences and relationships which resemble philosophic speculations, and, like the latter, they may be regarded either as forerunners of exact knowledge, as preliminary formulations, or as satisfactory projections of the actuality on a distinct and different plane. Viewed as the precursors of exact knowledge, they have a value only in relation to exact science. Viewed as satisfactory projections of the actuality, they have a value in and for themselves independent of any correspondence to objective reality.

Considered as anticipations of the exact knowledge of the historical occurrence, the historical laws are but the first steps. We are forced to stop first at certain regularities on the surface of historical life until the laws which describe the actual relations between the smallest elements are known. Without further investigation these regularities are formulated in abstract rules which in a sense explain

[1] *Probl. der Gesch.*, pp. 77–85.

nothing but give none the less a first orientation in the manifoldness of the historical occurrences. But an inquiry aiming at exact knowledge cannot be satisfied with a correlation between phenomenological complexes formulated in terms of a historical law. It cannot accept the presupposition of a special momentum for a particular social institution or for a special aspect of social life, nor can it assume a unitary force for those institutions which is different from and independent of the sum of the forces of its elements. It has to continue its process of analysis and differentiation of phenomena until it approaches the actually effective laws of the single elements. It has to explode the artificial unity of the complex, restore the independent efficacy of the elements within the complex, and take cognizance of the efficacy of elements outside of the complex.

In this approach toward the actually effective forces and factors, the specific concept of "historical law" will finally dissolve. This is only natural. The formulation for relations between occurrences within a special field must lose all validity when it becomes recognized that this special field is in actuality not separate from and independent of the composing factors within and the cosmic circle without. Human history does not occur as a separate, self-contained chapter of which only the beginning and end are influenced by cosmic forces. It develops in continual endosmose and exosmose with these cosmic forces. It is continually influenced by forces from the outside which cannot be determined from preceding history, and, as these forces and factors are not constant, the so-called historical law cannot give an adequate explanation of historical development. This inadequacy of the historical law is most clearly visible in the laws of the development of the special fields of socio-historical life.

A history of art which aims at a full and fundamental understanding of phenomena cannot hope to develop the artistic form out of the preceding form alone. Social relations, religion, intellectual levels, individual predilections would all have to be taken into consideration. It is the same way with the historical development of economic life. The phenomena observed in sequence may be purely economic, but the energies and factors which bring about the change from one form of production to the next are by no means purely economic. Personal, ethical, cultural, and physical factors all contribute in shaping the succeeding stage. The so-called materialistic interpretation of history is but an exaggerated form of this tendency to view economic situations as a unilateral causal series. Not only is the fact ignored that each succeeding economic occurrence is influenced by innumerable non-economic factors, but the self-sufficiency of the economic series and its freedom from the others is now conceived as a mastery over the others. The totality of historical development is now traced back to this series as its cause.[1]

The approach and approximation to exact knowledge of the actual factors and forces by means of the preliminary formulations in terms of historical laws has therefore an internal boundary. A further differentiation finally dissolves the concept of historical law and leaves nothing but the investigation of the historical fact and the timeless law. By the time the historical inquiry has become exact, its task is merely to determine the content of the historical actuality, which is the starting-point of all knowledge and without which no knowledge is possible.

The difference between the exact historical and the exact scientific inquiry lies in the fact that the first is interested in the individual occurrence and the latter in the law. Both are needed, because the knowledge of a timeless

[1] *Probl. der Gesch.*, pp. 94–101.

correlation between two elements is not a knowledge of their actual existence. The timeless relation which binds B to A is incapable of determining that A exists. To ascertain that A exists, to ascertain the individual case, which determines through its own qualities what laws apply to it, is the task of history. Science asks for the law, history asks for the specific instance of the law, for the specific case— and not as a means of reaching inductively a knowledge of the law, but as a final goal.[1]

But the historical laws may also be regarded as satisfactory projections of the actuality on a different mental plane. In that case the independent epistemological requirements really demand that the original syntheses and collective structures in which the actuality seems to shape itself shall be treated as unities without further analysis. From the point of view of exact science, they are not unities. But as they are then used for the purpose of historical knowledge and not for the purpose of exact knowledge, there is no valid objection. History, then, does not go down to elements, is not directed toward basic occurrences and individual forces. Its material is different and lies in a different mental plane.

A great many historical laws may be viewed as tentative formulations for relations to be further determined by natural laws. Examples of these are the following: that historical evolution tends toward an ever increasing differentiation of individuals or an ever narrowing collectivism, that the moral culture develops in a fixed relation with the intellectual culture or independently of it, and that social liberty is accompanied by the building of an objective spirit and a treasure of superpersonal cultural products. But, on the other hand, on the plane of conceptual syntheses they are in and for themselves satisfactory projections of actu-

[1] *Ibid.*, p. 147.

ality. In that case the demand for knowledge asks a type of question which can be answered in terms of such abstract and phenomenological categories. The answer does not have to be more exact and does not have to go down to single factors and causes. It may be changed if it is found to be erroneous, but it will then be replaced by an answer which consists merely of other contents of knowledge in a similar form. The new answer will remain methodologically at the same distance from causality as an ideal of exact science as the answer which it replaced.

History, whether in the form of a narrative or in the form of historical laws, builds out of that which is given of the historical actuality a theoretic structure on the basis of categories which have no place in an investigation which aims at exact knowledge. But these categories spring from fully autonomous needs of organization and create a self-sufficient picture of the historical actuality. That this picture is not a pure reproduction of the actuality is not a shortcoming, but its essence. It has dimensions and a style of its own which bear no relation to the requirements for a scientific picture of the socio-historical actuality.[1]

From the foregoing considerations it may be seen that neither the philosophy of history nor the search for historical laws is identical and synonymous with sociology. Whether one considers the historical law as a forerunner of exact knowledge or as a self-sufficient interpretation of historical development does not influence the fact that it does not reach objective validity.

Sociology is an exact science and has to apply the method of science. The philosophy of history and the search for historical laws are forms of inquiry which result from different and independent needs of cognition and produce a type of knowledge that is speculative and not exact.

[1] *Probl. der Gesch.*, pp. 108-20.

CHAPTER VI

THE METHOD AND TECHNIQUE
OF FORMAL SOCIOLOGY

AS WAS mentioned in chapter iii, the socio-historical actuality, society as content, may be regarded from three distinct viewpoints. The social sciences have divided society into different fields on the basis of a differentiation in content, and within these special fields there is therefore also room for three points of view. This may be illustrated by a social situation which is of interest to an economist—that, for instance, in which a number of men who have combined on the basis of a common interest refuse to work any longer for another number of men who have also combined. An analysis of this social situation from the three points of view will yield the following:

1. With reference to the individual bearers, it will yield certain specific motives and emotions bringing the individuals into the situation described.

2. With reference to the formal aspect of the reciprocities, it will yield two specific forms of association in conflict and opposition.

3. With reference to its factual aspect, it will yield a labor union on strike in conflict with an employers' association.

The importance of these three viewpoints for an epistemological inquiry has been referred to in chapter iii. What is of importance here is their methodological significance. The three viewpoints are three modes of approach toward an understanding of the actuality. The fact that each regards merely an abstraction from the actuality im-

plies that no single one of them by itself alone can lead to
a fundamental understanding of this social actuality. Any
one science resulting from these viewpoints cannot, in and
for itself, explain society. When the object is to understand the social actuality, the three viewpoints are mutually supporting and complementary to one another. They
are not self-sufficient. A fundamental understanding of
the actuality requires the application of all three modes of
approach.

The first category of cognition regards the social content as the product of processes in the individual consciousness of the elements. It aims at a psychological explanation of that content. In case of an economic content, it
would search for the impulses, desires, aims, and purposes
which lead men to economic activity.

The second viewpoint regards society with reference to
the interrelations and interactions between individuals.
It views the social content as the product of the socialized
group of individuals. It leads to an investigation of the social products apart from the individual contributions and
the objective factual significance. This mode of approach
might be called the sociological method.

The third category of cognition regards the social content, not as a product of individual contributions nor as a
product of the socialized group, but with reference to its
objective factual aspect.

All social activity which manifests itself in certain material must adapt itself to the laws and inherent characteristics of that material. The forms of political organization and economic production, the law, the arts, and language have laws and a logical development of their own.
It is through these inherent characteristics that they bind
the social forces within certain limits and guide them in
certain directions. Society, like the architect, is limited by

the character of the building-material. This has in and for itself a significance and value which are apart from all individual or social life and which require a special investigation. This factualness of the social content is, of course, in relation to the full actuality, also a mere abstraction. The economic and political contents do not develop through their own logic alone, but through the totality of mental and historical forces.

The social sciences in the usual sense of the term aim at the investigation of this factualness of the social content. The social actuality cannot be grasped in its immediate totality. It can only be made intelligible when resolved through abstractions into special fields of scientific investigation. There is therefore no science of society, but only a series of social sciences, just as there is no science of nature, but only a series of natural sciences.[1]

The dependence of our thinking on two mutually supporting thought forms, already referred to in the Introduction, becomes again manifest in the special field of the social sciences. A complete understanding of the factual objectivity of social situations can be reached only by an application of both the historical method and the method aiming at general laws. It is to be understood both in its genetic aspect, as a phase in a historical development, and in its timeless aspect. The first is to be obtained by studying it as a development from the preceding situation. The latter is to be obtained by a comparison with all similar situations independent of time and place.

The political or economic aspect of the present situation can be understood only on the basis of a knowledge and understanding of the past. The past, however, is intelligible only through our experience of the present. An economic occurrence can be explained only on the basis

[1] *Grundfr. der Soz.*, pp. 24–26.

of a specific historical-psychical constellation. But this deduction is an explanation only if we assume definite fixed correlations. We could never deduce a historical development if we did not assume above the individual case general relations, permanent tendencies, and regular correlations. Without these assumptions the totality would fall to pieces into a series of atomic occurrences. But these general laws which enable us to relate the situation or occurrence to the determining factors and conditions are in themselves the product of historical combinations. Forces and occurrences in the past have brought the things around us into forms and relationships which now appear as of general and superhistorical validity. It is because we consider them as of superhistorical validity that we are able to view the historical appearances of later date as special illustrations of general laws. Each method must therefore search for a justification in the other at every point of its application. Only through the reciprocal relation between the two can we hope to obtain an understanding of the objective actuality.[1]

A fundamental understanding of the economic or political aspect of a social situation would therefore require a psychological, a sociological, and a factual understanding, the latter to be obtained by the alternative application of the historical and the general inductive method.

The aim of sociology is an understanding of the processes of socialization. In this case the second category of cognition loses its methodological significance. The phenomena co-ordinated by means of this viewpoint have now become the central problem. The other two categories of cognition, however, maintain their methodological function. The process of socialization can still be regarded from these two viewpoints. It may be viewed as the product of

[1] *Phil. des Geldes*, p. 79.

processes in the individual consciousness of the elements. This view will result in an investigation which will yield the psychological explanation of the process of socialization. On the other hand, it may also be regarded with reference to what might be called its factual aspect. This view will result in an investigation which will yield the identification of the different forms of socialization and their inherent laws and characteristics. The first asks how the specific socialization comes into existence and how it is continued as the product of individual psychical processes. The latter asks: What are the characteristics of its form, and what is its inherent logical development as independent of the individual contributions? This latter question regarding the forms of the socialization will have to be answered in a fashion similar to that in which we answer the question regarding the factualness of the social content in the social sciences. It requires an alternating application of the general and the historical method. The first, which aims at the determination of timeless uniformities, is purely inductive. It finds its data in all countries, in all ages, and combined with all kinds of social contents. The latter, which is purely historical, investigates the development of the different forms of socialization.

A sociology which aims at a fundamental understanding of the processes of socialization must therefore find the psychological explanation and determine the general laws and the historical development of the different forms of socialization.

To illustrate the task of sociology with reference to a concrete example, we may formulate some of the fundamental questions which it would have to answer about competition.

Competition is found in countless varieties in the most varied connections—in politics and in economic management, in the history of religions and in that of art. The first point to be determined, therefore, is what competition means as a pure form of human behavior, what kind of relationship between individuals it really is. But, apart from this, sociology must be able to answer the following questions: Under what circumstances does it come into existence? How does it develop? What modifications does it undergo through the peculiar character of its object? Through what contemporary formal or material delimitations of society is it intensified or retarded? How does competition between individuals differ from that between groups?

The method of sociology is therefore like the method of the social sciences, but applied to a field of investigation which is obtained by abstracting the forms of socialization from the total social actuality. It is because this abstraction must precede that in the application of the method there arise difficulties of technique. There is no unquestioned technique available by which this process of abstraction can be guided and the fundamental sociological concept applied. The technique of the investigation is therefore not free from intuitive and subjective aspects.

The methodological necessity for keeping the three aspects of the social phenomena separate and distinct is crossed by the difficulty of maintaining the series independent of one another and by a desire for a composite picture of the actuality which shall harmonize all three. Some problems will seem to belong now in one category and now in another, and even when they are definitely recognized as belonging to the one or the other, the complete abstraction is perhaps never possible. Poverty may be regarded merely as a material condition of certain separate individual existences, but it may also be regarded as a sociological phenomenon. It may be viewed as the result of certain formal relations within the group resulting from general dislocations occurring in the contacts of human beings.

The difficulty involved in the abstraction may be seen from the following illustration. Toward the end of the Middle Ages certain guild masters were forced through an extension of their trade relations to new means of obtaining material and new ways of attracting customers which were inconsistent with the older guild principles. The ancient tradition that all masters should have a similar business organization was no longer followed, and they sought to place themselves outside of the narrow unity. With regard to the purely sociological form abstracted from the special content, this signifies that an expansion of the circle with which the individual is connected goes hand in hand with a more pronounced expression of individual peculiarity and a greater personal freedom. There is, however, no absolutely effective method for wringing this sociological meaning from the complex phenomena. The questions asked are: What purely sociological configurations are contained in the historical occurrence? What special interactions between individuals are involved, abstracted from the interests and impulses and from the factual conditions? Not only are these questions answerable in various ways in a given case, but the historical facts within which the actual sociological form is realized must be cited in their factual totality. There is no definite guide for the decomposition of the actuality into form and substance. Until the technique of this decomposition can be formulated in precise concepts, a certain amount of intuitive procedure will therefore be inevitable.[1]

It would seem that therein lies the fundamental difficulty. This difficulty is, however, not insurmountable. The natural sciences did not start with a perfect technique,

[1] *Soz.*, pp. 13–16.

and there is no reason to believe that sociology will not perfect its technique as it grows. Besides, in dealing with the great objectified social structures there is less chance for a purely subjective treatment in the abstraction of the form. Also, where this danger is greatest, namely, in the treatment of the minute processes of socialization, there is a safeguard in the great number of data on which the induction may be based.

The complexity of social life and the relative crudeness of the technique of sociology prevent in the present stage a fundamental clarity regarding its basic questions and a perfect validity of its answers. But in many fields of scientific investigation, the so-called foundations are less secure than the superstructure erected upon them. Scientific procedure, especially in new fields, can scarcely dispense with a certain amount of intuitive performance. Only subsequently do we become fully conscious of its motives and norms and can we subject them to a conceptual criticism. Scientific labor will, of course, never be satisfied with a vague and intuitive treatment of details, but science would be doomed to sterility in new fields if it had to wait for a completely formulated methodology and technique.[1]

[1] *Soz.*, p. 97.

CHAPTER VII

THE PREREQUISITES OF
SOCIALIZATION

AS WAS mentioned in chapter iii, sociology as an exact science is flanked on one side by a field of philosophic inquiry in which the basic assumptions and fundamental concepts of the science have to be investigated. The study of the actual forms of socialization has to be preceded by a determination of the ideal logical presuppositions of socialization on the basis of a logical analysis of the elements of experience. This investigation must answer the question as to how society is possible in the same way as Kant answered the question as to how nature is possible. But the two questions have a very different methodological significance.

Nature is a subjective synthesis, existing only in the mind of the observer and resulting from categories of thought and perception with which the subject shapes the disconnected elements of immediate experience into a unity. Society, however, is an objective unity, resulting immediately from the functional psychical occurrences within the composing elements and realized independently and outside of any observer. The society may of course be observed, but this process in the consciousness of a subject neither conditions nor contributes to the socialization. Socialization, the growing into a unity, is immediately the result of the mental activities of the entities involved. Each of the elements performs the function which, with regard to external nature, is performed by the mind of the observer. Society is a psychical process, and the conscious-

ness of constituting with others a unity is the only unity
in question. The consciousness of socialization is immediately its vehicle and inner significance, not in the sense
of a consciousness of constituting society in the abstract,
but in the sense of an awareness of the innumerable actual
relationships and a feeling and knowledge of influencing
and being influenced by others. The question as to how
society is possible is therefore a question as to the conditions that must be fulfilled to enable the procedures in the
individual consciousness to be processes of socialization.

To a certain extent that problem is the problem of
sociology. It searches out the processes, occurring in the
last analysis in individuals, which condition the fact of
their socialization. These procedures are not conceived as
temporally antecedent to and causing the socialization,
but as partial processes which in their synthesis are called
socialization. But there the method is inductive and the
emphasis lies on the synthesis and its form. Here the question must be understood in a more fundamental sense.
The problem is: What lies universally and a priori at the
basis of society, what presuppositions must be operative,
what prerequisites fulfilled, in order that concrete processes in the individual consciousness may actually be processes of socialization? What elements must be contained
in them in order that they may create a social unity out of
individual elements? This problem may be called the fundamental epistemological problem of sociology.

The aprioristic conditions which make society possible
cannot be indicated by single terms like the Kantian categories. They must be described somewhat in detail.
Three sociological a priori conditions will be enumerated
by way of illustration, but there are probably a great many
others.

The first might be roughly indicated as resulting from a

peculiar distortion in the ideas and representations which individuals have of one another. The pictures which human beings form of one another are not the result of pure sense impressions, but modifications of the actuality. In the first place, there is a tendency toward generalization which makes us see another as a type. We think of a man, not primarily in terms of his individuality, but in terms of a group or a class, in terms of a category which does not fully cover his identity and with which he is not fully identical. We know a man, not in his pure individuality, but as exalted or degraded by the general type under which we subsume him. Even of his purely individual side we form a picture which is not identical with the actuality, but rather with what he would be were he completely his ideal self. We create out of fragmentary data about his personality the complete picture of a fully realized individuality.

This tendency operates within the already existing society as the a priori of further associations and socializations between individuals. Within certain social spheres, classes, or groups, individuals view one another, not from a purely empirical standpoint, but on the basis of the a priori that the fact of belonging to a certain group gives the individual definite mental characteristics. In the circle of scholars, officers, church members, civil servants, and members of families, each individual regards the other under the natural presupposition that he is a member of the group. We see the individual, not simply as an individual, but as a colleague, a comrade, or a fellow-partisan, as an inhabitant of the same specific world as ourselves. The same thing occurs in the relation between individuals of different groups. The civilian who meets an officer cannot divest himself of the thought that the officer is a military man, and views him in that light. These unavoidable, quite automatic presuppositions are the means by which the individual obtains in the mental picture of the other that quality and form which make the social relation possible. They permit the beginning of the socialization.

Owing to these tendencies toward social generalization, it becomes impossible within a differentiated society to discover the true individuality. They interfere with the ideal cognition of the actual individual, but they are the conditions which make social relations possible. In this they bear a resemblance to the Kantian categories, which reshape and transform the immediate data of experience, but none the less make the given world intelligible.[1]

Another presupposition which determines the way in which individuals view one another might be formulated as the apparently trivial theorem that each element of a group is not only part of the group, but, besides that, something else. This fact becomes operative as a social a priori in this form, that it gives to that part of the individual which does not enter into the social relation a positive significance for that relation. There are certain types whose sociological significance, even in their germ and nature, is determined by the fact that they are in some way shut out from the group for which their existence is significant. Instances of this are the case of the stranger, the enemy, the criminal, and even the pauper. But this form applies, not merely to the case of such general characters, but, in numerous modifications, to every individual existence. The whole relation between individuals would be different if each confronted the other only with that part of himself which is taken up by the interrelation. The officer is more than just an officer, the civilian more than just a civilian, and that other non-social part of the personality interpenetrates the picture we form of him as an officer or civilian.

[1] *Soz.*, pp. 31–35.

Social situations, professions, and classes might be classified and distinguished according to the smaller or larger part of the personality which remains outside of the social relation. There is on the one hand the Catholic priest, whose ecclesiastical function completely covers and absorbs his individual existence, and on the other hand the objective, impersonal function of the producer and distributor in the modern economic system. The knowledge that the social activity is something completely differentiated from the rest of the individual has even in this marginal case a positive influence on the attitude which people assume toward him and he toward them. An a priori of empirical social life is therefore that life is not entirely social.[1]

But the individual's existence is not only in subdivision of its content partially social and partially individual, but also as a whole that existence may be viewed on the one hand as a social existence and on the other as a completely individual existence. The social structure is composed of beings which are at the same time inside and outside of it. Latently or openly, there exists between the individuals and their socializations a relation like that between two parties. This relationship exists, moreover, not only between the individuals and specific forms of socialization, but also between the individuals and society at large. We know ourselves to be members and products of society, and we realize that our life-process is intimately interwoven with that of society. Yet, however completely we may trace its content from social antecedents and reciprocities, it still remains capable of consideration under the category of the individual life. It can still be viewed as experience of the individual and with reference to this experience. These are two categories under which the same content may be viewed.

[1] *Ibid.*, pp. 35–37.

The standpoint from which the individual may be understood may be taken either within or outside the individual. The totality of his life may be regarded either as the centripetal destiny of its bearer or as the product and element of the social life. Therefore the fact of socialization brings the individual into a double situation. He is included in it and is at the same time in antithesis to it. He is a member of its organism and at the same time a closed organic whole.

"Within" and "without" are not two determinations which exist alongside of each other, but they signify the whole unitary position of the social being. His existence is therefore not merely in subdivision of its content partially social and partially individual. It stands under the fundamental, formative, irreducible category of a unity, which cannot be expressed otherwise than through the synthesis of these two logically antithetical determinations. Society consists not only of individuals who are in part not socialized, but also of individuals who are conscious of leading a completely social existence on the one hand and at the same time a completely individual existence on the other hand. The social being is the synthetic category of the two, just as the concept of causation is an aprioristic unity which includes the two elements of cause and effect.[1]

This analysis enables us to see the second a priori of empirical social life. "It may be formulated as the ability to view society as the *terminus a quo* and the *terminus ad quem* of human beings who view themselves as a *terminus a quo* and a *terminus ad quem* of its qualities, developments, and destinies."[2]

The third a priori might be roughly formulated as a

[1] *Soz.*, pp. 38–41.

[2] *Ibid.*, p. 41.

condition of harmony between the individual and the social whole. Society as an objective structure viewed in abstraction from its individual bearers is a system of contents and functions. What holds good for a bureaucracy viewed as a system of correlated functions must hold good to a certain extent for the social system. Each individual entering a bureaucracy will have an assigned place awaiting him. But this place must none the less be in harmony with his individual energies. In the social system the positions and functions are not consciously planned and assigned, but they are created and found through and by the individual activities and experiments. The phenomenological structure of society appears, notwithstanding this difference, as a system of functions in which each element has a specific individual place. The life of society runs its course, not psychologically but phenomenologically, as if the position of each individual within it had been predetermined. The individual can therefore lead a social life only in so far as the position ideally belonging to him, that is, harmonizing with his individual tendencies, is actually available.

If this condition were unrestrictedly fulfilled, the actual society would be a perfect society, not in an ethical or eudemonistic sense, but in the sense of conceptual perfection. The group would be, not a *perfect* society, but a perfect *society*, perfectly socialized. In so far as the individual does not find the fulfilment of this prerequisite of his social existence, the socialization is incomplete. Complete socialization implies a thoroughgoing correlation between the individual and the surrounding circles, the full integration of his individual singularity with the life of the whole.

This is most clearly evident in the case of a vocation. On the one hand, society creates within itself a vocation which, although differing from other vocations, can none the less in principle be followed by many individuals. On the other hand, however, notwithstanding this general character of a vocation, the individual enters into it on the ground of what he feels as a personal calling. A vocation therefore requires a harmony between the structure and the life-process of society on the one side and the individual impulses and qualities on the other side. Upon such a general presupposition rests in the last instance the idea that there is a position and a function within society for every personality and that he should search until he finds it.

The empirical society becomes possible only if this condition which culminates in the vocational concept is fulfilled. Socialization means that the individual elements have become a unity, that they mutually influence one another, and that there is a reciprocal significance of the elements for the totality and of the totality for the elements. Socialization results from processes in the individual consciousness, and these processes can therefore be processes of socialization only if the condition outlined above is fulfilled. This causal interdependence which connects every social element with the existence of every other element, and in that way weaves the external tissue, becomes a teleological one when regarded from the side of the individual bearers, who view themselves as self-sufficient, self-determining egos creating these relations.

That this phenomenal totality adapts itself to the purposes of individuals who approach it from outside, that it offers them a position in which their individual singularity, which is internally determined, comes to play an inevitable part in the life of the whole, is one of the fundamental categories which give the individual consciousness the form which makes it a social element.[1]

[1] *Soz.*, p. 45.

The presuppositions, assumptions, and basic conditions outlined above are some of the a priori categories of empirical society. It may be a question of terminology whether the inquiry which determines them can be called epistemology. Judged on the basis of method, it does not belong to the empirical science itself, but to that part of the philosophic inquiry which investigates the basic assumptions on which the science rests.

SUMMARY

THIS first book gives Simmel's methodological analysis of the different forms of inquiry into the sociohistorical actuality. His relativistic viewpoint leads him to a conception of society which might be called an intermediate position between the nominalistic and the realistic view. He finds a certain amount of justification for both, but escapes the resulting antinomy by attributing only a relative value to each and by introducing a third way of looking at society. That third way is the functional, relativistic way.

If he is to be called a nominalist because in the last analysis only the individual has for him existential reality, his nominalism is of a special type. It results from the special type of analysis with which he works. It is not the analysis so often criticized with the trivial remark that the machine is more than its parts and the molecule more than its atoms. Society is analyzed in terms of component elements, not as individual existences, but as bearers of relationships. It is an analysis in terms of functions, not in terms of substances; it is an analysis in terms of relationships, not in terms of individuals. Society as content is the totality, is the sum of all individuals, together with all their interests and all their relationships and all the products which result from the transformations of these interests through their realization in socialization. But society as form, as association, is nothing but the sum of the integrating functional relationships. A machine as a going concern consists of component parts together with the functional relationships, the power that drives the machine, the raw material, and the product. But the machine as a pure mechanism, the pure mechanics of the machine, is nothing but the sum of the integrating functional relationships of the component parts.

Simmel conceives of sociology as a special, limited, and empirical social science, and determines its relations to the other social sciences and to the philosophical inquiries into the phenomena of the socio-historical world. He gives due value to social metaphysics as a fully autonomous form of mental activity, but denounces its claims to encroach upon scientific inquiries. If the philosophic method is a necessary procedure to give a first orientation in the manifoldness of the phenomena, it is a childhood procedure which is to be conquered, and until it is conquered, there is no social science. Only by following the method of science can the investigation produce results which have objective validity.

BOOK II

SOCIAL SCIENCE

FORMAL SOCIOLOGY

INTRODUCTION

IN THE preceding chapters we have dealt with Simmel's fundamental considerations regarding the methodology of the social sciences in general and of sociology in particular. Our next task is, therefore, to indicate to what his conception of formal sociology and of its method and technique leads in actual application.

The subject-matter of sociology, as will be remembered from the preceding chapters, is for Simmel the process of socialization as such. Sociology is the science of human relationships, the theory of association. Its task is to describe and explain the forms of socialization and to trace the tendencies of development and the conditions under which they arise.

The fragmentary character of his work prevents an inclusive treatment, and we are therefore obliged to limit ourselves to a short summary of his most important essays. Besides, a representation of his contribution to the study of sociology in this form illustrates better than any attempt at integration his opinion about the present early stage of the science. Simmel believed that a systematic presentation of sociology would be possible only in the distant future, and that for the time being the workers in that field would have to content themselves with isolated contributions. He explicitly states that even his great volume on sociology is not to be regarded as an attempt at a systematic presentation, but merely as an illustration of the application of its method to different phenomena within the field. This explains to a large extent the fragmentary character of the work, although that is undoubtedly also due in part to Simmel's intuitive fear and dislike of any structural rigidity.

The topics of the following chapters have, notwithstanding this fact, been selected with the view of giving at least a suggestion of unity. All unnecessary detail and expansion of irrelevant points have been omitted, and the choice of sequence and the special treatment of the material are due to the attempt to indicate with a few bold strokes what Simmel's sociology looks like. The aim has not been to give a comprehensive interpretation, but merely to indicate its skeleton structure. It is hoped that these chapters will suggest none the less what sociology according to Simmel purports to be. We feel justified in this attempt to suggest at least some kind of unity, notwithstanding the author's explicit warning, because only by treating it as a single unified field of inquiry can we indicate its right place between social methodology and social metaphysics.

CHAPTER I

SUBMISSION

SUPERORDINATION AND SUBORDINATION[1]

THE most important form of relationship in the whole social world is the relationship between the leader and his followers, between the superior and his subordinates. It is a form of socialization without which no social life would be possible, and the main factor sustaining the unity of groups. Superiority and subordination constitute the sociological expression of psychological differences in human beings, and wherever these are associated, there they appear in a more or less pronounced form.

This relationship between the superior and the inferior assumes oftentimes the appearance of a one-sided operation. It seems as if the superior exerts an influence which the inferior merely undergoes. But the latter is by no means a purely passive agent. The subordinate in turn exerts an influence on the superior, and it is only by virtue of this interaction of the two that in the relationship the one takes the position of superior and the other the position of subordinate. The relationship of superior to inferior is a form of interaction between individuals and therefore a form of socialization. It always allows a certain amount of independence and spontaneity on the part of the subordinate. In some cases of superiority and inferiority the amount of spontaneity and independence of the subordinate is great, in others small; but it is never wholly absent. Even in a case of the worst tyranny, the subordi-

[1] Adapted from *Soz.*, chap. iii, pp. 134-246.

nate has the choice between submission and punishment. However little consolation the existence of this alternative may bring to the individual in question, it shows none the less that the superior-inferior relationship cannot be established without some active participation on the part of the subordinate. This submission is not purely passive, but has an active aspect as well, and the resulting relationship is a form of social interaction.

What is called "authority" requires also a much more active participation on the part of those who submit to it than is generally supposed. To call a human being an authority means to ascribe to his judgments and decisions a certainty and an infallibility which are otherwise ascribed only to universal postulates and logical deductions. This authority can become established in two different ways. In the first instance, it results from the fact that a superior individual inspires in his group such a faith and confidence in his opinions and decisions that they obtain for that group the character of objective validity. In becoming an authority, his quantitative significance turns into a new quality with objective status. In the second instance, the authority becomes established by a different process. It occurs when a superindividual organization like the state, the church, or the school transfers to the individual a power of decision and a dignity which he could not inspire or obtain through his own personality. In the first instance the authority develops out of the individuality, in the second instance it descends into the individual from the outside. But in neither case can the transition occur without the active belief of those who submit to the authority. The transformation of the value of the individual into a super-personal value is brought about by the believers in the authority. Authority is a sociological product requiring the spontaneous and active participation of the subordinates.

Another variation of the superior-inferior relation is the relationship indicated by the word "prestige." This relationship, however, does not contain any superpersonal element. For that reason the existence of an active, spontaneous participation on the part of those who admit the prestige of an individual is more clearly visible. Like all other superior-inferior relations, it is a form of socialization involving an interaction between all the elements concerned.[1]

The superior-inferior relationships may be classified in three different types. The superiority may be exercised by a single individual, by a group, or by an objective principle in the form of a social or ideal superindividual power. Each of these three forms has certain specific characteristics which must be briefly enumerated.

Subordination to an Individual

The subordination of a group to a single individual leads to a strong unification of the group. It occurs not only if the group and its leader constitute already an internal unity, but also if the group is conscious of an opposition and antithesis between itself and its superior. In the first case, the group elements become conscious of their unity because their interests converge at a single point. In the second instance, they are forced to strengthen their unity in order to oppose more effectively the unified controlling power to which they are subordinate.

This is the case, not only in political groups, but in all other organizations. In the factory, the ecclesiastical community, and in the school class, wherever the organization terminates in a single head, there the common subordination leads to a strong unity independently of the fact whether the relationship be one of harmony or opposition.

[1] *Soz.*, pp. 134–37.

This significance of leadership for the group unity, although manifest in all associations, is most clearly visible, however, in political groups. History has shown innumerable instances where the death of the common superior resulted in a complete disruption of the political unity of the group.

The relationship between the group elements and the leader is usually a combination of submission and opposition. Human nature seems to be so constituted that it requires both elements in its social relationships. The individual seems to seek, on the one hand, a superior power which will relieve him of part of his responsibility and protect him, not only against others, but even against himself; yet, on the other hand, he seems to feel a necessity for placing himself in opposition to this same power. Opposition and submission seem in the last analysis to be only different aspects of relationships which are fundamentally of a unified character. Every subordination shows both aspects.

This process of unification of the group elements resulting from a common subordination appears in two different forms. The first might be indicated by the word "leveling," the second by the word "gradation." In the first instance the group elements are all on a common level with regard to the superior. In the second instance the group consists of series of different layers decreasing in size, but increasing in significance.

The correlation between despotism and equality has long been recognized. On the one hand, perfect equality leads easily to despotism, because a slight variation is sufficient to give an individual a position of superiority to all. On the other hand, the despot has an immediate advantage in keeping his subjects on a common level. He will thereby prevent other superiority-inferiority relations between different ranks from coming into actual or merely psychological competition with his own supremacy.

The process of gradation gives the group the form of a pyramid. In this case the subordinates are not an equalized mass, but they stand to the common superior in different strata of power and dependence. These strata grow constantly smaller in size, but greater in significance. They lead up gradually from the inferior mass to the superior ruler.

This group form may come into existence in two different ways. In the first place, it may result from a distribution of power from above. Here the ruler may intentionally create a juxtaposition of ranks and classes. In that case the result will not be a weakening of his power, but a better protection of his position. The quantity of submission remains the same, but it is unequally distributed over the subjects. The resulting type of social structure is apt to be strongly conservative, because every class or rank that has another class subordinate to it will be interested in the persistence of the existing form. The distribution of power from above is, however, only in rare instances the result of a voluntary relinquishment on the part of the ruler. What usually happens is that the ruler loses the substance of his power and allows it to slip downward, while retaining its form and titles. The orders nearest to the ruler will retain most of his power, while the rest will go to those farther distant. The result will be a gradual percolation of his power through the whole group and a continuity and gradation of superior-inferior relations among all the elements.

This is the process by which oriental monarchies have usually obtained their characteristic form. Indolence or ignorance of governmental technique on the part of the persons comprising their administrations has usually prevented them from preserving the supreme power, for the power which is exercised over a large group is never a constant possession. It must be constantly acquired and defended anew if anything more than its shadow and name is to remain.

② The second way in which a group may obtain a social structure consisting of graded classes is by the accumulation of power from below. This occurs if out of a group of comparatively equal elements a certain number gain a special significance and out of this group there differentiate again a smaller number of especially powerful persons and so on until the development accommodates itself to a single leader. This type of development is the characteristic form in the economic world and in political life, but it is also manifest in the world of science. In the first process the resulting pyramid of superiority and inferiority was developed from above downward. In this latter form it is built from below upward.

The classical example of a social structure resulting from a combination of both tendencies is the feudal state. As long as the full citizen—Greek, Roman, or Teutonic— knew no subordination to an individual, he was, on the one hand, on an equal footing with his fellow-citizens and, on the other hand, sharply differentiated from all below him. In the feudal state, the gap between the unfree and the free was bridged by a long series of intermediate classses. The king gave a part of his property and power to the nobles in exchange for service. There occurred a distribution of power from above downward. But, on the other hand, the free farmer gave his land to the lord in exchange for protection. There was also an accumulation of power from below upward.

These two sociological formations of unification through leveling and unification through gradation also occur in case of subordination to a group. The monarchy is, however, the archetype and the primary form of all superior-inferior relations. Its form seems so effective that it even continues to exist in situations and institutions which have arisen from reactions against monarchy. The American president, the Athenian archon, and the Roman consul were, with certain restrictions, the heirs to the royal power of which the kings had been robbed by revolution. Even the democracy of the French Revolution was nothing but an inverted monarchy, and Rousseau's "general will" had all the attributes of an absolute personal sovereignty.[1]

Subordination to a Group

Subordination to a group occurs in two different forms. ① The superior may be a crowd, a group of individuals actually assembled and in close spatial proximity. ② But the superior group may also be an abstract unity manifesting a more or less permanent existence in an objective social structure. In this class falls the subordination of an individual to his state, to his church, or to any organized association.

In subordination to an objective structure, the superior-inferior relationship itself obtains a more or less objective character. The participation of the superior in the relationship loses its subjective aspects and obtains a super-individual character. Sentiments, feelings, and emotions are excluded from the participation of the superior, and the relationship becomes more or less cold and factual. It depends, therefore, on the type of relationship that is advantageous to the subordinate whether subordination to a group is better or worse than subordination to an individual. In great modern enterprises which either are corporations or are administered in an equally impersonal man-

[1] *Soz.*, pp. 141–63.

ner, the employees are usually better off than those in the small private concerns who are subject to the personal exploitation of the proprietor. On the other hand, in special cases of distress the administration of the corporation cannot act as generously as the private owner who is not responsible to anyone for his management. Subordination to a group is therefore an advantage to the individual if he is helped by a formal, impartial, factual, and business-like relationship. It is a disadvantage if the individual is helped by a benevolent, altruistic, and merciful relationship.

Subordination to a crowd, to a group actually assembled, varies also considerably from subordination to an individual. In organized associations which function as legal persons, the participation of the superior in the relationship loses the personal elements and obtains more rational, superpersonal elements. In crowds, the participation of the superior loses also the personal elements, but this time it obtains infra-individual collective emotional elements. It is this fact that explains the merciless cruelty of the Roman circus public, of the medieval religious persecutions, and of the modern lynching parties. On the other hand, crowds are sometimes capable of great enthusiasm and magnanimity.[1]

Subordination to an Impersonal Principle

Subordination to an impersonal principle or a law does not involve a reciprocity. The individuals who do not obey a law are not really subordinate to that law. If they change it, they really abolish the old law and put a new one in its place. In so far as they are subordinate to the new law, they feel themselves determined by it, but they do not determine it. Modern people who have learned to differentiate between the field of spontaneous activity and that of

[1] *Soz.*, pp. 172–77.

obedience prefer, however, subjection to a law executed by
an impersonal power to the subordination to an individual. This was not the case in ancient times. People could
then maintain their self-respect only if they were allowed
a certain amount of spontaneous participation, and they
preferred personal obedience to the subjection to a rigid
objective law. There is a great difference between viewing
laws as substitutes and makeshifts for an ideal personal
government and viewing personal government as provisional to the government of law.

The one-sided relationship which is characteristic of
subordinations to impersonal principles excludes them as
such from the category of sociological forms. There is none
the less a sociological aspect to these subordinations in two
special instances. The first occurs if the ideal superior principle can be interpreted as a psychological condensation of
an actual social power. The second occurs if this principle
establishes specific and characteristic relationships between those who are subject to it.

The former case is illustrated in the moral imperative.
The individual who has a moral consciousness feels himself
subject to decrees which have apparently not been issued
by any human power. He hears the voice of conscience only in himself, but it speaks with such force and precision
against his subjective egoism that it seems to come from an
authority outside of himself. One has attempted to solve
this apparent contradiction by assuming that the content
of morality has been derived from social decrees. The
species and the group seem to breed into the individual
those characteristics that are useful for the social self-preservation. They obtain a certain instinctive character and
appear in the individual as autonomous impulses next to
or in opposition to the properly personal impulses. This
explains the double character of the moral imperative. It

appears on the one hand as an impersonal command to which the individual simply has to yield, while on the other hand no external power, but only his subjective impulse or instinct, enforces it. The norms originally derived from the will of all are now conceived as impersonal factual norms, and the individual reproduces within his own consciousness the external relations between himself and his group. Subordination to the moral imperative is therefore a peculiar form of interrelation between the individual and his group.

The subordination to an impersonal principle has also a sociological aspect if it leads to specific and characteristic relationships between the subordinate individuals. In this case also the subordination to an ideal principle has usually been preceded by a subordination to an actual power. Individuals and classes often exert their authority in the name of an ideal principle to which they are themselves subordinated. The latter may appear to be logically prior to the personal authority, but in the historical development the personal rule usually precedes the rule of an objective principle. The power and rule of the personal superior grows gradually into an objective power through ratiocination and through the extension and depersonalization of the relationship. The result is a situation in which the superior exerts his authority, not in his own right, but as the personal representative of that ideal power. This development can be easily traced in the history of the *patria potestas* among the Aryan peoples. The power of the father was originally unlimited and entirely subjective. His momentary desires and his personal advantage might be the sole basis for his decisions and regulations. But this arbitrary power gradually became limited by a feeling of responsibility. The unity of the family group embodied in the family spirit grew into an ideal power, and the lord of the family merely undertook to execute its commands. Customs and mores rather than subjective preference began to guide his acts and decisions, and from being the sole lord of the family property he became its manager in the interest of the whole. Thus the relationship between superiors and inferiors is placed on a new basis. The family as a whole is thought of as standing above all the individual members, and the ruling patriarch himself has become subordinate to its objective principle. He can command the other members, but only in the name of that higher ideal unity. This leads to a very interesting sociological constellation, the subordination of the superior to the laws which he gives himself.

The growth of an objective principle to which both the superior and the inferior have to subject themselves finds in modern times its fullest expression in the economic world. The personal element has largely been withdrawn from the relationship between employers and workmen. It is no longer a relationship of personal service, but it has become a sale of a certain amount of labor power. The results of this modern development have been, on the one hand, an objectivation of the actual relationship and, on the other hand, the growth of a production technique which sets objective norms and demands to which both employer and workmen are subject.

The subordination to an impersonal principle gives, therefore, to the individuals concerned a peculiar double relationship. The fact that as a group they are imbued with a single spirit or subject to a single objective principle gives them in their relations to outsiders a more or less equal position. Within the group, on the other hand, they stand to one another in different relationships of superiority and inferiority. This double aspect of their formal sociological situation colors their whole social life. An employee of a large store may hold a commanding position within the organization; in his relations to the public, however, he will be a servant, not a superior. On the other hand, even the individuals holding the lowest positions will feel themselves bearers of the objective principles and upholders of the dignity of the firm in their relations to the outside world. The members of the Catholic clergy are placed in a similar double relationship. The lowest order of priests is as far above the layman as the idea of eternity stands above all that is temporal. On the other hand, the highest church authority calls himself the servant of servants. The monk who may hold a position of authority in his order is devout and subservient in his relations to the outside world, but the lowest priest brings the authority of the church to his dealings with the secular prince.[1]

Subordination to More than One Superior

Complete subordination to different persons or groups may create a most unpleasant situation for the individual concerned. This will be the case, for instance, if the superiors are themselves in opposition or in actual conflict. Each superior will demand complete obedience and hold the individual responsible for what he does in obedience to the other, as if such acts were free and spontaneous. Such is the typical situation of the man who has to serve two masters. If this conflict between the two superiors is a conflict between two social circles, it may become entirely subjectified, that is, transferred to the individual consciousness. In that case it will appear as a conflict between duties and loyalties and will bring most suffering to the strong individual. If the conflict remains an external conflict, it will, on the other hand, bring most suffering to the weak individual.

[1] *Soz.*, pp. 197–212.

In case of an external conflict or opposition, the position of the subordinate becomes very different if his relationship involves only a partial submission and leaves him a great deal of freedom and spontaneity. In that case the subordinate is left the possibility of choosing between superiors, and through that fact he obtains in relation to each of them, and perhaps in his own feeling in relation to both, a certain independence which he would not have had with only a single master. A similar advantage accrues to the subordinate if the superiors succeed each other while the former remains. The Roman senate was theoretically subordinate to the high state officials. The officials, however, served for only a short period, while membership in the senate was permanent. The result was that in actuality this body had a far greater power in its dealings with state officials than it was legally given. This is only a special instance of a general correlation. In the relationship between groups and their varying members or outsiders there accrues a special power to the group through the mere fact of its persistence. This occurs not only if the group is subordinate, but also if the group is superior. It is manifest in the authority of the state and the church over their individual members, which is among other things also due to the fact that they have, compared to the short lives of their members, a relatively eternal existence.

A similar advantage for the subordinate may result if his superiors are themselves placed in some kind of juxtaposition. A subvassal immediately subject to the king has a certain independence and strength in his relations to the vassal which would be absent if the first relationship did not exist. If the form of the social structure is such that a combination between the highest and lowest elements against the middle group is impossible, there results a situation which is most unfortunate for the lower circles. If the structure allows at the same time for the passage of pressure from above downward, it means that the lower circles will have to bear the whole brunt of any additional pressure exerted anywhere along the line. Any additional burdens and duties laid on the higher circles will then simply be passed on downward until they have been completely transferred to the lowest circle. Another situation arises if the middle circles offer resistance to the passage of pressure and completely sever the highest circle from the lowest. In that case the isolating layer may in some circumstances harm not only the lowest level, but also the highest, while in different circumstances it may act as a shockbreaker and a protection to both.[1]

Superiority and Subordination in Their Psychological and Sociological Aspects

The quantity of superiority or subordination that exists within a group gives a distinct character to the group as a whole. Societies which contain a great number of superior-inferior relations, either in the form of a sociological pyramid or in the form of parallel and co-ordinated relationships, appear to have the general characteristics of subordinate groups. The predominance of subordination imposes its character on the group as a whole. This is, for instance, the case in bureaucratic states.

That a society as a whole bears the characteristics of a ruling group occurs only in rare instances. It is possible only if the quality of superiority which elements possess in relation to other elements comes to be conceived of as existing independently of that interrelation. That one is a ruler presupposes a subject. But this logical requirement can sometimes be dispensed with. A man may be a ruler independently of the fact whether he rules or not, if he has

[1] *Soz.*, pp. 177–86.

the qualities of a ruler. He is called a ruler on account of subjective, psychological characteristics which would fit him for the position of ruler in an actual interrelation. The history of Spain shows an interesting illustration of the persistence of the psychological characteristic long after the actual sociological relationships had disappeared. The Spaniards felt themselves rulers and had as a nation the characteristics of a ruling group long after the Moors and the Jews, whom they once actually ruled, had been driven out of the country. This occurs, however, only in exceptional cases.

The more prevalent form of a society having a character which contrasts with that of the subordinate group is the society which allows great freedom and liberty to all its members. Freedom and liberty, however, usually do not mean a static condition, a mere absence of subordination. Liberation from subjection has usually meant at the same time a gaining of superiority, either over existing groups or over new groups. Struggles for freedom have usually ended in struggles for supremacy. The liberation of the third estate in France has meant the gaining of superiority both over the new fourth estate and over the older circles to which it was once subordinated. Equality with the superior group is but the first step on the road to the desired dominion over the former superior. Gaining liberty therefore usually means gaining authority. A special instance of liberation through the gaining of authority occurs in the case where a smaller group obtains from a larger group the full jurisdiction over its members. In this case liberation means that the small group as a whole, as a superindividual unity, becomes master over its individual members.

A social structure free from all relationships of superiority and subordination has been for many an ideal. But their existence is justified by the fact that the psychological differences between individuals create them, and by the fact that the technique for the realization of social purposes requires them. The motive for abolishing them results from the fact that the social superiority or inferiority is felt as a personal superiority or inferiority. The superior or inferior position in one social relationship is felt as a superiority or inferiority of the whole personality. There would, however, be no reason to abolish the sociological relationships if this psychological by-product could be avoided. This might presumably be the case if the relationships within the social structure became wholly objectified and allowed a complete withdrawal of personal feelings and sentiments from the impersonal social functions. Something similar is already happening in the relationships in the economic world. The feeling of personal superiority and inferiority resulting from the social relationships may also disappear if a further social differentiation and integration creates a structure in which the individual is at the same time in a great many superior and inferior positions.

Apart from the foregoing difficulty resulting from the existence of superior-inferior relationships, there exists a problem of even wider import. Originally these relationships were the immediate expression of psychological differences between individuals. In modern society the organization of the group has taken definite shape, and a great many of these relationships have become objectified in a more or less fixed social structure. The result has been the formation of a relatively fixed system of superior and inferior positions which are to a large extent independent of the individuals that hold them at any given time. They have not created these positions, they merely fill them. On the other hand, the stratification of society in classes leads to a situation in which many individuals are born into certain positions merely because they belong to a specific class. This may lead to a discrepancy between the qualities which these positions as such demand and the subjective qualities of the individuals filling them. To avoid this discrepancy as far as possible is one of the great problems of all modern societies.[1]

[1] *Soz.*, pp. 213–47.

CHAPTER II

OPPOSITION

CONFLICT AND STRUGGLE[1]

REFERENCE has already been made to the fact that the unity of groups is not due solely to the convergence of interests and the harmonious co-ordination of elements. Societies require a certain proportion of attraction and repulsion, harmony and disharmony, association and dissociation, integration and differentiation, co-operation and competition among their elements to obtain a definite organization. Groups which are entirely harmonious, and which are composed of elements which have centripetal tendencies only, would not only be impossible empirically, but they would have no life-process and no structure. The acceptance of leadership and the subordination to authority are therefore not the only forms of interaction that make for social unity. The conflicts and oppositions between the elements fulfil that same function. They, too, contribute to the total process of socialization and must therefore be investigated with reference to that function.

That conflicts have sociological significance, inasmuch as they either produce or modify communities of interest, unifications, and organizations, has in principle never been contested. But apart from this sociological significance which accrues to conflict through its consequences and accompaniments, it has a sociological significance in and for itself owing to the fact that it is a positive form of inter-

---

[1] Adapted from *Soz.*, chap. iv, pp. 247–336.

action between individuals and, as such, a form of socialization.

Struggles and conflicts have a positive sociological significance in contrast with dissolutions and repudiations of socialization, which are both negative. An antagonism between elements may arise from different subjective impulses, wants, desires, envies, or hatreds. But once the antagonism has arisen, the function of the actual struggle or conflict is to overcome the existing dualism and to arrive at some form of unity, even if it involves the destruction of one of the parties. The conflict itself is but the resolution of the tension between the two elements. That a conflict eventually terminates in a peace, either in the form of coordination or in the form of subordination, is only the obvious expression of the fact that it is a special form of synthesis between elements. It is a higher concept which contains and implies both union and opposition.

The positive sociological function of tension and repulsion is most clearly manifest in social structures which consist of a hierarchy of classes. The caste system of India does not derive its form solely from the internal coherence of elements within each caste, but also from the external repulsion between castes. The opposition and enmity between them prevent the gradual disappearance of the class boundaries and are therefore positive contributing factors in the preservation of the existing structure. But opposition does not merely function as a means to the preservation of a total system of relationships. In many forms of socialization it is an integral part of the relationship itself. This is illustrated by the function of opposition, aversion, and antipathy in certain types of relationship.

Opposition between elements within an association is not merely a negative factor. It is often the only means of maintaining associations which would otherwise be unen-

durable. The power and the right to oppose tyranny, ego-
tism, and lack of tact make it possible to protect the integ-
rity of the individuality on the one hand, while maintaining on the other hand interrelations which would otherwise have to be dissolved. Opposition is then not only a
means for the preservation of the relationship, but is also
one of the concrete functions of which the relationship actually consists. Aversion and antipathy as the latent subjective forms of opposition serve in a similar fashion in
other types of socialization.

Although antagonism by itself alone does not constitute socialization, it is seldom lacking as a positive sociological element in human association. Socializations might
be classified in a series according to the proportion between
the unifying and opposing tendencies of which they consist. There are conflicts in which the unifying aspect of
socialization is wholly absent. Such a marginal case is the
conflict between the thug and his victim. When a struggle
of this sort goes as far as complete annihilation, then the
unifying element has become nil. But in such a case the
concept of reciprocal action is really no longer applicable,
because that annihilation means the non-existence of the
other party to the reaction. On the other hand, as soon as
any sort of consideration or any limitation of violence is
present, there comes into play by virtue of that fact a socializing factor, if only in the form of restraint.

Another marginal case appears if the conflict is stimulated exclusively by the love of fighting, if it is a struggle
for struggle's sake. The moment any other stimulus induces the struggle, such as contempt, revenge, a desire to
possess or to control, limitations are placed upon the struggle. The object desired or the condition to be attained will
impress upon the struggle certain norms and restrictions
which apply to both parties. Also the fact that the stake

is something external to the struggle itself, which might perhaps be obtained by other means, will give a distinct color to the struggle. Only if the struggle is prompted exclusively by the love of struggle is there no other alternative and can satisfaction result from conflict only.

The pugnacious instinct, however, is usually not the sole element in the struggle. It acts rather as a reinforcement to the other impulses that bring about the controversy, or as a foundation on which a conflict can be built. Even if a struggle is originally fought solely for the sake of the struggle, this situation will not remain. The interest in the struggle may at the outset have been impersonal and indifferent to the content of the controversy, but eventually hatred and envy will reinforce the original impulse. The purity of a struggle for struggle's sake, therefore, does not remain. It becomes mixed with other impulses and with objective interests.[1]

The Contest Game

A conflict and struggle exclusively for the sake of the struggle and without any other impulse or ulterior motive occurs only in the case of the contest game. In this case the purely sociological attraction of self-assertion and of predominance over others in skill is combined only with the purely individual pleasure in the exercise of purposeful and successful activity. The contest game in its sociological motivation contains nothing but the contest itself. The worthless markers, for the sake of which men often play with the same earnestness with which they play for money, indicate the purely formal aspect of this impulse.

But even in the case of the contest game there exists a socialization in the more narrow sense of the term. No contest can take place without some kind of unification.

[1] *Soz.*, pp. 247–64.

People unite to contest, and the contest takes place according to rules and regulations acknowledged by both and defining the form of the interrelation. These norms create the technique without which the contest would be impossible. A contest implies a form of association, and the norms for this association are usually much more strict and impersonal, and are lived up to with a finer sense of honor, than are the norms of co-operative associations.

The Legal Contest

The intimate correlation between the opposition and union which is the essence of conflict finds its clearest manifestation in the contest game. It illustrates how the one realizes its full sociological significance and efficacy only in and through the other. A similar sociological form, although not in such purity, joins the two parties of a legal contest. There is in this case an object of contest, but the form of the contest is purely impersonal and factual. The respective claims are asserted with relentless objectivity and pushed with employment of all available means, without being diverted or modified by personal reactions or extraneous considerations. Nothing enters into the contest which does not properly belong in the conflict and which does not serve the ends of the conflict. In other battles, including the most savage struggles, there is always the possibility of the intermixture of subjective elements or of the intervention of a third or of a freak of nature. From the legal battle all that is excluded. It is to be fought to the bitter end without any interference on the part of what is not immediately pertinent to the main contention; and it is this impersonal character which makes it so severe, sharp, and merciless.

On the other hand, the whole contest presupposes and implies a narrow unity between the parties. Their contest means a common subordination to the law, a common acceptance of its forms of procedure, and a common recognition of the fact that the decision can be made only according to the objective weight of the evidence. The parties to the contest are subordinate to a social power and a social order which give significance and security to that contest and make it rest on a broad basis of community and consensus between the opponents similar to the unity and consensus which are created by the parties to a contract or a commercial transaction through the realization and acceptance of the fact that, apart from the possible antithesis of interests, they are bound by common rules and regulations. These common presuppositions, which exclude from the legal contest everything that is personal, give a purely factual and objective character to the unitary aspect of the relationship, which is paralleled in the dualistic aspect of the relationship by the sharpness, bitterness, and relentlessness of the struggle itself.

The Conflict of Impersonal Interests

The conflict between individuals on account of impersonal interests bears a similar character. In such a case the interest in the struggle, and thereby the struggle itself, becomes differentiated from the person of the opponent. But the realization of being merely representatives of superindividual claims and of fighting, not for self, but for the cause gives to the struggle often a radical and merciless nature. Its character becomes analogous to the conduct of some entirely unselfish and idealistic people who, sacrificing their own lives for a cause, hold themselves entirely justified in sacrificing everybody else. Such a struggle for impersonal interests, but which is fought with all the strength and resources of the whole personality, bears the stamp of respectability. The respectable man is the man who, while being wholly personal, is capable of keeping his own person in the background. The impersonal and objective character of such struggles therefore lends them a certain nobility. But, once the differentiation is accomplished and the struggle objectified, there is no further reserve. Any moderation would be not only inconsistent, but a treason to the cause. On the basis of the consensus between the parties that each fights merely for the issue at stake and without personal considerations, the struggle is fought out without personal bitterness, but also without any moderation which might result from the intermingling of personal elements.

This form of antithesis between unity and antagonism intensifies conflict most perceptibly perhaps in cases where both parties actually pursue the same interest. This is the case, for instance, in scientific controversies, in which the issue is the establishment of some truth. In such a case any concession, any polite consent to stop short of the full exposition of the errors of the opponent, any conclusion of peace previous to decisive victory, would be treason against the factual objective issue for the sake of which the personal element was to be excluded.

Social struggles have often taken this form. This has, for instance, been the case with the class struggle since Marx. Since it has been recognized that the position of the wage-earner is determined by the objective forms and characteristics of the economic system independently of the power and the will of individual persons, the personal bitterness incident to the general struggle and the local conflicts has much diminished. The entrepreneur is no longer thought of as a bloodsucker and a damnable egoist. The laborer is no longer assumed to act merely from sinful greed. Each party is ceasing to interpret the other's tactics and demands in terms of mere egoism and malevolence.

In Germany this objectivation and increased factualness of the struggle has been greatly helped by the abstract impersonal treatment of the conflict in social and historical studies. In England the objectivation has been greatly facilitated by the fact that the conflict has from its early beginning been fought by an organized trade-union movement and more or less organized employers' combinations. In these collective organizations the purely personal element had no place. But with this objectivation the intensity of the struggle has not diminished. On the contrary, it has become more conscious, better organized, and more aggressive and severe than it has ever been. The individual has become conscious that he is not merely struggling for himself, but is struggling rather for superpersonal ends; and that gives him a fighting strength and perseverance which he did not possess as long as his purpose was merely personal.[1]

The Conflict between Factions

The peculiar sharpness and bitterness which the co-existence of union and opposition gives to certain conflicts is also illustrated in factional strife. In that case the union is the starting-point and the basis of the relationship, and the opposition and the dualism a later development superimposed on the original foundation. Such conflicts are usually much more passionate than those between parties which were not originally united in a common bond. This situation is illustrated in the conflicts between religious and political factions and in class struggles and civil wars.

There are apparently two forms of consensus which contribute especially to the bitterness and sharpness of conflicts. The first is the consensus which is due to the

[1] *Soz.*, pp. 265-70.

possession of a great many common qualities and characteristics. The second is the consensus which is due to a common participation and absorption in a unitary social group. The first contributes to the bitterness of the conflict because an opposition between elements which have otherwise much in common receives by contrast a strong light and leads to profound subjective reactions. The second contributes to the bitterness of the conflict because there arises a social hatred in addition to the personal hatred.

In some cases falling under this category the separation is not the result of a conflict, but the conflict is the result of the separation. There will then be an antagonism between the parties not only on account of the difference in attitude toward the issue in question, but also on account of the fact that each considers the other as an enemy of the group and a danger to its unity. The resulting bitterness will be strongest in the cases in which the actual dismemberment of the group has not yet taken place or is unlikely to take place. If the dissociation has taken place, it signifies a partial termination of the conflict. The individual difference has found its sociological termination, and the stimulus to constantly renewed friction is removed. The tension which results from the combination of this dualism and unity can be resolved only by complete unity or separation. Where the latter is impossible, the efforts to obtain the first will be made with greater strength. Hence the severity of the actual struggle. It is an ordeal to live in enmity with a person to whom one is nevertheless bound and from whom one cannot be freed even if one desires a dissociation. A similar situation arises if an individual is unwilling to give up or incapable of giving up his membership in a group whose unity he values as an objective good and for whose persistence he feels that he must fight and struggle. From a correlation such as this spring the bitter quarrels that are being fought within political factions or trade unions or families.[1]

Competition

A special type of correlation between unity and opposition occurs in the different forms of competition. Competition is distinguished from an ordinary struggle by the fact that it is an indirect conflict. In one form of competition, the object of the conflict is in the hands of a third person, and the mere victory over the opponent, although the first necessary step, is not the final aim. In the second form of competition, each competitor works immediately for the final aim without spending any energy on his opponent. This type of competition is illustrated in a track meet and in modern business.

The runner who succeeds by his speed, the merchant by the price of his goods, and the preacher by his oratory may be stimulated by the efforts of their competitors, but they proceed as if otherwise these competitors were non-existent and their own aim and purpose the only thing in this world. This complete concentration on the factual aspect of the issue leaves only an antagonism of a formal nature. The result is that competition can be used as a form of conflict which will be of benefit to both parties. Competition is often stimulated artificially, as between the regiments of an army or between subgroups of co-workers for a common cause. It will not only lead to an increased activity on the part of each competing group which will be for the benefit of the whole, but even the victory of the winner will indirectly benefit the losers.

This peculiar character of competition, the neglect of the opponent and the concentration on the objective re-

[1] *Soz.*, pp. 271–77.

sults, makes it also extremely valuable to the wider social circle to which the competitors belong. Conflicts which result from subjective pugnacity, or which are fought for something that one of the opponents possesses, are of no benefit to the group as a whole. But if a competitive struggle is fought without the intermixture of other conflict elements and for something the group has to give, the results will be most beneficial. For the group as a whole, the competition will then be a way to stimulate the creation of objective values by means of subjective motives. For the parties concerned, the competition forces an increased production of objective values as a means to subjective satisfactions. This is the situation in the modern business world, where the producers fight their competitive struggles by the production of better and cheaper goods.

But apart from these indirect advantages for the larger circle, competition has immediate sociological results of no less importance. As the objects for which the competition exists are in the hands of the group and can be obtained only by incurring its favor, the contesting parties are forced to establish intimate relationships with the group and to anticipate its wishes and desires. Competition is therefore a socializing force. It is a synthetic force weaving a whole network of threads through the social structure, and adds to the strength of its texture. It seems that since the breaking up of the small group and the resulting disappearance of solidarity, individuals act in the interest of other individuals only if they are forced or stimulated to it by competition. Competition produces results which could otherwise be brought about only through love and altruism. In its modern form it is not merely a struggle of all against all, but also a struggle of all for all. This latter formal synthetic aspect is often overlooked by the

critics of competition, who usually see only the factual results and advantages for the group and the formal anti-
thetic aspect of the relation between the competitors.

A competitive system is therefore not identical with a
system that is purely individualistic. The competitor
works, of course, for his own interests. But, as the contest
is fought by means of objective values or social services and
is usually advantageous to the group, it may be in the interest of the group to foster competition. With reference
to the final aims of social life, the question of the advantage or disadvantage of competition is a problem of social
technique, not a question of ultimate ends. The question
has been answered in different ways. On the one side stands
the group that advocates unlimited competition because it
believes in the efficiency of the competitive system. On the
other side stands the group of socialists, who deny that the
waste of energy and duplication which result from competition are counterbalanced by the advantages of the
competitive system. They advocate a social technique
which is to operate with a system of co-ordinated and integrated services directed from a central point, instead of
a system of competing individual efforts. In between
stand different groups advocating restricted competition
in some fields and organized and co-ordinated services in
other fields. A comparison of these different systems is a
comparison of means, not of ends. A judgment and valuation of their comparative merit should therefore be based
on their efficiency as means. But the intellectual capacity
for a theoretic valuation is usually lacking, and the result
is that in the controversies of the different groups sentiments and subjective preferences play a more important
part than differences of opinion about actual efficiency.[1]

[1] *Soz.*, pp. 282–97.

The Results of Conflict for the Internal Structure of the Group

Apart from the sociological significance which conflicts possess for the relationships between the opponents, they lead also to important modifications of the inner structure of the contesting parties. These modifications are, of course, of sociological importance only if the parties to the conflict are themselves social groups.

The outbreak of a struggle forces a group to concentrate its energies and centralize its activities. In time of peace it can allow a great amount of decentralization and local autonomy, but immediately the struggle breaks out, it becomes necessary to concentrate all the available energies and to place them at the disposal of the central authority. The result is that conflicts often lead to a purification of groups through the expulsion of inharmonious elements. In times of peace a group can allow within its fold a certain number of antagonistic elements. But a struggle pulls the elements so much together and binds them so closely that the divergent elements must either be forced to harmonize or be repulsed. This makes groups at war so intolerant toward their own members. They can allow only small deviations from the norm and must suppress or expel any member whose divergence threatens the harmonious unity on which the strength of the group depends. Especially the small group cannot allow any uncertain elements in its midst, and it gains in actual strength by expelling them, although it loses in numerical strength.

A struggle therefore strengthens the unity of groups. The influence of wars on the growth of nationalities and that of heretics on the strength of the Catholic church are only a few of the innumerable illustrations that might be cited from history. But a common opponent not only strengthens unity, but often creates a unity which did not formerly exist. Military alliances and political combinations are only two instances of this phenomenon, which is manifest in all aspects of human life. This blending force of conflicts is illustrated not only in the formation of new combinations, but also by the fact that the termination of the struggle often leads to a split in the victorious party. Combinations made especially for the purpose of fighting a common opponent often contain elements which could not combine for peaceful pursuits. As long as the struggle lasts, the individual differences are suppressed, but, once the conflict is ended, the divergence between the elements reasserts itself and leads to separation or even perhaps to a mutual antagonism.[1]

The Termination of the Conflict

The termination of a conflict is a special undertaking which differs both from the actual struggle and from a condition of peace. It involves more fundamental changes in the social relationships than the actual outbreak of a conflict. The latter is usually merely an outburst of a latent antagonism due to already existing frictions and oppositions. But the termination of the conflict involves fundamental sociological changes. The sociology of conflict demands therefore as an appendix at least a short analysis of the forms in which conflicts are terminated.

Among the many forms in which conflicts come to an end there may be distinguished three main groups, according to whether the termination is due to victory, to compromise, or to conciliation. The love of peace will be present as a subjective element in the termination of most conflicts, just as a certain pugnacity plays a rôle in the outbreak of most conflicts; but neither is an immediate determinant of form.

The simplest and most radical form of passage from

[1] *Soz.*, pp. 306–23.

war to peace is victory. Victories are more or less absolute and occur in different degrees of completeness. The type of victory that is of special importance for the succeeding peace is the one that results, not exclusively from the preponderance of the one party, but in part at least from the resignation of the other. This confession of inferiority and acknowledgment of defeat before actual exhaustion is not always a simple phenomenon. It may be induced by various motives, such as a tendency toward self-humiliation, a feeling that it is worthier to yield than to speculate on an improbable chance, and a feeling that the confession of defeat is a gift to the conqueror and, as such, a last act of strength.

The termination of a conflict by compromise is completely different from a termination by victory. The fact that certain conflicts can be terminated by compromise places them in a class by themselves separate and distinct from conflicts which must be fought for a victory. Conflicts induced by hatred or revenge allow no compromise. In primitive times, conflicts fought for a single specific object could not be terminated if the object was indivisible. That this is none the less possible today is one of the great advances of civilization. It has resulted from the differentiation between the value of an object and the object itself. It took the invention of exchange as a practical synthesis of gift and theft, the earliest forms of transferring values, to make this possible. Once this differentiation had been accomplished, the possibility was created of terminating conflicts about objects through an exchange of values.

In contrast to compromise, which is an objective means of terminating conflict, conciliation is a purely subjective means. What is referred to here is not the sort of conciliation that often follows a compromise or any other termination of the struggle, but rather the kind that leads to this termination. This tendency toward conciliation, which seeks to end the struggle apart from any objective grounds, is a specific sociological impulse. It is similar to the disposition to quarrel apart from any objective grounds which promotes struggle. This tendency toward conciliation is not identical with the general peaceful disposition. The latter avoids strife under all circumstances and never fights without longing for peace. The spirit of conciliation, however, often manifests itself most clearly immediately after a complete and most enthusiastic devotion to the struggle. It is usually strongest after the fighting energies have spent themselves in full.

Conciliation as resulting from subjective elements is relatively independent of the objective situation. It can occur after the complete victory of one party or in the middle of an undecided struggle or after the successful arrangement of a compromise. On the other hand, the struggle may terminate in victory or compromise without the conciliation of the opponents. Moreover, the conciliation itself is to be distinguished from the situation which follows it. This may be either a relationship of attachment and alliance or a mutual avoidance of all positive contacts. Conciliation is therefore a subjective means of terminating conflicts without reference to their probable outcome, be it victory or compromise.[1]

In the preceding pages different forms of conflict have been analyzed in their sociological aspects. It is evident from that analysis that a conflict is a synthesizing force. It means not only a synthesis between the contesting parties and a strengthening of the internal unity of opposing groups, but, in the form of competition, it also leads to a strengthening of the bonds between the opponents and the group as a whole.

[1] *Soz.*, pp. 323–36.

CHAPTER III

THE NUMERICAL RELATIONS
OF SOCIAL FORMS

THE QUANTITATIVE DETERMINATION OF SOCIALIZATIONS[1]

I T WILL be conceded without hesitation that a group of a certain size must build organs, establish forms, and maintain regulations which a smaller group does not need. Mere observation shows that small groups, on the other hand, develop forms of interaction which disappear when they grow in size. It is possible to undertake an analysis of this quantitative determination and to trace some of the more important correlations between the forms of the socialization and the number of elements that are socialized.

This quantitative determination has two aspects, a negative and a positive one. The negative aspect is evident when there exists a numerical limit above or below which a specific form cannot occur. In case this specific form is the result of, or is possible only with, a definite content, then, if there is a correlation between the content and the size of the group, it can be realized only in groups of a certain size. In such a case the content determines the size of the group and thereby the form. The forms of communistic societies, of secret organizations, and of certain religious sects, which are all limited in their membership on account of their doctrines, are illustrations of this negative determination. The positive aspect is evident when a change is directly required by a purely quantitative modification of

[1] Adapted from *Soz.*, chap. ii, pp. 47–133.

the group. In that case the size immediately determines the form.[1]

Definite correlations between characteristic sociological formations and arithmetically definable magnitudes appear only near the lower boundary of the numerical series. Higher up in the scale such a definite mathematical formulation is not possible, and the modifications must be formulated in terms of more or less. More precisely, however, the situation is this. To every definite number of elements there correspond, in accordance with the purpose and the spirit of their association, a specific sociological form, a characteristic organization, and a definite degree of firmness of texture. With every added or subtracted element these experience a modification, however small and indeterminable. There are, however, no special terms for these different sociological conditions, even in a case where the differences can be observed. This forces us to describe the situation as if it were a combination of two conditions with the one more, the other less conspicuous.

The Monad

The simplest structure which may be subsumed under the sociological category is the single individual, however paradoxical and essentially contradictory it may seem. The two phenomena, isolation and freedom, which appear in relation to the individual are distinctly of a sociological character. Not only are they characteristic of the relation between the individual and the group, but the amount of freedom and isolation which the group allows the individual elements is immediately significant for the structure of the whole.

The mere fact that an individual maintains no reciprocal relationships with other individuals is, of course, not

[1] *Soz.*, p. 47.

sociological. But the situation which is expressed by the concept "isolation" does not consist of this fact alone. Isolation does not signify merely the absence of all society. For the isolated individual, society exerts a long-distance influence either as echo of the past or as anticipation of future relationships, either as a longing for socialization or as a voluntary renouncement of it. He has not the same characteristics as a man who has been from his birth the only inhabitant of the world. Socialization, even if it be only with a negative sign, is also a determining factor even for his condition.

It is of importance for the configuration of a group whether it favors or allows isolation of individuals. Close and intimate communities do not permit such intercellular vacuums in their structure. But in larger groups a certain quantity and quality of social life will produce a distinct number of temporarily or chronically isolated existences. They form a social deficit in the same way as the forlorn, the criminal, and the suicide.

Isolation in these cases takes the form of a relationship within the mind of the individual between himself and a specific group or between himself and group life in general. It has sociological significance in another way when it occurs as a periodic differentiation or an interval within one and the same relationship. A monogamic marriage in which husband and wife occasionally enjoy the pleasures of isolation, even though happy in their relationship, is different from one in which such isolation would be considered as a lack of faithfulness or as a danger to the relationship.

Thus isolation, apparently confined to the single individual and consisting in a negation of socialization, is in reality a phenomenon of positive sociological significance. It is important for the agent in whom it is present as an experience which signifies a well-defined relation to society. But apart from this, it is important for large groups as well as for the most intimate relations to which its occurrence either as cause or as effect lends a distinct character.

Not only isolation, but also freedom, appears in the first place as a negation of socialization, as an absence of all social restraint. This may describe the position of a Christian or Hindu hermit or of a solitary settler, but for a social being freedom has a much more positive meaning. It appears as a continuous process of emancipation from social restraints, as a struggle, not merely for independence, but for the right to enter voluntarily into dependence, as a struggle which must be renewed after each victory. Freedom as a negative social attitude is almost never a permanent possession. It is a process of incessant liberation from restraints which limit in reality or attempt to limit ideally the independence of the individual. It is not a being, but a becoming, a sociological activity. It is a relationship, even if observed from the standpoint of the agent.

Not only in its functional aspect, but also with regard to the content, does freedom mean more than absence of restraint. Freedom from the influence of others would in numerous cases have no meaning or significance for the individual if it did not facilitate an extension of his will over others. While apparently negative in character, freedom has therefore in reality a very positive significance. Freedom consists to a large extent in a process of liberation, and it obtains meaning and significance as a reaction against restraint. But it also consists in a position of strength in the relations with others, in the possibility of self-assertion in these relations, and in the opportunity for making others tributary or subject. It is in these relationships that it finds its positive value and realization.[1]

[1] *Soz.*, pp. 76–80.

The Dyadic Group

That such apparently individual qualities as isolation
and freedom are in reality sociological relationships can,
however, be pointed out only by referring to indirect and
complicated connections. The simplest sociological formation is therefore the reciprocity which occurs in the case
of the interaction between two elements.

That the dyadic group has a typical sociological form
is evident from the fact that the most divergent individuals
uniting for the most varied motives will show combinations
of the same formation. And not only is this form characteristic for pairs of individuals, but it is identical in the case of
an association between pairs of groups like families, states,
or combinations of various sorts.

Its specific character is determined by the fact that
for the participants the relationship does not appear as a
special structure over and above them. It may appear to
an outsider as an independent, superindividual unity; this
is not the case for the individuals concerned. They are
aware of the fact that it rests immediately upon the one
and the other. The whole does not obtain a superpersonal
life independent of its bearers. The group ceases to exist
if one individual departs, which is not the case with combinations of more than two elements. The individual has
not beside him a multiplicity of other individuals which
ultimately constitutes a higher unity. He has beside him
only one other individual, and the dependence of the whole
upon himself and his co-responsibility for all collective
action is more clearly visible. He cannot hide behind the
group either in omission or in commission, and the result
is that the individual enters into the relationship with a
much greater part of his personality than is the case in
large groups. The dyadic group, in contrast with all other
groups of more numerous elements, is characterized by the

fact that it does not grow into a higher, superindividual unity.

There are, however, exceptions to this rule that the superindividual unity of the dyadic group does not obtain objective existence. The first example is the monogamic marriage. In this case the exception is due to the historical tradition which has given the marriage form a certain objective fixity and superindividual validity. This traditional element is projected into the relationship in the individual case and suggests the existence of this form as independent of the bearers. In that respect it is in sharp contrast with a friendship bond into which no traditional element enters. The second example is the business partnership. Although the formation and the functioning of the partnership rest on the co-operation of the two individuals, yet the subject-matter of this co-operation, the business or the firm, is an objective structure. With regard to this objective structure each of the partners has rights and duties which are in many respects similar to those of outsiders. But this objectivation has a very different sociological significance from that observed in the preceding case. The business is something separated from the beginning from the individuals who carry it on. And this is true whether the number of partners be two or more. The relationship of the business associates has its purpose outside of itself, whereas, in the case of marriage, the purpose of the relationship lies within it. In the former instance the relationship is a means to objective ends, in the latter everything objective appears really as a means to the subjective relationship.[1]

The Triadic Group

That combinations of two elements have specific traits is shown not merely by the fact that the entrance of a

[1] *Soz.*, pp. 80–92.

third modifies it entirely, but also by the fact that a further extension is not followed by a modification of corresponding degree. The dyadic group is the first in the numerical scale to show a unity and synthesis, but it also manifests an internal antithesis and opposition. The entrance of a third element causes considerable modification. On the one hand it makes for a superindividual unity, and on the other hand it changes the direct and immediate reciprocity. Added to the direct relationship there is now an indirect relationship which both reinforces and interferes with the immediate reciprocity. The new group is less dependent on the immediate participation of the elements than the dyadic group. It absorbs less of the total personality and can continue its existence if one element drops out.

The function of the third and the configurations of triadic groups are herewith largely indicated. The dyadic group showed synthesis and antithesis. The entrance of a third element means transition, conciliation, renunciation both of the immediate reciprocity and of the direct opposition. But it can also create oppositions formerly absent. The triadic group can therefore manifest three characteristic formations which are impossible in dyadic groups and which are likewise excluded from larger groups. Two of these configurations are known by the title of the third person, namely, the non-partisan arbitrator or mediator on the one hand, and the *tertius gaudens* on the other hand. The third configuration is usually indicated by the motto *Divide et impera.*

In the first instance, the non-partisanship of the third element serves the group as a whole. The conciliator or arbitrator aims to prevent a disruption of the existing unity between the opposing elements.

The non-partisan can, however, also use his advantageous position for his own selfish interests. In that case his position becomes that of the *tertius gaudens*. In the first case he serves as a means to the ends of the group, in the latter case he makes the relationship between the others and himself serve as a means to his own ends. In such cases the triadic relationship is often especially created by the non-partisan for his own advantages and not yet existent in consolidated structures.

In the last configuration, indicated by the motto *Divide et impera*, the third element plays an even more active rôle. While in the second configuration there usually is an existing antithesis between the two elements which the third element merely uses to its own advantage, in this third configuration the third element actually creates that antithesis. There are, of course, transition forms which are difficult to classify under one or the other. But the essential fact is that two elements originally united against a third, or at least mutually dependent in their relations to a third, are placed in mutual antithesis and opposition by this third element. The result is that they will mutually counterbalance each other and leave the third element free to pursue its own interests, or mutually weaken each other enough to give the third element a predominance which no other single element can dispute.

These three configurations are variations of the form of triadic groups. They are purely formal configurations. They can be found in social situations having the most varying content, and occur not only as relationships between persons, but also as relationships between groups. They are manifest in military alliances, in political combinations, and in economic associations. They appear in the relationship of the monarch to other monarchs as well as in the relationship of the monarch to his subjects.[1]

[1] *Soz.*, pp. 99–126.

The Large and the Small Group

For groups larger than triadic groups no correlation between specific formations and numerically definable magnitudes can be formulated. But a very clear distinction can still be drawn between the forms of small groups and the forms of large groups. The quantitative determination does not cease, although it can no longer be expressed in numerical terms.

The correlation between the size of the group and the form is apparent in the gathering that meets for a social function. A party for thirty guests requires certain standards of food, drink, dress, and behavior which do not exist for a party of two or three. In the greater social circle the more intimate contacts between individuals disappear, and this disadvantage has to be compensated for by other means. For that reason there is a close relation between the size of the social gathering and the amount of luxury necessary to make it a success. With the increase in size there will also be an increase of standardized polite behavior over spontaneous participation. In their purely sociological aspect, small groups are characterized by the fact that they require a larger participation on the part of the individual members, that they absorb a greater part of their personality, and that they are more clearly and sharply separated from one another. The larger groups show in these respects just the opposite sociological characteristics.[1]

The forms which are characteristic of large groups result from the fact that they are forced to build special structures to take over the function which the immediate reciprocity between elements fulfils in small circles. The social unity can no longer be produced and preserved by the immediate relationships between individuals, and the large group must therefore build special organs in which

[1] This point is more fully developed in Book II, chapter vii.

the reciprocal activities and relationships of its elements can crystallize. Out of that necessity are born objective structures and norms, official and representative bodies as means to preserve the social unity, which small circles can dispense with. The formation and function of these special structures will be dealt with in the chapter on social preservation. They are referred to here because their formation is immediately related to the size of the group, and because they are, as such, characteristic of large groups.

The formal difference between large and small groups is also manifest in the type of norm by means of which the group secures its self-preservation. This is most evident in the distinction between mores and law. In small groups the relationships between individuals are regulated by the mores; the large group needs, in addition to these, the law. The life of primitive peoples living in small communities was entirely regulated by the mores. The mores set the norms for the whole of the religious, political, and economic life, and covered the entire domain of what appear at present as the spheres of morality, convention, and law. With the formation of larger social circles and the combination of these small groups in single units, there occurred a differentiation in fields of different social content and a differentiation in different kinds of norms. The result had both a social and a sociological aspect. Out of the mores differentiated on the one hand individual morality, on the other hand law. In modern society all three forms of norms serve to secure an individual behavior in accordance with social requirements.

Society has an interest in the moral perfection of the individual only in so far as that moral perfection guarantees an adequate social behavior, that is, only in so far as it regulates social relationships. But in so far as it serves that function, it is a highly efficient instrument. It has a more immediate normative influence than the law and the mores, and it requires no contribution and support from the group to make it effective. Hence the tendency of society to urge moral perfection and to appeal to the conscience of the individual. A conscience that works effectively has this advantage for society, that the individual gives himself the reward for his adequate social behavior which would otherwise have to be guaranteed to him in one form or another by either custom or law.

The mores are the characteristic form of norm for the small group. Formerly they were the sole regulator of social life; today they function in conjunction with morality and law. Nearly all mores are class mores, that is, norms for small social circles. Non-conformity is punished by social disapproval and by the immediate reactions of those observing it. The sphere of the mores is therefore the small circle in which the immediate reciprocities between individuals still form the main basis of the social union.

In large groups these immediate reciprocities become less important and are in some cases entirely absent. The large group can therefore not rely on the mores to guarantee an adequate social behavior on the part of individuals. It must create on the one hand definitely fixed and clearly defined objective standards, and on the other hand special organs whose task it is to see that these standards are complied with. For the state this means the formulation of statute law and the creation of a judiciary and a police force.

The mores regulate a large part of the individual's existence, but their function is limited to a small social circle and their sanction is not always sufficient. The law regulates a small part of the individual's existence, but its function extends over a large social circle and its sanction is guaranteed by severe and forceful restraint. Morality regulates the whole of the individual's existence, but it has no sanction other than the dictates of conscience. These are the three special forms of norms which regulate the internal and external relations of the individual to his social groups. Their purely formal aspect is evident from the fact that the same content may at different periods be left to the mores, to the law, or to individual morality.[1]

The Size of the Group and Its External Relations

Apart from this determination of the internal relations by the size of the group, the number of the group elements gives also in many instances a special character to the group as a whole viewed in relation to the outside world. The significance of the numerical magnitude of the group for its external relations is manifest in two types of social situation. The first occurs in the subdivision of large groups into numerically defined subgroups. The second occurs if society as a whole prescribes a numerical maximum or minimum membership for certain kinds of groups and associations.

Social Organization on a Numerical Basis

In the first instance, the numerical magnitude becomes the principle of social organization. Parts of the group of a specified magnitude are considered as units. Numerical identity of parts becomes the form principle of the group. The group as a whole is then related to each of its parts as the parts are related to their individual members, that is, numerically. The numerical relationship is, of course, not the only relationship. The individual members must be relatives or neighbors or fellow-workers or fellow-fighters. They must have something in common on the basis of which they are combined in subgroups. But in so far as the structure of the subgroup is dependent on its size, it is not

[1] *Soz.*, pp. 53–62.

determined by that common bond, but merely by the formal exigencies of the large group. This numerical subdivision of large groups is a schematic, formal, and mechanical type of social organization. It makes possible the combination of smaller units into larger ones until social differentiation and integration shall have given the large group a unified organic structure instead of a mechanical unity.

The numerically defined subgroup may have been formed out of small organic circles, but its teleological significance does not lie in its own structure, but in its external relationships to the large group. Such an organization makes it possible to maintain the character and the structure of the parts independently of the growth of the whole. The central administration deals only with elements of identical sociological quality, and an extension of the group merely means a greater number of elements. This type of social organization finds its most complete expression in an army. Increase or decrease in size can be obtained by simply adding or subtracting a number of numerically fixed sociological forms. For that reason it has always been used in a more or less pure form for all warlike purposes. Nomadic peoples on a campaign of conquest have no other stable social content available as a basis for organization and must resort to a formal principle which will serve their purpose. The numerical principle is the most advantageous one and infinitely superior to the kinship organization in that it is less likely to lead to disruption through blood feuds. After the conquest, the numerical principle will often be projected into the administration of the conquered territory until a more factual or organic principle can supplant it.

The advantages of such a subdivision on the numerical principle hold, of course, for all magnitudes and are independent of any specific number. Certain specific numbers have, however, usually been chosen for such subdivisions, namely, the number ten and its derivatives. This is undoubtedly due to the fact that the number of the fingers of the hands suggests itself easily as an appropriate magnitude for numerical groupings of elements into units. Many secret societies have consisted of organizations of groups of five. In the older civilizations, many organizations shaped themselves as combinations of groups of ten with special duties and responsibilities. Of the larger derivatives, the classical example is the hundred. It was the numerical magnitude for subdivisions, not only in early German and Anglo-Saxon times, but also in the ancient American civilizations.[1]

Minimum and Maximum Qualifications

The second instance in which the numerical magnitude becomes of importance for the external relations occurs in case the group manifests specific characteristics only below or above a certain size. The distinction between the general character of the external relations of small and large groups has been referred to previously. But the same question can be asked in detail for the relation between certain specific characteristics and certain well-defined magnitudes. In the last analysis the internal relations of the group elements will be the basis for the character of the group as a whole, but in this case the interest is not in these internal relations, but in the group as a unit. The facts which point to the existence of a special significance of the size for the group as a whole all belong to one category. They are the legal prescriptions with regard to maximum and minimum membership for groups which are to be subject to specific rights and duties.

[1] *Soz.*, pp. 126–30.

These prescriptions are due to the fact that on the average a certain degree of solidarity, tone, force, or tendency will appear only with a certain group size. If these characteristics are desired, that size is prescribed as a minimum; if they are to be avoided, then that size is allowed as a maximum. In reality, no two groups of the same size will be identical in character, owing to the difference in individual elements. But legal regulations cannot make exceptions for individual variations. They must fix numerical magnitudes which conform to averages. Hence the minimum and maximum regulations for associations are expressions of average conditions, in the same way as the minimum age for suffrage is an expression of average conditions as independent of the relative maturity of a specific individual. But as expressions of average conditions they express correlations between specific characteristics and the size of the group. History is full of such regulations. Among regulations with regard to the maximum can be mentioned the limitation of street gatherings, of public meetings, and of religious revivals.

Among regulations with regard to a minimum are the stipulation of the smallest membership giving right to incorporation and the stipulation of the minimum number of judges or jurors required to pass a valid judgment. In the first instance, the minimum is required to guarantee a sufficient solidarity, without which corporations might be a danger to the public economy. In the second case, the minimum requirement aims at obtaining a number large enough to allow for a counterbalancing of mistakes and prejudices so that the collective opinion may be the true one. Where the law stipulates a minimum, it expresses a distrust in isolated individual action and a faith in collective action. Where it stipulates a maximum, it expresses, on the other hand, a distrust in the collectivity which it does not have for its single elements.[1]

The foregoing observations are sufficient to disclose a definite correlation between the number of the elements associated and the forms of their association. That correlation is more immediately visible in the internal relations of group elements, but it is also manifest in the character of the group as a whole and in the relations between groups.

[1] *Soz.*, pp. 130–33.

CHAPTER IV

THE SPATIAL RELATIONS OF SOCIAL FORMS

THE SPATIAL ORGANIZATION OF SOCIALIZATIONS[1]

SPACE as such is in the last analysis a subjective mental category, a form of co-ordinating discrete sense impressions in unitary perceptions. It is a synthesis which results from a specific psychological function and which, as such, has no immediate sociological significance. What appears as objective space is, as such, merely an irrelevant form.

But what is in reality a mere formal condition without which certain occurrences cannot take place has often been taken for an efficient cause. Certain interpretations of history have laid much stress on the spatial factor and have regarded the size of states, the dispersion or concentration of peoples, the mobility or stability of the masses, as if these factors were efficient causes emanating from space instead of mere expressions in spatial form of the actual forces and processes. What makes a state big is not the number of square miles of its area, but the forces and resources of its people. What creates the characteristic phenomena of neighborliness or strangeness is not the spatial proximity or the spatial distance, but a specific psychological content.

Notwithstanding this fact, the spatial forms of objects and occurrences are often of great importance, not as causes, but as effects that throw light on the character of

[1] Adapted from *Soz.*, chap. ix, pp. 614–708.

144

the actual forces. The spatial conditions of an occurrence are often very indicative of the processes which have brought it about. Such is also the case with the processes of socialization.

Interaction between human beings is conceived of and experienced as space-filling. If individuals live within certain spatial boundaries and are isolated from one another, the space between them is empty space. But if they enter into reciprocal relations, the space between them seems filled and animated. The term "between" has a double meaning. It is a spatial and a functional concept. The result is that the interaction between two elements, which in the last analysis consists of an immanent movement within each of the elements, comes to be conceived of as taking place between them in the sense of in a spatial location. The functional reciprocity is felt to be located between the two points in space occupied by the elements themselves. It manifests itself in space, and the spatial form becomes therefore characteristic of the reciprocity as a whole. An investigation of the spatial aspect of sociological forms will therefore throw light on the character of the processes of socialization.[1]

Spatially Exclusive and Non-exclusive Groups

The fact that social forms manifest themselves in space makes it necessary to view them first of all in relation to certain fundamental characteristics of space. One of these characteristics is its exclusiveness. Just as space in general is unique and exclusive, so each part of space has a certain uniqueness and exclusiveness. A specific localized part of space cannot be conceived in the plural. It is unique and exclusive. This characteristic of space makes it possible to conceive of a plurality of fully identical objects. The

[1] *Ibid.*, pp. 614–17.

fact that each fills a different part of space, which is not identical with any other part of space and which does not coincide with any other part, enables us to differentiate between fully identical objects. The unique character of space is therefore transferred to objects in so far as they are viewed in their spatial extension.

In case the spatial location of objects is significant as a point of reference, as in the case of the land or the soil, this transference of the characteristic of exclusiveness and uniqueness becomes of great importance. For social structures will then be unique and exclusive to the degree in which they are tied and related to a specific area of land. Such sociological forms are characterized by the fact that within their territory there is no room for an identical structure. Of other social structures there are a great many identical forms possible within the same area. Such forms are mutually permeable. As they have no internal relations to space, they cannot come into spatial collision. The best example of the first group is the state, of the latter, the church.

The relations between individuals which are created by a state, or rather which create a state, are so closely related to territory that a second state on the same territory is an impossibility. Within a certain area there is, however, room for more than one guild or more than one church. The life-principle of a church is non-spatial. It extends through all space and is therefore not exclusive within a specific part of space. Within these two extremes there are intermediate forms. Social structures vary in their spatial aspects from those that are territorially completely fixed and thereby unique and exclusive, to those that are fully superspatial and allow a plurality of identical forms within the same area. The proximity or distance, the uniqueness or the plurality which characterize the relations of social groups to their territory are therefore often the root and symbol of their structure.[1]

Sociological Boundaries

Another characteristic of space which is of significance for social structures is the fact that it can be divided into parts which appear as unities. These space unities are conceived of as framed by imaginary boundary lines. Not only the space filled by objects, but also the space occupied by the functional reciprocities of group elements, comes to be conceived of as a space unity framed by a border line. This space unity is on the one hand a spatial expression of the sociological unity of the group, while on the other hand the concept of its functional unity is reinforced by the unity of its spatial extension.

This border line has for the group a significance similar to that which a frame has for a picture. It fulfils the double function of separating it from the outside world and of closing it within itself. The frame announces that within the border line there is a world subject to its own norms, entirely divorced from the world outside. It symbolizes the self-sufficiency of the picture. A group is similarly characterized as an internal unity if its spatial extension is conceived of as bordered by a boundary line. On the other hand, the functional unity resulting from the reciprocities between the elements finds its spatial expression in that surrounding frame.

The existence of a boundary between two states is the spatial expression of such internal and external relations of the elements of the two groups. The spatial boundary is not the result of the fact that the territories, that is, the pieces of land, border upon each other, but it is due to the fact that the relationships between the elements involved

[1] *Soz.*, pp. 617–24.

are those of internal union and external opposition. The border is not a spatial fact with sociological consequences, but a sociological fact that expresses itself in spatial form.

The existence of a sociological boundary line between groups or individuals means the existence of a special form of interaction for which we have no single term. It means a relationship which contains in a latent form an attitude of both defense and offense. It may be a line delimiting the rights of the individuals at the end of a struggle, or a line indicating the delimiting of their respective influence preceding a struggle. In all human relationships there exists such a boundary line beyond which the individuals are not allowed to transgress. It shifts and changes and is perhaps never stationary, but where that line is drawn at a given moment is indicative of the character of the relationship.

The necessity for understanding the persons with whom one maintains social relationships forces one to probe into their individuality and to seek a more extensive knowledge than can be acquired from their mere fragmentary actions. Our sense impressions have to be reinforced by and interpreted in the light of other knowledge not freely placed at our disposal, in order to form a complete picture of their individuality. Yet, however necessary it may be to penetrate into their individual domain, there is a limit beyond which we are not allowed to probe. That limit is the border of their exclusive personal sphere. Where that border line is to be found is indicative of the character of the relationship and of social life in general. In primitive times, when individuals showed only small differences, the sphere of the exclusively personal was usually much smaller than in modern times, when people are highly individualized. In commercial relations the boundary line lies elsewhere than in the relations between parents and children, and in the relations between diplomats elsewhere than in those between war comrades.

Another instance of sociological delimitation is found in the case of associations which have different kinds of members participating to different extents in the duties and benefits of the organization. The distinction between those that are full members and those that are not signifies that there is a boundary line between the latter and the totality to which they none the less belong. Within the group, this boundary marks certain points along the centripetal lines of rights and duties, indicating the limit which exists for the participation of some but not of others. Within the personality of the member, that limit signifies the boundary between the part of his individuality that falls within and the part that falls outside of the relationship.

The difference between the two kinds of participation is not so much a difference in intensity as a difference in extent. The person who is not a full member has rights and duties which are carefully specified and relatively independent of the life of the group as well as of his own fate. For the full member, a similar separation between his own individual life and that of the whole is not màde. He partakes with the whole of his personality in the total life of the group, and that which will be required of him or which will be due him cannot be stipulated in advance.

The delimitation of the participation of certain members through a specific determination of their rights and duties gives to their relations to the group as a whole an objective character. The objective character of the social relations of modern times is due largely to such limitation of the individual participation. In the Middle Ages the group claimed the whole of the individual, but stood as a whole behind him in mutual solidarity. In modern groups, even in those which are not purely purposive associations, the relationship implies only a limited contribution on the part of the members in exchange for a limited service on the part of the group.

Apart from the significance of a boundary line for the reciprocities across the border, the existence of such a boundary is also of importance for the internal relations of group elements. It is characteristic for the social life of the group whether the surrounding frame is felt as compressing and hemming in the life-processes of the group, or as sufficiently wide to allow for expansion and growth. This sociological density is not identical with a mere density of population. It is not primarily the result of the number of people, but depends rather on whether their forces and activities have sufficient room for growth or whether any expansion throws them against the border. In oriental states, the spatial frames of groups leave plenty of room notwithstanding the density of population. In western commercial states, the framework may appear much more narrow notwithstanding a much smaller population density.

The history of Venice shows an interesting illustration of the existence of a narrow frame and its influence on the life of the group. Territorial growth being impossible, the expansion of the city had to take the form of a dynamic expansion into the world at large. This policy required a world-view and wide vision which was lacking among the masses, and therefore led to an aristocratic form of government. Although Venice is perhaps the best illustration, the formal sociological influence and significance of a narrow spatial frame is not limited to political constellations, but is manifest in all social groups and associations.[1]

[1] *Soz.*, pp. 624–30.

Spatial Fixation of Social Contents

Another important significance of the spatial relations of social groups exists in the fact that they allow the fixation of their content in a definite locality. It makes a great difference in the structure of the group whether the group as a whole, certain definite elements in it, or certain of its fundamental interests are definitely fixed to a specific locality or spatially entirely undetermined.

The difference in social structure between nomadic and sedentary tribes has often been pointed out. This territorial fixation apparently occurs in different degrees of flexibility. Some groups bind themselves absolutely to a definite area and prohibit their members from leaving that area. Others withhold certain privileges from members living outside of the specific area. Others, again, are entirely free from any territorial fixation and have no specifications about domicile in their membership requirements. The modern purposive association tends toward the latter type. The fact that the introduction of the money economy has enabled the participation and contributions of members in certain associations to take a purely monetary form has made the necessity for actual aggregation for such groups entirely superfluous.

The territorial restrictions which a group attaches to its membership requirements may appear at first sight as an expression of the great power of the group over its members. This, however, is not always the case. In many instances the group binds its elements with external restrictions just because it feels its power and its unity insufficiently secured by the mere subjective cohesion. Territorial restriction or its absence may therefore be an expression both of great strength and of weakness. The freedom with which a modern state allows its subjects to emigrate is an expression of its strength and of the security it feels about its own continuity as independent of the movements of its members. The local diffusion of the modern family in contrast with its centralization in the ancestral home is, on the other hand, an expression of the weakening of the family unity.

The significance of this spatial expression of the relations between the group and its individual members remains the same when the group as a whole is nomadic. Many nomadic peoples like the Arabs prohibited the personal ownership of land or the building of permanent dwellings. The fixation of the individual to a definite locality under such conditions of nomadic existence would also have meant a dissolution of the bonds with his group. The sociological unity of the group finds its spatial expression in this case in a prohibition of fixation, just as under certain sedentary conditions it finds expression in a prescribed fixation.

Another form of spatial fixation which is of importance for the social structure is the fixation which results from the creation of a focal point for the reciprocities within the group. The fact that the family, the club, the university, the trade union, and the religious community have a home and a definite meeting-place gives them a distinct character. All associations which have a home of their own are thereby differentiated from all those other associations, like mutual-benefit societies, political parties, unions for temporary or illegal purposes, and socializations which consist merely in a consciousness of common aims and ideals, which lack all spatial fixation. The word "home" is used here, not in the sense of a mere piece of property, but in the sense of a locality in which the group meets and lives its social life. In that sense it is the spatial expression of the unity of its sociological energies. But this objectivation

of its unity is not only a spatial expression, but also a powerful means of further strengthening and preserving that
unity. Not only is the men's house in primitive communities the spatial expression of the formation of a special
class, but this class formation could never have taken place
without the house as its objectivation and the focal point
for its reciprocities.[1]

Distance and Proximity

Not only the spatial relations to a focal point, but also
the spatial relations between the elements themselves, are
of importance for the form of the socialization. Socializations between persons at a distance would be greatly modified if the individuals were brought into spatial proximity.
A business combination, a friendship, a society of stamp-
collectors, and a religious community can temporarily or
permanently dispense with personal contact. But the ties
which unite the members would be quantitatively and
qualitatively modified if there were no intervening space
to be bridged.

The relationships of a purely factual and impersonal
character and the relationships of a purely emotional character apparently overcome the disadvantages of spatial
separateness in the most successful manner. In the case
of the former, such as scientific and commercial transactions, this is due to the fact that their content can be fully
expressed in logical forms and can therefore be transferred
in writing. In the case of the latter, such as relationships
whose content is a religious feeling or a personal love and
devotion, it is due to the fact that emotion and imagination often overcome the conditions of time and space in a
mystical manner. For relationships which are not of such
an extreme type, but which partake of both characteristics,

[1] *Soz.*, pp. 630–40.

spatial proximity is a direct advantage. It allows a reinforcement or a toning down of the purely emotional ties
through actual sensations and observations, and it enables
the insufficiencies of the logical formulation to be sup-
plemented by personal contact.[1]

Apart from the purely psychological effects on the immediate relationships, the proximity or distance between
the socialized elements is also of importance for the objective structure of the group as a whole. This is manifest in
the correlation between spatial proximity and centralization on the one hand, and between local diffusion and decentralization on the other hand.

A community whose elements live far apart will rarely
show tendencies toward centralization. When during the
Middle Ages the Swiss peasant communities constituted
themselves into political units, they repeated in their organization the fundamental traits of town administrations.
But the community life of the peasants was not entirely
transferred to the special administrative organs, as was the
case in the cities. The popular assembly remained the most
important organ for jurisdiction as well as for the general
guiding of public affairs. This was the result partly of the
distrust in central organs which cannot be adequately
supervised from a long distance, and partly of the lower
vitality of the social reciprocities in the rural districts.
Town communities, on the other hand, show a far-going
centralization entirely independent of their otherwise pronounced democratic tendencies.

Dispersed living in rural districts is a favorable condition for the development of aristocracies, and even de-
mocracies begin to partake of aristocratic characteristics
under such a condition. This is due to the self-sufficiency
of individuals and their freedom from and independence

[1] *Soz.*, pp. 640–46.

of the central administration. The history of the Germanic tribes is full of illustrations of this type of development.

The Spartans solved the antinomy between the agrarian character of their state, which predisposed it toward an aristocratic, decentralized type of structure, and the centralization which was required by their military organization in an interesting fashion. They left their agricultural estates in the hands of managers and lived in spatial proximity in the city. Something similar occurred, although in a different form, among the French nobility under the ancient régime. As long as the nobles had lived on the land, they had been practically autonomous on their own estates. The increasing centralization of the ancient régime robbed them on the one hand of their judicial and administrative independence, but, on the other hand, it drew them to Paris.

The correlation is therefore between spatial proximity or local compactness and centralization on the one hand, and local dispersion and decentralized autonomy on the other hand. It is a correlation that can be found in groups with democratic tendencies as well as in groups with aristocratic tendencies, and is therefore an illustration of a determination of sociological forms by purely spatial relations.[1]

Movement of Groups and Group Elements

The correlations so far referred to have been correlations between social forms and fixed spatial relations. The next question is: What forms of organization do we find in wandering groups, and what kinds of formation result if not the group as a whole, but only certain elements, lead a wandering existence?

[1] *Ibid.*, pp. 668–70.

The best illustration of the first instance can be found in the organization of nomadic tribes and in the special formations of otherwise sedentary peoples during their actual migrations. The effect seems to be a suppression or a dissolution of internal differentiation, often accompanied by a strong personal despotism.

The patriarchal organization of the family among nomadic people finds its counterpart in a despotism of the group over the individual in times of actual migration. It resulted immediately from the fact that these migrations, even if not directly for war purposes, required none the less a military form of organization. But it was a military organization of a character different from the one that is found among sedentary people. The latter means a special fixed organization intersecting all existing group formations, and presupposes a far-going differentiation and an advanced division of labor. A differentiation and division of labor presupposes, however, either a narrow spatial contact or an intensive functional contact of elements. Those conditions did not exist among primitive nomadic tribes. They consisted of dispersed families which were largely self-contained and self-sufficient and in no functional relations with one another. The food conditions drove them to spatial dispersion and forced them to separate. Only the need of mutual protection drove them to spatial contraction and brought them together. Their actual combination during such periods of migration was therefore not based on an organic synthesis, but it took the form of a mere mechanical aggregation of equal elements held together by a more or less personal despotism.

The members of a wandering group are very dependent on one another, and this temporary but immediate common interest overshadows the existing differences which a sedentary life would bring to full expression. A certain fundamental equality and lack of differentiation is apparent among the elements of all moving groups. The traveling merchants of the Middle Ages had communistic types of organization as long as they were actually on the road, and sometimes continued their communistic form of living even during their stay in foreign parts. The organization of the factories of the Hanseatic league is an illustration of this tendency. On the other hand, the despotic element is usually not entirely lacking, as is manifest in the absolute and unlimited authority of the caravan leader and the captain of a ship.

The wandering of certain elements in otherwise sedentary groups presents two important phenomena. The first is the movement of elements which contributes to the unification of the group. The second is the wandering of elements which is harmful to the preservation of the group.

The groups which are dispersed over a wide territory maintain their natural unity in modern civilization by means of different dynamic relationships between their elements. The similarity of objective culture which is accompanied by the knowledge that it is identical for all points of the area, the uniformity of law and language, the functional organizations and the scientific associations, all contribute to the creation of a sociological unity. In so far as these socializations are effective, they need only to a very small extent the actual movement of individuals. Modern life succeeds in creating a consciousness of social unity through factual similarities, knowledge of common interests, fixed institutions, and written communication. But in periods when such an objective organization and technique have not yet been developed, the movement of individuals through the territory of the group is of great significance for an effective unification.

During the Middle Ages the merchant, the scholar, the

monk, the artisan, the artist, and the civil servant were all more peripatetic than they are today. Their wanderings brought the different corners of the territory into contact with one another and contributed greatly to the unification. The political centralization could be maintained under such conditions only by an actual movement of the center by means of traveling civil servants. The journeys of the king or of the king's judges and magistrates were for a long time the only means of overcoming the spatial dispersion of the group elements and of maintaining at least an approximate political unity.

An entirely different effect results if the wandering is done by elements whose life-principle is that of mobility while the life-principle of the group is that of territorial fixation. Such harmful effects result from the wandering of tramps and vagabonds who express in their spatial relations their internal restlessness. Their wandering is an expression of their nonconformity to the sedentary principle of the group, and serves forces which are antagonistic and dangerous to a harmonious unity.[1]

Other Spatial Expressions of Sociological Forms

The sociological interest in the phenomena so far referred to arises only after the spatial configuration has fully appeared. In another set of phenomena the sociological importance lies mainly in the processes immediately preceding and in the sociological structure and energies determining the spatial configuration. To this group belong the organization of groups on a territorial basis, the rule over territory as an expression of the rule over people, and certain sociological configurations which find expression in a strip of intentionally depopulated land.

[1] *Soz.*, pp. 670–81.

Social Organization on a Territorial Basis

The significance of the organization of a group on a territorial basis is best illustrated in the change from a tribal to a political organization. It means the substitution of a spatial principle for a kinship principle, of spatial relations for blood relations in the subdivisions of the group, and of administrative areas for clans. Apart from this, it means the dissolution of formerly internally coherent subgroups and the combination of their elements in a single large structure which appears more mechanical, but also more rational, than the biological and emotional bonds of the tribal system.

The territorial principle is the immediate expression of the unity of the state. The danger of a suborganization for the state lies in the fact that its basic principle may be hostile to spatial relations. Blood relationships are superspatial and do not fit into a political system based on territory. A political organization based on kinship must crumble after it has grown to a certain size, because the subdivisions have a strong organic unity which is entirely independent of the common territory. The unity of the state can be preserved only if its subgroups are formed on a principle that is indifferent to that unity and at the same time less exclusive. The organization of the state on the basis of administrative territorial subdivisions fulfils these requirements. It enables genetically and qualitatively different elements which are spatially related to function as units without thereby endangering the unity of the whole. Such territorial subdivisions are much less likely to develop particularistic tendencies than subgroups consisting of closely related elements held together by kinship and forming strong unitary structures. This is the advantage of a subdivision according to a spatial principle. The complete impartiality and the identity of relationships between the state and its subjects find thereby an expression and a correlative in the complete impartiality and identity of the relationships between the spatial subdivisions and their occupants.

Dominion over Territory

Another spatial configuration which is an expression of sociological relationships is the dominion of a state over its territory. This is in the last analysis nothing but the dominion over people expressed in a specific relationship to a spatial area. The dominion over a territory is the result of and an expression for the dominion over people. The state rules over a certain area because it rules all the people in that area. In whatever spot of the area the individual may be, he will still be subject to the state's authority. This infinite number of possible points comes to be conceived of as a plane and hence gives rise to the concept of a dominion over territory. The function of the state can only be a dominion over people, and a dominion over territory in the same sense would have no meaning. It is merely the expression of the legal fact that there is no exception to the dominion of the state over all actual and possible subjects within its boundaries.

There have been many historical instances in which dominion over people was the result of an actual ownership of the soil. Such was the case in feudal times, when individuals were immediately bound to the soil and change of ownership meant change of dominion. But even under those conditions the dominion over people does not follow from the ownership of the soil in the same sense as does the right to the product of the soil. The relationship between the two must even then be established by separate and specific norms and forces. The dominion over people is even then a separate purpose and not a self-evident result.

The dominion over the land is, in relation to the dominion over people, of a secondary importance. The dominion over land is, however, of immediate importance if in the form of ownership or otherwise it means the right to the products of its soil. It is only when confusing the two meanings of the term dominion that the fact of the fundamental sociological nature of the concept becomes obscured.[1]

The Function of Empty Space

Another spatial expression of specific sociological formations is the use of empty space for the purpose of expressing neutrality. Primitive peoples often laid waste a small strip of land between their territories and agreed that neither of the two groups was to enter that borderland. They relinquished the advantages which such an occupation would have in the case of an offensive for the advantages which accrued from the non-occupation by the opponent for their own defensive. The empty strip between them was the spatial expression of a relationship of armed peace, which might be formulated in the words: If you do not harm me, I shall not harm you.

The neutrality of empty space obtains a different significance if, instead of merely separating the groups, it is used for positive services. Its function can be, not only to separate, but also to unite the groups. Meetings of individuals which cannot take place on the territory of either group may be arranged to take place in a neutral area. The neutral area in primitive times is the uninhabited region between the territories occupied by the tribes. It is the place where the trading is done and where individuals potentially at war meet under conditions of peace. And the existence of that unoccupied empty space is the most char-

[1] *Soz.*, pp. 691–96.

acteristic expression of their peculiar relationship of potential antagonism.[1]

The foregoing illustrations of the importance of the spatial conditions for the forms of socialization must suffice. Numerous other examples might have been cited, but the instances given are fully representative. They show that many social forms express their essential character in specific spatial configurations, and indicate the value of a study of these spatial conditions as a means to an understanding of their underlying processes of association.

[1] *Soz.*, pp. 703–8.

CHAPTER V

SOCIAL CONSERVATION

THE PERSISTENCE OF SOCIAL CIRCLES[1]

SOCIAL groups, once formed, have a tendency to persist. This persistence of the group unity results from the permanence of the interactions between the group elements and manifests itself in the continuity of the life of the group. This permanent coherence between the composing elements suggests the existence of a special vital force.

But an understanding of the life-process of the group requires more than the mere assumption of the existence of a vital force. Upon further analysis, the apparently unified force appears to consist of a great many separate and distinct processes of interaction. The apparently unitary process of social self-preservation must therefore be analyzed and resolved into the actual primary processes. These primary processes will by no means prove to be conservative processes only. At all times there are destructive forces which menace the persistence of the group both from within and from without. If these could operate unhampered, the group unity would soon be destroyed. But, apart from these destructive forces, there are conservative tendencies which produce permanent interactions between the elements and thereby maintain the group unity. This unity persists for a longer or shorter time, until it yields at last to the disintegrating forces.

The group appears to have a life of its own relatively

[1] Adapted from *Soz.*, chap. viii, pp. 494–613.

independent of the individuals who compose it. The group can remain identical while the members change. We still speak of the same state, the same army, the same association, when not a single original member survives. The persistence of the group is therefore by no means identical with the persistence of its members. It is a different phenomenon. The members may perish while the group remains, and the group may dissolve while the individuals remain.

At first sight it would seem as if there were a great similarity between the phenomenon of group persistence and that of group existence. But the process of socialization as it takes place in the temporal order is not fully identical with the process that takes place in the spatial order. The group exists at a certain time because the mental bond between the individuals overcomes their separation in space. It is the process of interaction between them that creates and maintains the unity of the group. But in the case of individuals separated from one another in time, the group unity cannot be maintained in the same manner. In that case a complete reciprocity is impossible. The earlier members may indirectly influence the later members, but the later members cannot influence the earlier ones. Hence the persistence of the social unity in spite of shifting membership presents a peculiar problem which is not solved by explaining how the group has come into existence at a certain moment.

Among the different factors which contribute toward this persistence of the group may be mentioned the following: the fact that the change in membership occurs only gradually; the permanence of the locality; the objectivation of the group unity in symbols; its protection by means of law, honor, and morality; and the formation of special organs. The function of each of these factors and its contribution to the conservation of group life will require a short explanation.[1]

Permanence of Locality

The first and most obvious factor which contributes to the preservation of the group unity is the permanence of the locality or of the soil on which it lives. The state, the city, and numerous other associations owe their persistence first of all to this abiding substratum. This permanence of the locality alone is not sufficient to guarantee the preservation of the group, but it forms an important contribution. It is of a physical character, while the life of the group is of a psychical character. But it functions as a permanent point of attachment. Permanence of locality, however, is only one factor leading to the preservation of group life, and it fulfils this function only for special groups. There are a great many associations which are entirely independent of any attachment to a definite locality.[2]

The most characteristic example of this function of the permanence of the locality for the persistence of the group is seen in the case of the feudal state. That state as a particular kind of association of human beings derived its permanence from the indestructibility of its soil. The inhabitants were subject to the authority of the state because they were immediately attached to the soil. It was in and through the soil that the unity of the feudal state existed and persisted.[3]

---

[1] *Soz.*, pp. 494–97.   [2] See Book II, chapter iv.

[3] *Soz.*, p. 498. In a modified form, this theoretical attachment to the soil is still one of the basic characteristics of the state. It is still a territorial organization. Since the feudal period, however, different functional groups have differentiated from the territorial group. This gives the modern state an entirely different aspect. The recent literature on the pluralistic state is in the last instance but a subsequent justification of this process of differentiation. See Book II, chapter vi.

The Gradualness of Change

More important for the persistence of the group unity is the physiological concatenation of successive generations and the element of kinship. The significance of this factor lies in the fact that the displacement of one generation by the following does not take place all at once. The number of individuals that leave and enter the group at any given time is relatively small compared to the number of those that remain. The change takes place so gradually that the group persists as a unit in a manner not unlike that in which the organism persists in spite of the change in its cells.

This physiological concatenation and the fact of inheritance, which is immediately related to it, are practically the only factors in modern times which preserve the family in the larger sense. Of all the elements that formerly contributed to the persistence of the family, such as occupation, religion, tradition, etc., only the physiological factor remains.

The gradualness of this change and its contribution to the persistence of the group unity is most evident in case the latter rests on procreation. But the same form of change occurs in cases where the physical agency is excluded. The Catholic clergy is an illustration of such a case. Here the continuity is secured by the fact that enough individuals are in office at a certain time to initiate the neophytes. The physiological basis gives place to a psychological one. The old members belonging to the group at any given moment separate from the organization only after the new members have been fully assimilated to the form and the spirit of the group. It is this fact that makes bureaucracies so tenacious and that preserves their character and spirit in spite of all the shifting of individuals. The persistence of this kind of group depends, therefore, also on the fact that the change is sufficiently slow and gradual.

This form of gradual change not only is operative in case of shifting membership, but functions in a similar manner with regard to the other elements òf group unity. We still speak of "the same group" even when its political organization, its laws and customs, have altered considerably. This is possible because the alterations do not affect all the vital elements of the group life simultaneously, but only a minimum at a given moment.[1]

Objectivation of the Group Unity in Symbols

The group unity and its persistence may find objective expression in personal, material, and conceptual symbols. If the life of the group becomes intimately bound up with the existence of leadership, special arrangements are required to secure the self-preservation. In national groups this finds expression in the principle that the king never dies. It involves the very significant sociological conception that the king is no longer king as a person, but that his person is only the irrelevant vehicle of the abstract kingship. The group will then reflect its immortality in a hereditary kingship.

This hereditary principle is purely formal in nature and may bring to the throne the most capable as well as the most incapable leader. This principle is possible only if within the group a relationship between ruler and ruled has become fixed and permanent, only if it does not depend any longer on subjective relationships, but has become a status. As long as this aspect of the group form is still uncertain, the supreme leader can hold the group together only through definite personal qualities. But if this form has become established and secure, the personal ele-

[1] *Soz.*, pp. 501–4.

ment can withdraw in favor of the formal principle. That formal principle is the hereditary kingship.[1]

The objectivation of the group coherence may dispense with this personal form and become attached to material symbols, such as crown jewels, a flag, a banner; or it may find expression in a maxim or motto.[2]

The importance of a material symbol becomes much greater if it serves as a common possession. It may be that the material interests of the individuals converge in this symbol, or that the centralized functions of the group depend on it. In that case it is of importance to secure its permanence. This is usually obtained by the "dead hand," the provision that the property of the association, which, as such, is eternal, cannot be alienated. For the church the eternity of her tenure was a symbol of the eternity of her life-principle. That her possessions were chiefly real estate strengthened the usefulness of her material properties for the preservation of her group unity. Modern associations and corporations try to secure the same ends by different means. In some cases the provision is made that no restitution of contributions shall be made to those who withdraw, and in other cases the constitution stipulates that in case of dissolution the funds shall not be distributed, but shall revert to another association of similar purpose. In the latter case the provision aims, not at the physical per-

---

[1] *Soz.*, pp. 511–14. This formalistic sociological aspect of the hereditary kingship is, of course, not the whole story of its historical development. Simmel would not have us believe that. But it is none the less to be regretted that he did not refer to the reverse side of the medal. The kingship did not only become hereditary because it reflected the immortality of the group, but also because the princes conceived their *imperium* as a *dominium*, as a permanent possession in their own family.

[2] For an extensive account of the importance of the symbol or the emblem for the group unity, see Emile Durkheim, *The Elementary Forms of Religious Life* (translated by Swain), p. 236.

sistence of the group, but at the protection and the continuity of its purposes.[1]

Law, Honor, and Morality

Another factor which is important for the preservation of the group is of a purely subjective character. It manifests itself in a feeling of patriotism for the state or city and of devotion to the family or to the religious community. Different from this factor, which remains entirely subjective, are the elements of morality, honor, and law. The moral action may derive its force from the freedom and autonomy of the individual. The individual himself may give it a specific content. That content has for him, none the less, an objective aspect. It faces him as a norm to which his actions should more or less conform. The law, in a similar fashion, apart from its special organs, faces the individual as an ideal objectivity which binds him morally, but which has none the less a superindividual aspect. Between these two kinds of norm which contribute to the social self-preservation lies a third form, honor. Law aims at objective ends by objective means, morality at subjective ends by subjective means, while honor aims at objective ends by subjective means.

In the series, morality, honor, and law, each preceding sphere includes the succeeding sphere, but not the reverse. The moral imperative commands what honor and law demand. The standard of honorable conduct commands what the law demands. The sphere of law is the least extensive sphere. Legal regulations apply to the minimum necessary for social self-preservation, and for that reason conformity is secured by physical restraint. Conformity to the moral standard has no stronger sanction than that of

[1] *Soz.*, pp. 526–31.

good or bad conscience. Honor takes an intermediate position. Nonconformity is punished by means which are neither of a purely subjective character, like moral discomfort, nor of a purely external character, like the physical ‚restraint in the legal sphere. With the formation of an honor standard protected partially by subjective moral consequences and partly by objective social consequences, society creates a guaranty for an adequate individual behavior in spheres which lie outside the field of legal provisions and which cannot be left to individual morality.[1]

Honor originally refers to a class standard. It sets the norms for the preservation of smaller circles contained within a larger group. It preserves both the unified character of the social circle and its distinctions from the other circles within the large inclusive organization. What is sometimes referred to as human honor in general, or individual honor, is an abstraction. There is no human honor as such. There is family honor, military honor, honor among thieves, but no individual honor. Honor is a factor in the self-preservation of a group and can be understood only as such.[2]

Concentration and Objectivation of the Social Coherence in Special Organs

The factors contributing to the social self-preservation mentioned thus far were the objectivation of the group unity in a spatial form, a personal leader, material symbols, or in ideal norms. Another important factor is the objectivation of the group coherence in a special organ composed of a number of persons. In that case the factor exhibits in itself a sociological character. It is sociological not only in function, but also in structure. A religious

[1] For the formal aspect of these restraints, see also Book II, chapter iii.

[2] *Soz.*, pp. 532–35.

community embodies its unity and purpose in its priest-hood, a political community in its bureaucracy or in its army, permanent unions in their officers, and transitory associations in their committees.

The formation of such special organs is the result of a sociological division of labor. The interaction between individuals, in which in the last instance all socialization consists, appears at first as an immediate reciprocity between the elements. The whole group of individuals partakes at first immediately in the religious, military, legal, and economic activities. The individual activities become unified in social activities on the basis of common agreements and mutual adjustments. The religious worship is the result of the religious needs common to the individuals. The administration of justice is cared for by an immediate judgment of the community as a whole. The economic life is made possible by a direct exchange of producers who are at the same time consumers.

These interactions which create the social unity and thus become functions are in a later stage no longer exercised by the persons immediately concerned, but pass over to special functional groups. The previous immediate reciprocities make room for a situation in which each individual element comes now into contact, not with all other elements, but with the newly developed organs. In a group without specialized functional organs, only the individuals have an actual existence; the coherence between them, that is, the group unity, has only a functional aspect. But if these organs have been formed, the group coherence becomes embodied in a structure of its own. That structure is not only separate and apart from the members of the group, but it is even relatively independent of its individual bearers.

The church, the bureaucracy, and even the industrial

system are objective structures relatively independent of the individual priest, civil servant, or merchant. As individuals, they carry out the functions which these structures possess as organs of the group, but they do not produce them. Although the bearers of the special social structures, they remain none the less subject to the group as a whole and to the special conditions which the functioning activity of these organs imposes upon the group as a whole. The merchant must buy the articles of his personal use, the judge is subject to law, the tax-collector to taxes, and the priest to confession. But over and above their individual elements, these special organs embody and objectify the forces that hold the group together. They further consolidate the group elements into a unit and give to the group coherence, apart from its functional aspect, an objective structural existence.

The formation of special organs has great advantages and contributes considerably to a better preservation of the group. It permits a greater flexibility in policies and a quicker and more efficient adaptation to changing conditions. The transference of special functions to smaller groups opens the possibility for the use of expert knowledge and a higher average intelligence, while, on the other hand, it reduces the dangers of emotional excesses resulting from increased collective suggestibility.[1]

These specialized structures for the fulfilment of specific social functions contribute, therefore, greatly to the preservation of the group. But, on the other hand, this preservation also requires that the differentiated organs shall not attain complete independence. They serve their purpose only if they remain structural condensations of the formerly direct reciprocities between the elements of the larger group. They fulfil their function only if they give

[1] *Soz.*, pp. 537–56.

practical form to the forces and tendencies of the larger group and remain the vehicles for the attainment of its aims and purposes. Though relatively independent, these organs must serve none the less as a means to the ends of the larger group.

If the process of differentiation goes too far, if they attain a complete independence of the group and exist only for themselves, then their useful function ceases and they become the seat of destructive tendencies. There then arises an antagonism and opposition between the whole and the parts which endangers the life of the group. The examples of this danger are numerous. Bureaucratic and legal formalism have many times placed their own requirements above the ends of the group. In the case of legal formalism it has found its characteristic expression in the maxim *fiat justitia pereat mundus*.

A certain amount of dependence is necessary, not only to avert the danger of antagonism and opposition, but also to enable the group to take back in certain cases the already differentiated functions. In the evolution of society it often becomes necessary, for the self-preservation of the group, to throw out of service the existing organs. This may be because the specific function is no longer required, or because the rigidity of the structure prevents an adequate fulfilment of the function under changed conditions. When the organ proves unequal to its task, recourse must be had to the immediate reciprocities between the elements as a temporary substitute for the differentiated functional structure.

Many social structures are adjusted from the beginning to such alternations between the immediate reciprocity and the fulfilment of functions by special organs. In business corporations the relation between the general meeting and the board of directors, and in political organizations the relation between parliament and the cabinet, provides for a sufficient dependency of the special organs upon the group. Every revolution which disposes of the government in power and returns the legislation and administration to the immediate initiative of the individual members shows this form of sociological change. But not every group can perform such a reversion to the original type. In large groups which live under complicated conditions, the administrative function cannot be taken over by the group as a whole. Under those conditions special organs are inevitable, and their immediate response to and dependence on the larger group is usually limited to a possible substitution of different individuals as bearers of the structure. These facts constitute the essential difficulty of all group life. The social self-preservation and the protection of the group unity require, on the one hand, functional differentiation and the formation of relatively independent structures, while, on the other hand, too large an independence or too rigid a structure immediately threatens the safety of the group form.[1]

[1] *Soz.*, pp. 563–73. For the larger aspect of this conflict between the objective structure and the living forces of social life, see also Book III, chapter ii. Simmel touches here upon the fundamental sociological aspect of some of the great problems represented in controversial literature on social reform. What shall be the relation between the special social organs and the group as a whole; what degree of independence and autonomy shall be given to them?

Revisionist socialism, guild socialism, syndicalism, Marxism, and anarchism have each a different answer to that question.

The revisionist sees in the system of production, considered as a structure, a functional organ of the group, and he wants that structure to be fully controlled by the group as a whole. The structural aspect of the group as a whole is for him the state. He is a social absolutist and wants complete dependence of the organ.

The guild socialist conceives not only of the system of production, but also of the state, as a functional organ of the group. He wants the independence of the latter curtailed, its dominion abolished, and the independence of the economic organ increased. His ideal is a functional organization. He renounces social absolutism. The organs are to be equally independent, but are to function in co-operation. They will be mutually dependent in their external relations on

The Functional Forms of Social Self-Preservation

Up to this point the process of social self-preservation has been treated mainly from its structural aspect. The structural elements, personal, material, ideal, and social, by means of which the group secures and protects its persistence have been enumerated and considered. But apart from this structural aspect, there is a purely functional aspect. The life-processes of social groups show, namely, two clearly distinct types. They can be distinguished on the basis of the rhythm of the sociological changes within the group.

On the one hand there is the conservative, the stable group. It preserves itself by conserving its form with the utmost tenacity and by an absolute rigidity of structure. It meets any opposition with active resistance and tries to maintain the same forms of interactions between the elements throughout all the changes in external conditions.

On the other hand there is the unstable group. It preserves itself by its flexibility of form. It adapts itself to changes in external conditions by corresponding changes in internal structure. It is capable of immediate and important changes in its sociological form without disrupting its unity.

---

account of their functional relationships to the group as a whole, but fully autonomous in their internal relations.

The syndicalist and the Marxist also consider the structural aspect of the system of production as an organ of the larger group. But because it is the most important organ and includes all individuals, it should dominate the group as a whole. Their ideal group organization is another social absolutism, with the economic structure successor to the political structure as absolute sovereign.

The anarchist, being an extreme individualist, ignores the functional relationship between associations and the larger group. Associations are for him only voluntary combinations of free individuals, not structural elements functionally related to a larger group. As they have only internal relations, they should be fully autonomous and independent, free from any external restraint. His organization is an individual absolutism.

The first type of social self-preservation is character-istic of groups which contain widely divergent elements. If these divergent elements are not sufficiently integrated and not adjusted to a harmonious co-operation, there is a dan-ger that any change or innovation will drive them farther apart. That danger is especially great in cases of rigid social stratification and complete separation between the social classes. The reason for this is that any change is likely to begin in one social class, or at least to affect that one class more immediately and more strongly. If inter-mediate classes exist, the change can spread gradually through the whole group, extending slowly over wider circles and at the same time decreasing in intensity. If such classes fail, the change will attack also the classes least disposed to it in a much more violent and ruthless manner. The middle class or classes fulfil the function of buffers and shock-breakers. They absorb the inevitable dislocations which result from sudden changes, reduce them, and distribute them over the whole group. This is one of the formal sociological reasons why aristocracies, in so far as they are based on sharp class distinctions, are also essentially conservative. A social group consisting of clearly separated castes, or a political combination con-sisting of distinct ethnic groups, is also faced with the same problem.

A similar conservatism is found in groups or structures which have lost their actual functional relationship with the larger social unit. Changes and innovations in the sociological forms can be borne and sustained only by liv-ing social forces. Obsolete social structures have long lost that sustaining force. They persist as empty forms, as hol-low husks which even the smallest change might destroy and demolish. The life has gone out of them. The vital or-ganic relationships have disappeared, and they can maintain themselves, even if merely as empty frames, only on the basis of a rigid conservatism.[1]

The opposite type of social self-preservation is characteristic of groups that live within larger groups, either tolerated or opposed and suppressed. The self-preservation of these groups and the persistence of their social unity require an extreme elasticity and variability of sociological forms. Their offensive and defensive strength lies just in the variety of forms under which they can operate. They must be able to expand and contract at any moment and avail themselves of any type of organization that circumstances permit.

Bands of brigands and conspirators can maintain their social unity only if they can instantly subdivide into smaller groups, act separately under different leaders, and instantly reunite again for larger enterprises. Great flexibility of form is the indispensable condition of their persistence. The Jews in Central Europe have lived for centuries under conditions which have been similar from the formal point of view to those of brigands and conspirators. They have been small suppressed minorities within larger social groups. They have maintained their social unity in the face of these oppressions by a great variability of sociological form. Their social solidarity has been a religious solidarity, an economic solidarity, or a political solidarity. It has attached itself to each of these forms according to circumstances and conditions. Here again the flexibility of form has been the means of persistence and the strength of their defensive and offensive against the larger group.

Apart from such cases as the existence of a smaller group within a larger group, there is no immediate corre-

[1] *Soz.*, pp. 574–80. For a more elaborate treatment of structures that have outlived their social usefulness, see G. D. H. Cole, *Social Theory*, chapter xiii, "The Atrophy of Institutions," pp. 193–200.

lation between the form of the self-preservation and the size of the group. The type and the amount of flexibility that are most conducive to the preservation of the group unity depend on a great many factors other than size. Small groups will, however, usually show a more pronounced type. They will preserve their unity either through a rigidity of structure or through flexibility of form. The large group has an opportunity for combining the two processes which is denied to the smaller group. It can maintain a great stability of general institutions by allowing a certain flexibility for small local variations.[1]

The foregoing considerations of the structural and functional aspects show clearly that social conservation is not a single simple phenomenon. It is not the result of a single vital social process, but the result of a great many different factors and a great many different processes which combine in various forms according to varying circumstances.

[1] *Soz.*, pp. 598–606.

CHAPTER VI

SOCIAL DIFFERENTIATION

The Intersection of Social Circles[1]

THE history of human associations shows a tendency similar to that of the association of ideas. The sociological development seems to repeat the psychological development. In thought, association by contiguity generally precedes association by analogy. The accidental coexistence of objects in space and time is at first sufficient to bring about an association between the ideas of these objects. The complex of characteristics of these objects appears at first as a unitary totality. Only when one of these characteristics is observed in a great many other combinations does it become differentiated from the rest. The similarity between various objects is then observed detached from the individual combinations, and the association based on the relations between the contents of ideas succeeds the association based on their temporal or spatial coexistence.

The Historical Aspect of Social Differentiation

The development of human relationships shows an analogous tendency. The individuals are at first associated with others in their immediate environment, and this association is relatively independent of their individual peculiarities. At a later stage there arise associations between the homogeneous elements out of the different heterogeneous groups.

[1] Adapted from *Soz.*, chap. vi, pp. 403–53.

179

The individual is at first more or less completely absorbed in the family group. It is a community group, an inclusive association of widely divergent elements. Later each individual enters into relationships with persons outside of his circle on the basis of a similarity in character, tendencies, and activities. The association based on objective coexistence is replaced by one which is based on subjective relations. The higher concept synthesizes what is common in a great many different phenomenal complexes. In the same way the practical viewpoint brings together from different and unrelated groups individuals with similar interests. There arise new social circles which intersect the existing "natural groups" at different angles.

Examples of this development may be found in many fields. The relatively independent groups which originally combined into universities were based at first on the nationality of the students. Later the students combined on the basis of common study, and the university became a combination of "faculties." This was a radical replacement of a local or racial solidarity by a solidarity based on a common interest and purpose. A similar development, though more complicated in form, is visible in the history of trade unionism. The local organizations of workingmen have practically disappeared, and in their place have come organizations based on the common trade or industry.

This change is accompanied on the one hand by an increase in individual liberty. It does not abolish restraint, but it leaves the individual an element of choice as to what he shall be bound to, as to the association that shall exert that restraint. On the other hand, the new type of association requires a greater active participation and thereby allows a more conscious expression of individual characteristics.

These results are clearly visible in the changes in the

social life of the individual during the latter part of the
Middle Ages. Originally the individual was bound up in
his village community. The feudal period created a new
basis for union, namely, subservience to the same lord.
But these two bonds of union were both of an external
character. They were determined by factors which lay
outside the will of the individual. Only with the rise of
free associations did the individual become a more or less
free and active participant in the social life. Motives for
association lying within the individual came to replace or
to co-operate with the external accidental factors which
up to that time had alone determined his place in the social
structure.

In modern times there exists a vast superstructure of
such social circles above the more natural and primary
groupings and intersecting the latter at different angles.
The family group is no longer an all-inclusive association
fully closed, independent, and self-sufficient, but it is inter-
sected by the numerous associations to which the individual members belong. And these associations intersect not
only the family group, but all other primary groupings,
such as the local community and the nation.

These new social circles are of a very different kind
from the original primary groups. They are purposive
associations, associations for specific factual purposes.
The individuals do not co-operate in these associations
with the whole of their personality, as was characteristic
of medieval corporations. They do not become entirely
absorbed in these associations, but merely co-operate by
means of definite factual contributions conducive to the
specific factual purpose. This gives the new type of association a much more rational character than that of the
primary groupings. They may be associations based on
emotional interests, like religious sects, or on economic,

political, or military interests; but in all these cases their content is created by more or less conscious deliberation and according to a rational design. This formal character of secondary formation finds its most complete expression in associations of intellectuals. Rational intellectuality is in that case not only the formal characteristic of the group, but it has become the content itself.

The number of social circles to which an individual belongs is to a certain extent a measure for the development of civilization. In modern times a man belongs to his paternal family, to his own, and to that of his wife. He is related through his profession to a great number of professional and business circles. He may be an officer in the reserve army and a member of half a dozen social clubs. Many of these circles are concentric circles. In that case membership in the smaller circle leads more or less automatically to membership in the larger circle. But membership in a great many other circles is the result of a differentiation from primary groups on the basis of individual characteristics and a combination with others having similar characteristics. In many instances the original relationships with the primary groups remain effective notwithstanding these partial differentiations. They do not disappear; they merely appear less important than the relationships with those circles which are expressions of individual characteristics.

The importance of this type of association lies in the fact that it brings about a social integration of individual differentiations. It does not combine similar individuals, but it yields a combination of divergent elements on the basis of a differentiated similarity in these elements. It enables individual differences to become significant for the life of the group, a goal that could not be obtained as long as corporations absorbed the whole of the individual.

And it also enables the individual to participate more fully in the social life with all sides of his personality.

During the Middle Ages the individual was also in many cases a member of different associations, but his relationships were much less determined by his individual characteristics. The Hanseatic League united different towns and enabled the individual citizen to participate in a field which extended far beyond the city limits. The guilds offered the individual a membership in associations which extended and co-operated throughout the country. But these social circles were concentric circles. The individual did not participate in the larger circle as an individual, but as a member of an existing group. The new participation was not on the basis of any individual characteristic and did not lead to any intersection with existing circles. For that reason the result of these new associations for the individual existence was different from that of additional associations in modern times. They did not lead to a fuller determination of the individual's place in society, as they did not result from differentiations out of primary groups. This is accounted for partly by the fact that the individual devoted himself much more fully to his corporation, and partly by the fact that the principle of union was a principle of equality. Only equals could combine and unite in corporations. Therefore the larger combinations were at first combinations of towns with towns, of convents with convents, and of guilds with related guilds. As members of corporations the individuals were equal, and only in so far as they were equal did the common bond exist in the larger groups. It did not exist in so far as they were individually differentiated. The individual as such in his individual uniqueness remained outside the larger union. It was not an association that attached itself to a differentiated individual characteristic.

The system of concentric circles was a transitional form between the participation of the individual in one narrow exclusive corporation absorbing the whole of his personality and the modern form of participation in a great number of intersecting social circles. The old corporation demanded from the individual his exclusive loyalty. The new association touches only a certain aspect of his personality and leaves him free to enter into innumerable other associations. The transitional form of concentric circles, although not permitting that full sociological freedom which the individual has obtained since the invention of the purposive association, enabled him none the less to participate in a greater number of social circles and in a wider area of social life than had been possible up to that time.[1]

Social Differentiation and Sociological Determination

From the foregoing observations it becomes evident that there is an immediate correlation between the extent of social differentiation and the extent of sociological determination. That is, the more different social classes and groupings there are, the more is the individual sociologically determined by his membership in these classes. The groups or circles to which an individual belongs form a system of sociological co-ordinates. Each new circle added to the ones in which he participates determines more fully his place in the sociological structure. The more associations he participates in, the less chance there is that there exists for another individual a fully identical system of co-ordinates.

This sociological determination will, of course, be more definite in the case of overlapping and intersecting circles than in the case of concentric circles. If he merely partici-

[1] *Soz.*, pp. 403–12.

pates in concentric circles, there may be a greater number of individuals in an identical sociological position. The gradually decreasing circles like nation, social class, and subdivision of the latter do not give the participating individual a specific and unique place. But if he participates in a number of social clubs and scientific societies apart from his immediate business relationships, his position becomes pretty well defined.

Such a participation in a number of intersecting circles has also important consequences for the individual himself. It allows him to express in his social life a greater part of his personality. He regains in the manifoldness of his associations some of the individual uniqueness which is lost, as far as his social life is concerned, as long as he is a member of only one association.

Such a position at the intersection of different social circles means not only a more complete determination, but also new tasks. The complete certainty which results from membership in a single group is replaced by a situation which is not free from waverings and uncertainties. Membership in a plurality of social circles may even lead to an external and internal conflict that may threaten a dualism and disruption of the individuality. This does not contradict the fact that a pluralistic participation strengthens the individuality as such. The dualism and the unity are mutually supporting. On the one hand, there arises the problem of disruption just because the individual is a unity. On the other hand, the ego will become more conscious of its unity if it is the meeting-point of divergent group interests. The membership in different family groups which results from modern marriage will make the lives of the individuals richer, extend their interests, and force them not only to internal and external conciliations, but also to energetic self-assertions.

A unique and exceptional case of sociological determination through the intersection of social circles is that
of the Catholic clergy. No social group or class is excluded
from providing priests and monks. The Catholic clergy is
a social circle which in theory intersects all existing circles
in so far as they are primary groups. But its peculiar characteristic is the fact that it lifts the individual fully and
completely out of his former circles. With his entrance into
this circle the individual loses all connections with his
former associations and renounces his former sociological
identity, including his name. The intersection does not
exist for the individual priest, but only for the class as a
whole. As a whole it is a group to which former members
of all classes and circles belong. As a whole it is sociologically determined by the fact that it has identical relations
to all other classes. But the individual priest does not possess an individuality in the general sense of the term. Because he is *entirely* priest, he must be entirely *priest*.

The most radical means by which the individual priest
is kept out of the intersection of social circles is celibacy.
Marriage leads to such a complete and binding sociological
fixation that a married individual can often not fully realize his logical position in his other social circles.

For that reason certain associations have refused membership to married men. The journeymen guilds of the
Middle Ages were often closed to married individuals
who were otherwise fully eligible. The reason for this was
that their group unity could be preserved only by a complete equality and homogeneity and by a free circulation
of members throughout the whole area over which the
group extended. The acceptance of married men would
have created inequality and impeded the liberty of action
of a part of its members.

But apart from the actual content of the associations,

the sole fact of participation in more than one group is sufficient to give the individual a more conscious realization of his individuality. Even in cases where this effect is merely negative, plural participation removes at least the feeling of the inevitableness and the obviousness of his original association. Certain organizations have therefore sometimes opposed the mere formal fact of participation in other associations quite independently of their content and purpose.

The amount of sociological determination which the individual receives from his participation in different social circles will be greater if his relative position in each of these associations is a different one. He may hold in one circle a place of authority, in another a subordinate place; in one group a central position, in another a position on the outskirts. He may be economically interested in one organization and personally attached to another one. The structures of these organizations may make it impossible for another individual to hold a similar place. All these factors would lead to a sociological determination which would be impossible in the case of participation in a single group or even in the case of participation with identical position in different groupings.[1]

The Two Aspects of Social Differentiation

Social differentiation shows itself in a variety of forms. But, in the main, two basic types can be discovered which appear in various combinations. The first type is manifest in the formation of large superordinated circles out of smaller, more specialized circles. The second type is manifest in the differentiation of more specialized circles out of more co-ordinated and more inclusive circles.

Perhaps the most interesting illustration of the first

[1] *Soz.*, pp. 412–21.

type is the formation of a labor class. It has required a very high abstraction over and above all individual characteristics before this integration of individuals in a unitary class-conscious group could come about. Independently of what the individual produces, whether guns or toys, the formal fact that he works for a wage is sufficient to make him a member of a group which includes all those who work under similar conditions. The identical relation to capital permits a differentiation of this similarity out of the different occupations and a combination and union of all those who participate in such a relation.

The concept "workman" is the result of a logical process which has been in intimate interaction with the socio-historical process which created the wage-earner. The growth of large-scale industry placed thousands of workers in identical factual and personal situations. The complete penetration of the money economy through all social life depersonalized human service and reduced its significance to a monetary value. The increased demands for a higher standard of life brought about an increasing discrepancy between real wages and desired comfort. All these factors yielded on the one hand a special emphasis on wage work as such and the formation of the concept "workman," while on the other hand they created the actual social conditions which enabled these workmen to combine. The term "workman" has not remained a mere logical concept; it has become a legal concept. The existence of workmen's compensations and workmen's insurance is indicative that the mere fact of being a workman gives an individual certain legal rights.

The correlate of the labor class and the result of the same differentiation is the class of manufacturers or entrepreneurs. As a logical concept, its formation synchronizes with that of the labor class. But, owing to specific reasons,

the actual group formation and the rise of a class consciousness has come much later. The number of entrepreneur
associations has none the less been increasing rapidly during recent years.

As long as the formal relationship between employer
and employee was not observed separate and apart from
the content of their activities, this differentiation could
not take place. In other words, as long as the main emphasis was on the fact that the ones were metal workers
and the others metal manufacturers, the stress was on the
common interest in the metal trade. They formed a small
social circle between them, as in all other trades and indus-
tries. But once the emphasis was placed on the formal relationship between employers and employees, there developed a social differentiation which created two large
social circles intersecting all existing ones and placed in formal opposition in relation to each other.

The formation of a merchant class resembles in many
aspects the sociological genesis of the laboring class. Like
labor, the merchants form a group partly real, partly ideal.
They constitute an association of individual merchants
quite irrespective of their trade. In this case, however, the
differentiation of the general out of the more specific has
been facilitated by the fact that the form of the merchant's
activity is more independent of its content. The activity
of the workman depends to a large extent on what he
makes. The concept of activity as independent of its content is therefore not easily formed. The activity of the
merchant is relatively independent of what he trades in.
It is buying and selling in all cases, and this fact has greatly
simplified the formation of the general concept and of the
general class.

A third example of the formation of a large superordinated circle out of smaller circles is the growth of the femi-

nist movement and the sociological evolution of the concept "woman." The original position of the woman was in the home. She was absorbed in the family. Her special functions, though common to all women, prevented her from forming the large superordinated circle including all women. Her functions kept her fully bound to the small family group and led to an exclusive devotion to a few individuals. Her sociological position was that of an individual fully tied up in a small, highly individualized circle.

The modern industrial development has completely changed this situation. Among the working classes, the girl and the married woman have been drawn into the factory. The process for them has meant an external liberation from the complete absorption of the home. The same changes have brought for the middle-class woman an internal liberation. A great number of activities formerly carried out in the home have been taken over by industry, and this has resulted for her in a greater freedom within the home.

This difference in the results of industrialism for the two social classes explains the difference in the immediate practical aims of these groups of women. The first wants to go back to the home, the second wants to go out of the home; the first wants to be more a "family woman," more wife and mother, the second wants to be more a social woman, more a political woman. But for both groups the binding ties with the smaller circle have been dissolved. The complete absorption in the small group has been abolished, and the barriers against a practical solidarity of women have been removed. The concept "woman" is no longer a purely logical and abstract concept. It has become a guiding principle for unitary associations including all women, as is manifest in the different branches of the feminist movement. In these associations they can work for interests which are common to women of all classes and which concern themselves with such facts as legal status, the administration of property, and the guardianship over children. A large superordinated social circle has been formed intersecting the family circles and uniting in a common group what has been differentiated as homogeneous out of these heterogeneous smaller groups.[1]

Another form of social differentiation, or at least another aspect of social differentiation, is manifest in the splitting up of co-ordinated circles. It leads to the formation of a number of different circles out of what formerly has been one group. In the Middle Ages such a separation was unknown. The guild did not only regulate the trade activities of its members; it regulated their whole lives. The apprentice was not only a vocational student of his master; he was one of his family. The different aspects of life were intimately integrated, and if the emotional and political life centered around the vocational life, regulation of the latter implied and included regulation of the former.

In modern times the different sides of the individual's life have become more clearly differentiated, and he expresses each of these sides in separate associations and relationships. This differentiation has been due to a large extent to the division of labor. The division of labor has led to a type of activity which becomes on the one hand increasingly mechanical, but which on the other hand absorbs much less of the total personality and allows other interests to assert themselves more freely. Besides, the increasing professional differentiation must show that similar life-interests can be combined with different professions. The multiplicity of such other interests which is characteristic of an advanced civilization leads also to similar results. The similarity of interests among those in

[1] *Soz.*, pp. 436–45.

different professions and the difference in interests among those in similar professions ultimately lead to a psychological differentiation and a sociological separation of the original all-inclusive group into separate and distinct associations.[1]

These two types of group formation, these two aspects of social differentiation, are manifest in all group life, but in our modern world more than ever before. New social circles are being formed incessantly, sometimes as superordinated circles out of smaller groups, sometimes as separations from existing circles, as new groupings within existing groups. Social circles with a specific content, like religious associations, have sometimes been formed by the latter process, sometimes by the former process. The religious life has at one time differentiated itself from the whole life of the community. At other times religious sects have been formed by individuals out of the most divergent social circles.

In a complicated social structure with a great many concentric and intersecting circles, new circles are usually formed by a process of differentiation which partakes of the two aspects. Viewed in relation to existing smaller circles, the new circles look like superordinated circles. Viewed in relation to existing larger circles, they look like separated, specialized circles.

It is this incessant process of differentiation and integration that is the purely sociological manifestation of the vital dynamic character of social life. It creates the manifold complexity of the modern social structure and gives the individual a chance to express his individual peculiarity in his freely chosen place at the intersection of selected social circles. He differentiates himself from some and combines with others, he combines with some against the

[1] *Soz.*, pp. 445–48.

combinations of others, and he even differentiates himself from and opposes those with whom he combines for other purposes.

This latter combination finds its most characteristic expression in the merchant class. The merchant combines with other merchants in an association for common interests like commercial legislation, class prestige, and the maintenance of prices. These common interests unite the class as a whole in its relations with outsiders. But, on the other hand, the merchant is in competition with and thereby in opposition to his fellow-merchants. Membership in that social circle means at the same time a co-operation with others and a competition against others. It means a position similar to that of others and at the same time a position apart from others. The individual guards his own interest by waging a severe competition against those with whom he is strongly united for the purpose of safeguarding their common interests. This internal opposition is most clearly expressed in the merchant class, but it is present in nearly all associations. Even the ephemeral polite society that gathers for an evening function is not free from it.

Human nature seems to show a fundamental need for both types of association, a fundamental desire for both co-operation and competition. The individual wants to feel and to act with others, but he also wants to act against others. A certain proportion between the two is apparently a necessity for the full expression of his individuality. He can satisfy that desire by a participation in associations which have these formal characteristics quite irrespective of what their content is. In many cases the participation in certain associations is due, not to their factual significance, but to the fact that they give the individual a certain proportion between competition and co-operation in his associative life. It is often due to this fact that the individual will select for himself a point of intersection of social circles from which he can satisfy both needs of his nature and in that way realize the full expression of his personality. Within circles characterized by much competition, the individuals will search for circles which are entirely free from competition, and within groups that are entirely free from competition, the individuals will search for opportunities for competition. For that reason the merchant class finds its compensation in a great number of societies and clubs which are of a purely sociable nature, while the aristocracy, which is comparatively free from competition, finds its compensation in clubs and societies in which the sportive element and the individual competition are strongly developed.[1]

Social Differentiation and Individual Liberty

The modern highly differentiated social structure with its numerous groupings and associations partakes both of the collectivistic and of the individualistic ideal. On the one hand, it enables the individual to find for each of his tendencies and inclinations an association, or at least a social circle, which makes satisfaction of these desires easier and offers him the advantages of belonging to a group. On the other hand, it enables him to express the uniqueness of his individuality in the specific combination of circles and groupings. The combination of individuals creates the association, but the combination of associations recreates the individual.

In an advanced civilization, the community group to which an individual belongs with the whole of his personality has become so large that he is robbed of the advantages and support which membership in a small group could give him. The bonds of association in that group

[1] *Soz.*, p. 424.

have become so attenuated that he practically lives in isolation. But the formation of purposive associations creates a compensation for this isolation which has resulted from the ever growing extension of the community circle.

The degree of compactness or sociological density of such associations can in a way be measured by the extent to which they have developed a special group honor. The existence of a family honor, a military honor, or a business men's honor is indicative of the fact that a strong consciousness of group unity has been developed. Only a strong consciousness of group unity and a fairly close-knit association can make the individual feel that the group as a collective personality has a special honor and that any dishonorable behavior on the part of one member involves a loss of honor for all members. Only such groups can secure a socially desirable behavior on the part of their members without having recourse to methods of force and external restraint.

The formation of such groups in our modern social structure has led to an entire redistribution of freedom and restraint. The small community in which the group as a whole or its centralized authority regulated the life of the individual in nearly all of its aspects has disappeared. In the modern state the centralized authority limits its regulative function to what is the inevitable minimum necessary to protect the group as a whole. The individual has become free and unrestricted in a wider and wider field.

This field does not remain a field of unrestricted individual activity, but it becomes occupied by new group formations and purposeful associations. But the interests of the individual and his own free choice determine to which of these he shall belong. The result is that they can dispense with methods of forceful external restraint for the preservation of their group unity and rely on an honor spirit or mere social disapproval to maintain a conformity to desired social behavior.

The undifferentiated authority of a group over its members, however far it may extend, must always leave a large part of the individual life outside of its scope. This field is left to the individual's free arbitrary will, and he is often the more free in that field in proportion as he is restricted in his group life. The Roman or the Greek citizen was severely restricted in his political life, but as master of his house he had unlimited power. The primitive savage was completely bound up in his tribal community, but completely free in his behavior to outsiders. Tyranny finds its correlative in a complete license in those fields which it does not reach.

The modern social structure yields a better proportion of freedom and restraint. The arbitrariness of the centralized authority and of the individual have both diminished. The latter was at first a compensation for the undifferentiated restraint of the collective power. With a decrease in the first, there followed a decrease in the latter. The more the individual as a whole was freed from social restraint, the more did he voluntarily bind himself in the separate aspects of his personality. The more he became freed from the authority of the all-inclusive group, the more did he freely bind himself in other social circles. He found social bonds and lived a social life with those sides of his personality which up to that time had expressed themselves in a purely individualistic behavior. This correlation is of a formal sociological nature. It holds good for all aspects of social life independently of their content. It is illustrated by the fact of the existence of a vigorous associative life in countries with great political freedom, as well as by the fact of the formation of numerous sects among religious communities which lack a strong hierarchical system.

It is the social differentiation which has brought about this better distribution of freedom and restraint. It has destroyed the forced combination of heterogeneous individuals and of heterogeneous interests of individuals in all-inclusive groups, and has created a social structure made up of associations that unite the homogeneous elements of heterogeneous circles. As a sociological form, this process of differentiation and integration manifests itself in the most varying social contents. But in the last analysis it is itself only a specific manifestation of a basic mental function which is operative in all fields of mental activity and most clearly manifest in the association of ideas.

CHAPTER VII

THE INDIVIDUAL AND THE GROUP

THE EXPANSION OF SOCIAL CIRCLES AND THE INCREASE
IN INDIVIDUAL DIFFERENTIATION[1]

IN SOME of the paragraphs of the preceding chapter we referred to the correlation between the extent of social differentiation and the extent to which the individual was sociologically determined within the group. The general process of social differentiation and integration leads also to another interesting correlation between certain aspects of group life and certain aspects of individual existence. It may be formulated as a correlation between the extension of the social circle and the degree of individual differentiation.

The wider the social circles in which individuals participate and the larger the groups of which they are members, the greater will be their individual differences. The extension of groups and associations leads on the one hand to a growing similarity in the sociological form of these groups, while on the other hand it leads to an increased individual distinctness of their members. The group loses in individual distinctness what the individual gains.

The simplest form of an expansion of the social circles of an individual is the amalgamation of two separate and distinct groups. Even if these groups are composed of homogeneous elements and have a distinct sociological form, their amalgamation will none the less lead to a sharp

[1] Adapted from *Soz.*, chap. x, pp. 709–75.

individual differentiation on the one hand and to a greater similarity in sociological form to other groups on the other hand. The quantitative increase in the size of the group leads to a qualitative differentiation on the part of the individuals. The small existing differences in disposition and occupation between individuals become larger because increased competition necessitates individual specialization. On the other hand, the new group as a whole will resemble existing groups more closely than the groups out of which it was formed. There is only a relatively small number of sociological forms available, and this number can be only slowly increased. The greater the number of sociological forms within a group, that is, the more complex its sociological structure, the more will it therefore resemble other complex sociological structures. In the amalgamated group, the sociological counterpart of the individual differentiation will create a set of sociological structures which are already found in other groups. The more fully the process of individual and social differentiation reshapes the new group, the more fully will it therefore come to resemble existing groups.

But not only is an extension of the social circle followed by an increased individual specialization. An increased individual differentiation is also followed by the creation of wider social circles. The differentiation of the individual from his fellow-group members seems accompanied by a tendency to make social contacts with individuals in other groups. It seems to create a need for transgressing the spatial, economic, political, or spiritual boundaries of the former group. In so far as this tendency leads to the formation of superordinated circles out of smaller groups, it has been treated in the preceding chapter. Here the tendency is of interest in the light of the full correlation between individual differentiation and the extension of the group.

An example of this correlation is manifest in the history of the guilds. Originally the guild prescribed stringent rules and required absolute uniformity of trade activities on the part of all members. Later it became impossible to maintain this condition of undifferentiated uniformity. The master who had become prosperous refused to be bound within the narrow limits of guild regulations. When he finally secured the right to employ more journeymen and to sell articles not manufactured in his own shop, there resulted two important changes. On the one hand, the originally homogeneous group of guild members differentiated into rich and poor, capitalists and workers, traders and craftsmen, and the possibility of unfolding personal characteristics led to an increased differentiation and specialization. On the other hand, there followed a great extension of the market and a great increase in the number of customers. The differentiation of the functions of merchant and craftsman gave the former a greater freedom and permitted him an extension of business relations which had been impossible under former conditions.

This division of labor which appears in correlation with the extension of the group is not confined to the content of the activity, but it also manifests itself in a sociological direction. As long as a group is self-sufficient, there exists at least this similarity, even in case of professional specialization, that the service of each individual is functionally related to the group. This service has from the sociological point of view a centripetal direction. When the group ceases to be self-sufficient and begins to trade with other groups, there occurs within the group a differentiation between those who work for internal consumption and those who work for foreign trade.

The same correlation is manifest in numerous other developments and situations. With the decline of the feudal system there developed a similar increase in individual differentiation and enlargement of social contacts. The serf, bound in a narrow circle, was partly owner of his own land, partly laborer on the lord's demesne. The decline of the system brought a sharp differentiation between individuals who were entirely owners and those who were entirely laborers. But both groups obtained contacts with wider social circles. The laborers enlarged their social contacts by working for different employers; the owners enlarged their social contacts by their increased commercial activity.

A similar observation may be made for all periods of social history. Among primitive tribes, the individuals show marked similarity and are strongly united in small social groups. The groups as a whole are dissimilar and antagonistic. The stronger the synthesis within the group, the stronger the antithesis to other groups. The growth of culture brought on the one hand a differentiation within the group, and on the other hand an approach to other groups. Among civilized peoples, the uneducated masses show less individual differences than the more educated classes, but the masses in different nations seem more unlike than the more highly educated classes. The medieval corporation fully absorbed the individual, but the corporations remained clearly distinct and separate. The modern association touches the individual only in certain aspects of his personality and leaves scope for wide individual differences, but the associations themselves are integrated in one wide, all-inclusive unity, which is manifest in the uniformity of legal norms, the universal penetration of the money economy, the mutual dependence through the division of labor, and the common interest in the national economy.

This lack of differentiation among the elements of small

groups and the manifold differentiation among the elements of large groups may be observed in coexisting social circles as well as in the subsequent phases of the development of one group. It seems to result from a general and fundamental principle which can be expressed in the following formulation: /The individual appears to maintain a certain fixed proportion between the social and the individual aspects of his existence, which merely changes its form. If he is a member of a small group, he has little opportunity for the expression of his individual uniqueness. But his little group has an individuality of its own. If the group or the circle extends, the individual can express his individual uniqueness, but the group loses its individual distinctness. The personality of the individual gains in individual uniqueness, but loses in social uniqueness. As part of a whole, he is less characterized by membership in the larger group than by membership in the smaller group. In other words, the elements of differentiated groups are undifferentiated, while those of undifferentiated groups are differentiated. /This is not a formulation of a natural law. It is merely a formulation of a phenomenological correlation. It is a synthetic formulation in one single concept of the uniform results of uniform series of contingent events. The formulation does not indicate the cause of the phenomenon, but merely the phenomenon which results from a specific co-ordination of a great many formative forces.

The first part of the formulation is exemplified in the social organization of the Quakers. The group as a whole is extremely individualistic, as is manifest in its religious principle. It separates itself sharply from other groups and lacks an understanding of the higher political unity and its purposes. On the other hand, it binds the individuals strictly to a uniform type of group life that leaves little or no room for individual variations. The strong individualistic character of the group prevents an expression of personal individuality on the one hand and an approach to other groups on the other hand.

Both aspects of the correlation are exemplified in the political life of the American people before the Civil War. The southern states were populated mostly by adventurous individuals with no particular tendency toward local self-government. Their counties were large but colorless administrative units, and their real political unity resided in the state. The people of the northern states settled mostly in groups. They formed small local townships, which absorbed and regulated a large part of the personal life. But these narrow local structures possessed as a whole a much more individualistic character. The New England states were not combinations of individuals, but combinations of townships.

The apparently existing need for a fixed quantum of differentiation and conformity which seems determined by personal, social, and historical circumstances can evidently be satisfied in different forms. The individual leads in a way a double existence. In his private life he is conscious of his delimitation from his other group members. In his social life, that is, as a group member, he is conscious of his delimitation from everything that lies outside of his group. It is for this reason that the differentiation within the group can compensate for the lack of differentiation between groups, and vice versa, thus maintaining the fixed balance between variation and conformity.

Although membership in a small circle is in general much less favorable for a complete development of the individuality than membership in a large group, there is an interesting exception. In the large and wide cultural communities of modern civilization, the membership in a family group appears to give a definite support to the individualization. The single individual is apparently unable to face the large community alone. Only by giving up a part of his absolute ego to a few others and by uniting with these others in a small circle can he guard and maintain his individual uniqueness. He has to devote himself and his interests to a few others in order to be able to face the whole community on a broader front. In this way membership in the smallest circle within the widest group can support and protect the differentiation, although it usually serves this purpose only during the period of preparation and transition.

The modern family fulfils this function in an ideal way. As a collective unity it offers its members on the one hand the opportunity for a preliminary differentiation which prepares them for later, fuller differentiations. On the other hand it offers them a certain protection under which the individual differentiations can develop until they are capable of asserting themselves in the social totality. Modern civilization gives definite rights both to the individuality and to the widest possible circle. In such a social structure the family takes an intermediate position and partakes of the characteristics both of the small group and of the large group. It appears as an extension of the individuality, as a unity acting as one, distinct and separate from all other social units. But it also appears as a complex plurality within which the individual is differentiated from all others and develops his self-realization and self-sufficiency.

This double function leads to a sociological ambiguity. The family appears sometimes as an individual unit in the larger circles, sometimes as an intermediate circle between the individual and the larger circle. Both these functions may be found in the different phases of the evolution of

the family. It appears at one time as an inclusive social
circle absorbing the whole of the individual, but clearly
separate and distinct from all other families. Later it appears as a more narrow social circle capable of functioning
as an individual unit in a wider social circle. The patriarchal family, despotic and closely knitted, was self-sufficient from the economic and the military point of view.
The modern small family is more highly individualized,
but combines as a unit in the wider social circle, such as
the state or the nation.

In the modern complicated social structure, consisting
of a great series of ever widening social circles, there arises
with regard to each of these circles a similar problem of apparent sociological ambiguity. If there exist only two different social circles, the respective positions of the individual in these circles can easily be compared. In case of a
great many circles, the situation becomes more complex.
In that case, each circle except the largest has an intermediate position between a larger and a smaller one. It
functions in its relation to the larger circle as a unit with
individual characteristics, in relation to the smaller ones
as a complex of a higher order. The correlation formerly
referred to was a correlation between the individual element, the small circle, and the large circle. In the complex
social structure of modern civilization, we observe that a
single social circle can partake of the characteristics of all
the three factors in the correlation, depending on the relation in which it is viewed. This does not impair in any way
the truth and the value of the correlation. On the contrary, it proves that it is of a purely formal sociological
character completely independent of any specific content.

If there exist in social structures, apart from the individual units, small but complex circles and also large circles, the first and the last appear to be drawn together in

a common antithesis to the intermediate circle. This is manifest not only in the objective relationships, but also in the subjective attachments of the individuals to these factors. Personal devotion and attachment usually go to the smallest circle or to the largest one, but not to the intermediate circle. The man who sacrifices himself for his family may do the same for his country or even for humanity, but he will rarely do so for his province. This drawing together of the most individual and the most general structure over and across the intermediate one is the actual fundamental factor in the observed phenomenon that the larger circle favors individual liberty, while the small circle restricts it.

This common antithesis of the individual unit and the larger circle to the intermediate circle is manifest in history in innumerable instances. The medieval knight combined an individualistic and particularistic life with cosmopolitan tendencies. The individual self-sufficiency found its counterpart in a European knighthood which transgressed all national boundaries. This same antithesis is manifest in the destructive forces which destroyed the Holy Roman Empire. It declined and finally crumbled because of the particularistic tendencies of its parts and because of the efforts to bind it in close ties with all other parts of Europe. The forces of expansion and contraction finally disrupted it as an intermediate national structure.

This particularism had already been stimulated in another constellation which had different dimensions. If differentiated elements or elements which are apt to differentiate are combined in an inclusive social circle, there often result increased intolerance and friction and repulsion. The large common framework, which requires on the one hand a certain amount of differentiation among the elements as a condition of its existence, induces on the other hand an increased friction and opposition among these elements. The full realization of the potential contrasts and oppositions would not have resulted were it not for this compression within a unitary frame. In this way the world-policy of the medieval empire stimulated the particularism of kings, tribes, and peoples. The attempted and partially realized synthesis created and stimulated the individualism which finally destroyed it.[1]

The most suggestive example of this correlation between social expansion and individual differentiation is to be found in economic history. The introduction of the money economy has had results both for the form and for the content of social and individual life which illustrate perfectly the general correlation. The natural economy shows small, relatively self-contained economic circles. The difficulty of transportation limits their size, and the technique of the natural economy, therefore, does not permit a far-going differentiation in occupations. The introduction of the money economy changes this situation in two aspects. The general acceptance of money, its easy transportation, and finally its transformation in a credit system enable it to function over an ever expanding area until it unites all peoples in one economic circle with interlocking interests, supplementary activities, and similar usages. On the other hand, the money economy permits a far-going differentiation and specialization. The money wage makes the worker more independent of his employer. The possession of money gives the individual a greater freedom of movement. As the result of the full penetration of the money economy, the individual is brought into free competition with all other individuals within the larger circle and is allowed an amount of overspecialization and one-sidedness which is possible only within a very wide frame.

[1] *Soz.*, pp. 709–32.

In the economic world, money fulfils the sociological function of correlating the maximum extension of the circle with the maximum differentiation of the individual, not only with regard to the factual division of labor, but also with regard to his formal freedom and autonomy. It changes the small, homogeneous, self-contained circle of the natural economy into a group which manifests both extension and differentiation.

In political developments, the same constellation is found in a great many different forms. It occurred in the field of agrarian policy when, after the abolishment of collective ownership, the commons became partly public domain, partly private property. It occurred in the field of internal politics when, after the abolishment of the semi-public corporation, its functions were taken over partly by the state, partly by private associations.

Further illustrations of the correlation may be cited from the domain of law. The absolutism of the Roman state had a correlate in a certain absolutism of the individual. There was a *jus privatum* next to the *jus publicum*. There were norms for the all-inclusive totality, but also for the individuals whom it included. There existed a law for the larger community on the one hand and for the individual on the other hand, but not for the intermediate group. The old Roman law did not recognize the corporation as a subject of special law. In medieval Europe, on the other hand, there was no distinction between private and public law. But the communities of that period were not large inclusive unities like the Roman Empire, but small social circles which arose out of the needs and interests of individuals. There was no necessity for a separation of public and private law, because the individual was more intimately bound up in the community and expressed his individuality in his community life.

The correlation appears again in the development from blood feud to public justice. The blood feud was based on a strong internal solidarity of externally clearly separated and autonomous kinship groups. The revenge was directed against the whole group of the offender and executed by the whole group of the victim. With the rise of a large inclusive political circle, absorbing the different kinship groups, the blood feud disappeared. The rights of the particularistic groups were replaced by the rights of the superior authority of the larger group on the one hand, and the rights of the single individual on the other hand. The collective responsibility of the kinship group was replaced by the collective responsibility of the larger circle and the individual responsibility of the single person. Public justice and the immediate social restraint of the individual by the larger group replaced the blood feud and the restraint of one small group by the other.

An entirely similar development is manifest in the decline of the patriarchal family. When civil rights and duties in war and peace came to apply to the son as well as to the father, there began a gradual disintegration of the *patria potestas*. The results were on the one hand an increased power of the larger group over the individuals, on the other hand an increased liberty of the individual and a greater independence of the despotic ties of the small circle.

The subjective reflex of this correlation appears in the field of philosophy, ethics, and religion in the form of a high valuation of the individual on the one hand and a tendency to cosmopolitanism on the other hand. The philosophy of the eighteenth century was individualistic and humanistic. It stressed the rights of the individual, but conceived them as the "rights of man," as the rights of a member of a common humanity. The ethics of the Stoics was, in comparison

with that of their predecessors, individualistic and cosmopolitan. Their aim was a complete development and self-
realization of the individual. They conceived of compan-
ionship with others only as a means to that end. On the
other hand, however, they conceived a fundamental equality and fraternity which united all individuals in a common humanity. The socio-historical process had disrupted
the small social circles of Greek life. The ethical interests
formerly devoted to the city-state now attached themselves to the individual on the one hand and to an all-inclusive humanity on the other hand. Christianity is but
the religious formulation of this same fundamental formal
relationship. It gave the human being a fully independent
and autonomous individual soul, but bound him, on the
other hand, in one inclusive circle with all humanity. It
held him individually completely responsible for all his
acts and tried to instal in him at the same time a spirit of
self-sacrifice and a devotion to the largest possible circle.

The expansion of the social circle in which the individual participates will destroy, on the one hand, his provin-
cialism, his sectarianism, and his narrow group egoism.
On the other hand, it will stimulate both an individual
egoism and a wider social sympathy and solidarity. But
if, owing to peculiar circumstances, the latter cannot develop, if the social circle has become so large that all direct
personal relationships practically drop out, then there remains only an unrestrained individual egoism and ruthless
self-assertion. The introduction of money has brought
about such results in the economic world. It has liberated
the individual from the narrow bonds of his guild and even
from those of his national group and has created a world-
economy; but, on the other hand, it has favored an economic egoism in all degrees of ruthlessness. The wider the
economic sphere for which a man produces, the less does

he know his customers and the more is his interest exclusively directed toward the price that he can make them pay. The more impersonal his relations are with the consumers, the more are his efforts directed toward the purely financial results of his labor. Apart from the widest spheres for which the work can be done only with labor that derives its stimulus from an abstract idealism, the worker will put less of his own person into his work and have less of an ethical interest in it in proportion as the relation to his customers becomes less intimate. With the expansion of the group for which he works, he becomes more indifferent about his personal relations to that group, and there disappear a great many factors which might counterbalance his individual economic egoism.

It seems that human nature and human relationships are so constituted that the individual must rely on himself and is thrown back on his own resources if his relationships surpass a certain number. This holds not only for the quantitative extension of the circle, which must necessarily reduce the personal interest of the individual in each point of the circle. It holds also for the qualitatively increasing manifoldness within the circle, which also prevents the personal interest from attaching itself to one point. This mutual paralyzation of conflicting demands on the social sympathy leaves the individual egoism as sole survivor in the field. It is, however, an exceptional case, which occurs only if the group surpasses a certain limit.[1]

It will be sufficiently evident from the foregoing examples that the correlation between individual differentiation and sociological expansion is manifest in countless social situations. The relationships which it synthesizes may be found coexisting, in sequence, or alternating; but these are but minor variations of the same fundamental correlation.

[1] *Soz.*, pp. 746–59.

Everywhere the intermediate group appears as the mean between the individual unit and the larger group. It is sociologically self-sufficient because it offers the opportunity for the satisfaction of the formal need for differentiation and homogeneity which the individual can otherwise express only in the relationship between his private life and that of the wider social circle.

SUMMARY

THE preceding chapters illustrate the skeleton structure of Simmel's sociology. Apart from the topics selected, his works contain a great many other essays on specific social forms and general sociological problems. The phenomena dealt with are, however, sufficiently representative to suggest a more or less unified picture of the task of formal sociology.

It will be evident that, although drawing its data from the social life of all ages, its subject-matter is not the factual content of the social situation, but its purely formal aspect. Its aim is to find correlations between determinative factors and sociological forms. Its purpose is not to find correlations between determinative factors and social conditions.

Sociology is concerned with kingship and the state as forms of social organization, not as political institutions. It deals with the competitive system and large-scale production as types of social structures, not as phases of economic development. It is interested in law and morality in their formalistic aspect, as norms for specific relationships, not in their legal or ethical content.

—The subject-matter of sociology is therefore not the social actuality as such. It rests upon an abstraction from the actuality like that of any other science. In sociology this abstraction results from a differentiation between the form and the content of the social actuality. This mental process of differentiation is its essential technique. As long as this technique is not mastered, the correlation problems of the science will appear in the form of contingency problems. The difference in social content will then over-shadow the similarity in social form, and the full meaning of Simmel's illustrations and inductions will escape us. But once this process of differentiation has been mastered, there are no insurmountable obstacles of technique. The task of the science will then reveal itself as identical with the task of all other sciences within their special field. That task is to find the laws or, avoiding all metaphysical implications, to find phenomenological relationships with sufficiently high degrees of correlation to give a high probability of repetition.

The correlations of sociology are correlations between social forms and determining factors, and only by increasing the number of such correlations can we build a theory of the processes of socialization which will result in a science of association.

BOOK III

SOCIAL PHILOSOPHY

METAPHYSICS

INTRODUCTION

IN THE preceding books we have dealt with the philosophic inquiry into the presuppositions of the social sciences and with sociology as one of the empirical social sciences. There remains for us, therefore, to deal with that part of Simmel's work which lies in that other field of philosophical inquiry flanking the empirical sciences of the socio-historical actuality, namely, social metaphysics.

In this field the results of the different social sciences are correlated with the results of other sciences and brought to completion. In this field the metaphysical need for a unitary picture satisfies its demands by synthesizing the fragmentary results of the empirical inquiries or by interpreting a whole range of phenomena in terms of a selected phenomenon as their symbol and essence.

In this sphere lie Simmel's characteristic contributions to the philosophy of culture. They have this formal similarity, that they are all attempts to reach a fundamental understanding of a sphere of life by viewing a selected phenomenon of that sphere as its characteristic expression. In all these studies the thought movement proceeds from the sphere to the specific phenomenon and from there back to the totality of the sphere. In this way Simmel proceeds from a single religious phenomenon to the meaning of religion, from Kant, Schopenhauer, or Nietzsche to the significance of philosophy, from Rembrandt and Rodin to the meaning of art, from money to modern civilization, and finally from Goethe to the meaning of life itself. In this manner he searches in the single appearance of each sphere for the meaning of the whole.

For the purpose of this study Simmel's *Philosophy of Money* is best suited to illustrate his conception of the function of a social metaphysics as distinct from the function of a social science or a philosophic inquiry into the presuppositions of the social sciences. As metaphysics, it traces the relations of money to all the phenomena of social and cultural life and interprets modern civilization in terms of money as its functional category and symbol.

CHAPTER I

MONEY AND INDIVIDUAL LIBERTY

The Historical Aspect of Liberty

D UTY, claim, right, and obligation are in the last
analysis only names for a one-sided aspect of dual
relationships. Every duty has as its correlative
the right of another subject. This right or claim may have
for its content the personal services, the immediate result
of these personal services, or merely a specific object. This
series is also a scale for the amount of liberty that is left to
the person thus bound. The extreme form of the first instance is slavery. In that case there is no objective speci-
fication of the service demanded, but the individual is
bound with the whole of his personality and all his energies.
The transition to the second phase begins with the speci-
fication of the labor time or of the character of the work.
The third phase is reached if, instead of a quantum labor
time or labor force, a specific product is demanded. In
that case the claimant is interested only in a specific objective obligation. How that obligation is met becomes a matter of indifference to him, and the personality of the servant can withdraw from the service.

But as long as the natural economy lasts, a complete
liberation cannot be obtained. The intimate relationship
between product and producer prevents a complete withdrawal of the personality from the service demanded, although the substitution of a factual service for a personal
service means increased liberty. Full liberation becomes
possible only after the money economy has succeeded the

219

natural economy and the money payment the factual obligation. The personality is then completely divorced from the product and at full liberty to obtain that money in whatever way it may choose.

But the introduction of the money economy means not only an increased liberty in social life, but also an enrichment of social life, an increase in social values. What the objectivation of culture obtains in a substantial form, money obtains in a functional form. The objectivation of culture means the creation of objective values in which all can participate without depriving one another. The introduction of money means the mobilization of values, the possibility of transfer by exchange without loss to either party.

This enrichment began with the invention of exchange as a substitute for gift or theft. Gift and theft meant only the satisfaction of subjective impulses. Exchange means an objective valuation and a reciprocity between subjects instead of a mere one-sided possession and a one-sided desire. It means an exchange of possessions under conditions of justice. But it means more than a mere relative formal justice. It means also an increase in subjective enjoyment, an increase in subjective values.

The substitution of buying and selling for primitive barter allows a more complete realization of these two principles implied in exchange. The fact that money can be subdivided into minute parts makes it possible to weigh the value of an object in terms of money more precisely than in terms of other objects. Again, the new form of exchange gives to the one what he needs specifically and to the other what everybody needs in general and what he can therefore immediately exchange for what he needs specifically. Money creates a form of exchange which permits the realization of a maximum of subjective enjoyment.

The significance of the money economy for modern civilization becomes more apparent if we view the resulting liberation in connection with the resulting restraints. It creates, namely, a specific form of impersonal mutual dependence which allows full scope to personal independence.

During the period of the natural economy, a person depended on a small number of individuals, but his dependence was a dependence on personal services. The complicated technique which could develop after the introduction of the money economy makes a single person dependent on countless individuals, but these individuals have a significance for the subject only as bearers of an economic function, as possessors of capital, producers of goods, retailers or merchants. What they are outside of their economic function is of no concern. The totality of their personality remains outside of the economic relationships. The tendency of modern economic life which results from the division of labor is to make a person dependent on an increasing number of individuals, but to free him more and more from the personalities behind their functions.

The small circle on which a person was dependent in a natural economy was a personal circle. The large circle on which a person is dependent in the modern economy is not a personal circle, but a circle of objective economic functions. He depends on more people, but much less on a specific individual. Because he is dependent on the function and not on the bearer of the function, he can change and select the latter according to his own choice. This gives him an inner independence, a feeling of individual self-sufficiency. His freedom consists in his ability to change the individuals on whom he shall depend. Not dependence as such is the opposite of freedom, but dependence on specific persons, and if liberty means freedom from others, it has to begin with freedom from specific others.

The money economy shows this same tendency throughout the economic system. It is manifest, not only in the relationships between man and his fellow-man, but also in the relationships between man and economic goods, and finally in the relationships between man and money itself. Man has become less dependent on individual persons, but more dependent on his group and its objective functions. The large increase in goods and in the number of goods and their decreasing marginal utility have reduced the value of the single object and sometimes even made it worthless. But not only does the whole species of such objects retain its value, but with advancing civilization man becomes more dependent on objects and dependent on more objects. A single pin is practically without value, but modern life could not be carried on without pins. The cheapening of money has made the single quantum less valuable, but the function of money as such becomes increasingly important and inclusive. In all these phenomena within the economic world, the single elements, in their singularity and individuality, lose their specific significance and become interchangeable, while the factual functions which their species fulfil become increasingly important and make man increasingly dependent.

This development of economic life is but a parallel of the development of mental life. In its original form it lacks a sharp distinction between the personal and the factual aspect and shows no clear differentiation between the subjective and the objective side. It is only later that the contents of life—property, labor, duty, knowledge, social position, or religion—become differentiated from the psychological experience and are conceived as having a self-sufficient, independent existence, be it actual or conceptual.

The mental life of primitive men and of children does not distinguish between the objective or the logical truth and the subjective, psychological structure. For the child and the savage, the psychological content of the moment, be it imagination or fantasy, is immediate reality. The differentiation in contrasts and opposites is the result only of a slow process of development. This development which creates the individuality on the one hand and the objectivity on the other hand is the genesis of freedom and liberty.

The concept of individuality develops as the opposite and correlative of the concept of factualness and parallel with the latter. A great development in the latter also leads inevitably to a great development in the former. This is illustrated in the history of thought in the last three centuries. On the one hand there has been a growing feeling of the factual order of things, of the objective necessity of occurrences, and an extension of the concept of natural law. On the other hand there has been a growing emphasis on the self-sufficiency of the individuality, on its liberty and independence over and against all those external natural forces. Whatever difficulty metaphysics may have in reconciling the objective determination of things with the subjective freedom of individuals, as cultural contents the development of these two conceptions is the result of one single process.

The same occurs within the economic world. Here also there is originally no differentiation between the personal and the factual aspect of a service. Gradually there occurs a differentiation between the production and the product, and finally the personal element withdraws. This process also means the beginning of individual liberty. And here, too, individual liberty increases with the increasing objectivation and depersonalization of the economic world. Only after the economic system has developed into an objective system of integrated reciprocities and factual functional relationships has man become dependent on the functions of all other men and completely independent of their personalities.

Money is the ideal and most adequate bearer of such relationships. It creates relationships between individuals, but it leaves their individuality outside of these relationships. It is a perfect equivalent for factual services, but a very inadequate substitute for what is personal and individual, and the factual relationships which it creates form an excellent background from which to differentiate and distinguish the individuality and its liberty.[1]

Possession as Activity

The increased liberty which is brought to the individual by the introduction of the money economy is also manifest in the new form of property which it makes possible.

The acquisition of objects and, in a wider sense, the labor involved in obtaining them, and also the enjoyment of objects, have often been thought of in terms of movement. In contrast to these two forms of activity, possession was then thought of as a situation of rest related to the former as being is to becoming. But a full understanding of the significance of possession can be reached only if it, too, be thought of in terms of movement and activity.

It is a mistake to think of possession as a purely passive relationship and of property as an object which, in so far as it is possessed, requires no further activity on the part of the possessor. This conception is the result of a fictitious abstraction which could be made only after property had reached a fairly high stage of development. Possession in its original form was something labile, not some-

[1] *Phil. des Geldes*, pp. 297–321.

thing stable. The right to a part of the product of common land was under primitive conditions dependent on an active participation in the cultivation and the harvesting of crops. For other forms of property, efficient use was the only basis for a title. If the child wants to possess an object because it stimulates his interest, he is usually satisfied with looking at it attentively and touching it. If that desire is satisfied, he usually discards it. Among primitive tribes, possession usually does not involve more than a brief relationship of action or enjoyment, and the object so possessed is thrown away the next minute with complete indifference.

A concept of possession which does not imply some activity or other is a mere abstraction. It develops out of the former merely because the relationships between the possessor and his possession become more certain, more fixed, and more durable. The mere momentary relationship changes into a permanent possibility of realizing these relationships, into a certainty of being able to enjoy the object anew each time it is desired. But possession is not something qualitatively and substantially new over and above the single cases of actual enjoyment. Property as a juristic concept stands for something more than the single rights to and enjoyments of the object, but the totality of all possible and all actual enjoyments covers the concept completely. It means the absolute sum of all possible rights, and for that reason possession, not as abstraction but as actuality, has as a necessary correlative an active participation on the part of the possessor.

These various forms of subjective movement and mental participation which are in their totality called possession are dependent on, and in a way determined by, the qualities of the object possessed. Acquisition and fructification of non-monetary objects require specific qualities and capacities, and a specific possession exerts therefore also a specific influence on the possessor. Actual possession involves a reciprocal interaction between the qualities of the possessor and those of the object possessed. This interaction and mutual determination can be more or less close. The possession of objects which have a purely aesthetic significance or a highly specialized intellectual significance, or which can be obtained only with great difficulty, will involve a close interdependence. There will be a scale of objects involving for their possession a decreasing interdependence, until the final stage is reached in the possession of money. The possession of money requires no specific qualities and leaves the possessor completely free and independent.

This independence is manifest first of all in the acquisition. The peculiar abstract character of money makes it possible for all forms of activity and all kinds of talent to lead to its acquisition. It does not require a special dexterity, but can be obtained by dexterity in the handling of other objects. As all roads once led to Rome, so all economic roads now lead to money.

But this independence is also manifest in the aspect of enjoyment. All other forms of possession demand specific qualities and characteristics on the part of the possessor. Money makes no such demands and places no such limitations. It therefore increases the liberty and the freedom of the individual, not only in the negative sense, but also in the positive sense.

To possess an object means to be able to do with it what one wants, to be able to express one's will in and through and with that object. We possess our body in so far as we express our will in and through and with our body, in so far as it obeys our will. We express our tendencies and characteristics in our surroundings by means of our possessions. They mean an extension of the ego, an enlargement of the sphere of the individuality. An external object would be without significance if it could not obtain value, and the ego would be a point without extension if it could not express itself in external objects.

One may say that the acquisition of property means the growth of the individuality beyond the individual. If liberty means a state in which the will can realize itself unhampered, an increase in possession will mean an increase in liberty. But this liberty is restricted by the characteristics and the properties of the objects possessed. Our will is usually sufficiently adapted to life's conditions not to demand from objects what they cannot perform and not to consider that limitation as a positive restraint, but it would be possible, none the less, to arrange objects in a series according to the amount of obstruction which they place in the way of the expression of our will. The last item of that series would again be money. It lacks all structure of its own and adapts itself immediately to any demand or purpose. The objects which stand behind it may exert limitations; money itself adapts itself immediately to our will.

But because of its lack of structure it is also the most unadapted object. Because we possess it so completely, we cannot obtain any more from it than possession. Only in so far as an object is something in itself can it be something for us; only in limiting our freedom can it allow an expression of our freedom. This logical opposition reaches a maximum tension in money. It is more for us than any other object because it belongs to us without reservation, and it is less for us than any other object because it lacks any content which can be actually possessed apart from the mere form of possession as such. We possess it more completely than any other object, but we possess in it less than in any other object.

That money takes this extreme position in the scale of functional relationships between possessor and possessions is also manifest in another direction. The sphere of objects which I fill with my personality because I express my will in and through them is limited not only by the inherent characteristics of the objects, but also by the capacity for expansion of my ego. The sphere of objects can become so great that I cannot realize my potential dominion over them. In this respect also money takes a special place. It requires less effort in its administration, enjoyment, and dominion than any other object, and the quantity of dominion and possession that can be actualized is much greater than with other forms of property. In the former case the inherent characteristics of the objects themselves set the limits to the dominion and the freedom of the ego; here it is the capacity for expansion which limits the dominion; but in both cases money is the form of possession which allows the greatest self-expression and the maximum individual liberty.[1]

Money and Social Differentiation

The increasing differentiation already referred to between the subjective and the objective aspects and the personal and factual sides of life is also manifest in the historical development of property. Possession is an extension of the ego, a phenomenon of mental life. Its significance consists in the conscious realization of the existing relationship between subject and object. What is done with the object is a function of the subject, is a projection of the will or the feeling or the thought of the subject into the object. But this differentiation is a historical appearance. Originally practical possession, like theoretical possession, was a state of indifference, a situation in which the

[1] *Phil. des Geldes*, pp. 322–56.

subject and its objects were not viewed in contrast and opposition; and even when differentiation in consciousness
began, it was long before it resulted in actual independence.

Possession among primitive people was an immediate
activity of the individual; feudalism tied the individual to
the possession; hereditary professions and caste and guild
systems signify an intimate connection between the possession or the economic function and the whole of the personality. With the advance in civilization there begins a
differentiation which results in the growth of self-sufficient economic processes, in the development of an impersonal technique on the one hand and a growth in individual
independence on the other hand.

In this process of differentiation, money exercises the
function of enlarging the distance between the possessor
and his possessions. The shareholder of an industrial concern and the landholder who leases his farm leave the run-
ning of their property to a purely technical administration.
They merely enjoy the fruits without participating in the
actual production. This is possible only in a money economy. Money allows the possessor and the possession to
exist each according to its own laws, and drives them completely apart.

This completion of the process of differentiation
through the introduction of money is manifest, not only in
the receiver of rent or interest, but also in the producer
of goods or of services. It means in all cases a differentiation between the personality and the object or the service,
and the entrance of one of these into the economic system.
The money economy allows the substitution for personal
services of an objectively defined function, either in terms
of objects for a market instead of for a client, or in terms
of a definite amount of labor power. In this case only the
function enters into the economic system and finds its

equivalent in money received. But the money economy has also permitted the growth of the free professions and made possible the functioning of civil servants. For these individuals there is no immediate relation between a specific task or a specific service and the money received. The payment and the salaries of these classes are directed rather toward giving the individual as a whole a sufficiently high standard of living to enable him to fulfil his functions. In this case the function has also differentiated from the personality, although not so completely, and the maintenance of the individual becomes part of the economic world, while the single service or function does not find its immediate and specific equivalent in money.

But, in the last analysis, this differentiation between the person and the object or function is still a differentiation within the latter. The money economy merely gives the different spheres of interest and activity of the individual a relative independence of each other. If money lifts the economic function out of the totality of the personality, it remains none the less an activity of the individual. The opposite of the economic activity is merely the totality of the personality minus the economic function. What money does is to atomize the mental life of the individual, to individualize the different spheres within the individual. This is merely a continuation of the process of individualization and the growth of individual liberty within the group. The money economy has given the individual a relative independence of the immediate interests of his group, a relative self-sufficiency which finds expression in the pronounced individualism that accompanies all money economy and that was as characteristic of imperial Rome and of Florence as it is of the present-day Western world.

But money does not only lead to a liberation of the in-

dividual from his group as a whole; it also leads to a liberation of the individual from his immediate associates.
This is the result of the differentiation between the different
spheres within the individual. He can now participate in
an association with only a small part of his personality.
The medieval corporation embraced the whole of the personality. The money economy has created a form of association which demands only a money participation on the
part of its members and leaves the rest of the personality
untouched. It is an organization which unites people by
combining what is impersonal in them, while leaving out
everything that is personal and specifically individual.
Money has made possible the complete development of
the purely purposeful association. That does not only
mean that the individual can fully maintain his individual
identity while yet being united with others; it also means
that association has become possible between innumerable
persons who are radically different in character. The small
economic circle of the natural economy allows little specialization and little individual liberty. Money creates large
economic circles and allows complete specialization and
full individual liberty. It allows in the economic world the
full working out of the general sociological process which is
manifest in the correlation between the expansion of the
group and the development of individualism.[1]

[1] *Phil. des Geldes*, pp. 357–86.

CHAPTER II

MONEY AND THE STYLE OF MODERN LIFE

Money and Intellectualism

THE phenomena of the money economy are born primarily of that type of mental energy which is called intellect as distinguished from sentiment and feeling. The latter forms of mental energy predominate in periods of natural economy and in fields and spheres not yet invaded by the monetary system. This predominance of the intellectual function in modern life is due to the peculiar character of money which makes it both a means and an end.

The number of means, of intermediate steps, between the first activity and the final goal develops in the same ratio as our knowledge, the latter being the subjective correlate of the objective world-order. As every means is, as such, fully indifferent, the emotional values can in practice attach only to ends or purposes. The more of such ends or final stopping-points our lives contain, the more will the emotional function predominate over the intellectual function. The impulsive and emotional character of primitive people is undoubtedly due in part to the shortness of their teleological series. Even during the Middle Ages, with their production for home consumption and their handicraft technique, life contained a great many points of definite final satisfaction of purposeful activity. The technique of modern life, with its endless preparation and roundabout methods, has created teleological series of infinite length, so that the purpose of an hour's activity lies far beyond that hour and sometimes even beyond the sphere of the individual's vision.

This extension of the teleological series is in the first place due to the introduction of money. It creates a central interest over and above otherwise unrelated activities and thereby brings them into mutual relationships. After the introduction of money, the gains of one undertaking, and thereby that undertaking itself, can become the means to another enterprise—a thing which was impossible as long as the two were unrelated. On the other hand, money, because it is generally conceived as a purpose and an end, thereby degrades many things to means which are really ends in themselves. Money, because it is everywhere and for everybody both an end and a means, links all the contents of life into teleological relationships.

These relationships come to be expressed in terms of objective exchange values, and thereby come to be woven into a large system of factual contents which resembles the system of the causal relationships of the natural order. It is held together by the function of the all-pervading exchange value as the latter is held together by the all-pervading energy. In the relations between man and the natural order, objective knowledge and impersonal intelligence have taken the place of emotional attachments and personal feelings, and in a similar fashion the practical social world has since the introduction of money become more and more a problem for intelligent activity and less and less an object for emotional attachments.

This correlation between the significance of money and of intelligence for modern life is first of all manifest in a negative aspect. Both lack character. Both are merely functions. Intelligence is the indifferent mirror of the actuality in which all elements are pictured with complete indifference as to their values. In their relation to intelligence, all elements have equal rights as long as they are actual. Money is an indifferent mirror in which all elements are pictured with complete indifference to all nonmonetary values. In their relation to money, all elements have equal rights as long as they have an economic value.

This lack of character which is the essence of both money and intellect is also manifest in a more positive aspect. Money shows its complete indifference to other values in being available for all purposes. It serves the noblest pursuits and the basest desires; it functions in enterprises for human welfare as well as in enterprises for human destruction. In a similar fashion intelligence is used both for the welfare of humanity and for theft and murder. In the case of money, this lack of character is once more manifest in another direction. What is sold for money goes to him who pays most; what is bought for money is bought from him who asks least. Money and intellect are forms, functions, the one of economic life, the other of mental life, and, as such, they are relativistic and objective. That objectivity, that lack of character, is not a new quality in addition to other qualities, but it is their very essence. They are the only forms and methods of dealing with the world which exclude personal reactions and subjective responses.

This objective and impersonal character of money and intellect is also responsible for their importance in the development of individualism. To understand this double rôle, it becomes necessary to distinguish between content and function, between the factual aspect of these forms and the use that is made of them. The specific quality of the factual aspect of money causes it to transform the subjective impulse into an objective superpersonal activity which is subject to factual normalization. But that same quality of its factual aspect allows the individual to realize his per-

sonal ends by impersonal means. In its functional aspect
it has become the basis of economic individualism and the
grossest egoism. Because it has no character of its own,
but adapts itself to any purpose, it allows the individual
who makes use of it the expression of his full individual
peculiarity. The case of intelligence is not different.
Knowledge of the actuality in its factual aspect is impersonal, open to all, but it can be used for the expression and
the full realization of individual differences and for the satisfaction of the egoistic impulse.

Both money and intellect are indifferent to the individual peculiarities of life's contents. But because they
give form and direction to these contents to which they are
in principle indifferent, they create the contradictions of
practical life. Because of the formal equality of their relationships to all contents, they become a means for the
realization of the grossest factual inequalities.

There is another characteristic of modern life which is
also closely related to both rationalism and the money
economy. That is the tendency of man to deal with his
world in terms of arithmetically defined magnitudes. Modern man is above all else a mathematician, a statistician,
and an accountant. His theoretical world is to be understood in terms of mathematical formulae. His practical
world is to be weighed and measured in terms of quantities
of pleasure and pain. His political world is to be run on the
basis of counting votes.

This whole tendency is in intimate causal relation with
our economic world. The money economy has made our
daily life a series of mathematical operations. Most of our
acts involve monetary considerations, and their values are
to be calculated with minute precision and compared in
their minute details. It is the money economy which has
given us a practical world which is to be dealt with by

means of mathematical calculations, and this fact has been of great influence on our ideals of knowledge.

In this respect the money economy is merely the sublimation of economic life. Money relates the purely economic aspects of objects just as logic relates the aspects of objects which are intelligent and conceptual. The money economy creates an abstract structure or system which consists of the purely economic values differentiated from objects. This structure or system can be dealt with in terms of mathematics, and this fact reflects back on the objects from which it has been abstracted. If it is true that the predominant style of art influences our way of viewing nature, then the quantitatively definable superstructure of monetary relations above the qualitative actuality must influence strongly our way of viewing that actuality. Thus the calculating intelligence which expresses and manifests itself in the money economy receives back from that same money economy some of the characteristic mental energy with which it masters modern life.[1]

Money in Its Relations to Subjective and Objective Culture

The differentiation between the subjective and objective aspects of mental life already referred to becomes once more manifest in modern times in the separation between subjective and objective culture. But in this particular field the separation has apparently become so complete that there is not even a parallel development. In certain fields of life the objective culture outruns the subjective cultural development, while in other fields the subjective development outruns the growth of its objective counterpart.

If we view the contents of life as elements of culture, we

[1] *Phil. des Geldes*, pp. 480–501.

ascribe to them a value which they do not possess in their mere factual significance. They can be elements of culture only if their properties and qualities have been developed and extended beyond their natural stage. Natural objects become elements of culture only if they have been given a form and structure which they did not possess by nature. They must give expression to our will, our emotions, our intellect, and react back on our subjective, mental life. In so far as they are elements of culture, they are the embodiment of our thoughts and feelings; and this holds good whether they are cultivated plants or works of art or machines. And it holds good, not only for that part of culture which develops out of man's relations to objects, but also for that part which develops out of man's relations to his fellow-men and to himself, such as language, religion, morality, mores, and law. In cultivating things we cultivate ourselves.

Cultivation means increasing the total value beyond that of the natural mechanism. It is a value-increasing process which works both on nature outside of us and on nature inside of us. If we view the contents of life as cultural elements, we deny the self-sufficiency of their aesthetic, moral, or scientific value. To view them as elements of culture is not to view them in any of these static factual aspects, but to view them in their functional relationship to man. It is to view them as a phase in the process which goes from man through these values back to man, as elements which contribute to man's development beyond his own natural state. In so far as man cultivates objects, he cultivates himself, and in so far as the transnatural development of the energies of these objects is a cultural process, it is the visible and objective expression of the development of his own energies.

One of the characteristic phenomena of the cultural

life of our period is the fact that in many fields objective culture has outrun personal culture. The things which form the factual contents of our lives, such as household goods, means of transportation, products of science, art, and technique, have become much more cultivated, while personal culture, at least of the higher classes, has not advanced to the same degree. Our language has been greatly enriched; yet the writing and speech of individuals has become more careless, trivial, and worthless. The machine has become more intelligent than the workman. The advance of objective over subjective culture which occurred in the nineteenth century found expression in a change in educational ideals. The eighteenth-century education, in so far as it aimed at the formation of cultured individuals, was directed toward the development of inner values and personal qualities. The cultured individual of the nineteenth century was an individual with an extensive knowledge of the objectivity and of the forms of objective behavior.

This discrepancy is merely one of the phenomena which indicate the strange relationship between social life and its products on the one hand and the fragmentary contents of the individual existence on the other hand. In language, morals, political structure, religious dogma, literature, and technique, there has accumulated the labor of countless generations. They form the substantialized spirit of the past, the crystallized thought of our ancestors, in which a single individual participates as much as he will or can without ever being able to exhaust it. It is this objectivation of cultural values in special structures which guarantees their permanence and continuity, which creates the social heritage. But for that objectivation, each generation would have to start anew.

But it is also that objectivation of these cultural prod-

ucts in special structures which gives them an independence and a self-sufficiency which are in contradiction to
their real cultural function. Once objectified, they tend
to develop according to an immanent logic and a dynamics
of their own. They continue to grow independently of the
will of their real producers, and unrestrained by the limited
degree in which further absorption can still take place. In
their objective self-sufficiency they tend to lose their real
cultural meaning.

These cultural contents are produced by subjects and
are meant for subjects. But in their intermediate objective status they tend to estrange themselves both from
their origin and from their purpose. Their development
takes place independently of the meaning and significance
which it may have for the subject. There results a tension
between these forms and the continuous historical process
which becomes manifest in a historical dialectic. This historical dialectic is but one form of expression of the dialectic that is inherent in all life and which results from the
tension between the processes and the forms of life.[1]

This tension in the cultural subject-object relationship
may or may not lead to a rupture, but it is the fundamental
tragedy of all culture that it bears within itself the element
of self-destruction. If that rupture takes place, the objective forms lose their cultural significance and become mere
technique, mere civilization.

The essence of culture is that subjective mental energies obtain objective forms which are independent of creative life-processes, but which are reabsorbed into the life-
processes and so bring the bearer to a higher development
of his central ego. This flow from subject through object
to subject in which the metaphysical subject-object relationship becomes historical reality can, however, lose its

[1] See Introduction, pp. 19–20.

continuity. The object can break loose from its position as intermediary and destroy the bridge over which passes the road of cultivation.

The metaphysical question regarding the subject-object relationship finds here a historical answer. While the metaphysical answer to that question usually maintains that a sharp opposition and contrast between them is incorrect, the concept of culture implies a complete opposition of the two parties. It implies a supersubjective logic of these mental products by means of which the subject transcends itself in order to reach itself.

The great task of mind, to conquer the object by creating itself as object and to return to itself with this enrichment, often succeeds. But it must pay for this self-development with the tragic chance that these independent and self-sufficient worlds may develop with a logic of their own which will withdraw them farther and farther from the possibility of cultural reassimilation.

The style of social life is characterized by the relative proportion between objective and subjective culture. In small groups under primitive conditions, the relation is nearly a one-to-one correspondence. The objective cultural possibilities do not greatly outrun the subjective cultural values which are actually realized. With an increase in the cultural level and an extension of the culture circle, the two will grow apart. In large groups, only a part of the objective values become subjective values. The cultural possessions of the group are much greater than the cultural possessions of any single individual. The cultural creation of each single individual still enters into the objective social culture, but the totality of the latter does not enter completely into the former. The subjective culture lags behind the objective culture.

This differentiation and objectivation of culture is due

in the first place to the division of labor. It separates the laborer from his product. He makes only a part of an object, which, as such, has no meaning. It allows no self-expression and does not react back on the individual. His product is a fragment of an economic good, but not a cultural element; his production is an economic function, but not the creation of a cultural value. He becomes divorced from his product. In the field of consumption something similar occurs through the standardization of consumption goods. The cultural contents appear more and more as the embodiment of an objective spirit which faces as something external not only those who consume them, but also those who produce them. The immediate intimate reciprocity has disappeared, and so the personal culture can lag behind the objective culture.

In certain fields of cultural life the opposite tendency is manifest. That discrepancy is visible in social institutions which develop only slowly and gradually and thereby lag behind the development of individuals. These cases are summarized in the following formula: The forms of production are overtaken by the forces of production which they develop themselves, and therefore no longer allow an adequate expression and functioning of these forces. The latter are largely of an individual character. What people are capable of producing and can rightfully demand can no longer be realized by the existing forms of technique. The transformation will follow only after these forces have amassed a sufficient energy to break through the inertia of the old forms; until that moment, the factual organization of production lags behind the development of the individual economic energies.

But these discrepancies are made possible by the division of labor and therefore, in the last analysis, by the money economy. Money makes possible a complete division of labor, a far-going specialization, while yet maintaining the functional unity of the economic system. It is only after the introduction of money and the full development of the money economy that the factual contents of life reach their complete objective independence. And only after that stage has been reached can the objective culture outrun the subjective culture. But money also helps the realization of the other form of discrepancy. It places itself between man and this objective factual world and gives him a self-sufficient existence. It guards and protects his personal life from the immediate contacts with objects and thereby enables the personal energies to grow unhampered.

The function of money in these growing discrepancies is most important in the fields in which objective culture outruns subjective culture. That it also serves the opposite form of discrepancy merely shows its specific character as a historical force. It belongs to those forces which are characterized by the fact that they have no character of their own, that they are purely formal, functional, and quantitative, and can therefore serve the most divergent tendencies and paint life in the most varying colors. Its significance for the style of modern life is not diminished because it serves both types of relationship between subjective and objective culture, but rather increased; not denied, but rather proven.[1]

Money as the Symbol of Modern Life

Not only the quantitative relation between subjective and objective culture, but also the distance or proximity between man and his culture, is an important item in the style and perspective of life. Modern life is characterized by an increasing distance in the personal, subjective rela-

[1] *Phil. des Geldes*, pp. 501–33; *Philosophische Kultur*, pp. 240–53.

tionships and an increasing proximity in the impersonal, objective relationships.

The microscope and the telescope have brought the world of nature nearer to us in a purely rational sense, but this distance in its subjective aspect has become greater than it ever was in the days of anthropomorphism and mythology. The relations of man to his social environment show this same tendency. He differentiates himself more from his immediate circle and approaches the widest circles. The growing individualism means a weakening of family ties and a strengthening of purely rational bonds with the widest circles.

The function of money in this double process is visible first of all in its service in the conquest of distance. Only the transformation of values into money makes possible the existence of economic relationships which are independent of space. Only money makes possible and creates the situation wherein a German laborer or a German capitalist becomes interested in a change of cabinet in Spain, the production of African gold mines, or the results of a South American revolution. But the function of money for the opposite tendency is even more significant. The dissolution of the family is the result of the relative self-sufficiency of the individual members, and the latter is possible only in a money economy which can give them a subsistence even if they fully specialize their particular one-sided talents.

With regard to the distance between man and his cultural products, between man and the factual contents of life, money fulfils a function similar to that which it fulfils in the case of the distance between man and his fellow-man. This function of money has already been referred to in the preceding pages, and we need therefore only mention here that in that field of life the tendency to increase the distance entirely outruns the tendency to decrease the distance.

Another item which gives a distinct character to the style of life is rhythm. It plays an important part in nearly all aspects of our lives and is manifest in a great number of our activities. Rhythm satisfies the two fundamental needs for difference and similarity, for change and stability. The elements of each rhythmic period show quantitative and qualitative difference, ascent and descent, and the regular repetition of the periods shows uniformity and similarity. The individual, social, factual, and historical life-series express their style and abstract scheme in the simplicity or complexity of their rhythm, in the length or shortness of its periods, in their regularity or irregularity, and, finally, in the presence or absence of such periods.

In our modern culture a great many appearances which formerly followed a certain rhythm have now become continuous or irregular. Modern man through his conquest of nature and his relative independence of nature has become more and more independent of her rhythmic periods. Periodic famines so characteristic of primitive agriculture have completely disappeared. The industrial communities have become independent of the rhythm of agricultural life. The permanent middleman has made us independent of the weekly or monthly or yearly market.

But the development of the style of life is not a simple change from rhythm to an unaccentuated series from which all rhythm has disappeared. This is the case only in certain spheres of life. In other spheres rhythm is introduced where it was formerly absent. Manual labor among modern people is done in rhythmic periods of activity and rest. Primitive man shows irregular periods of great energy and complete laziness. Modern man has regular meal hours; primitive man eats when he feels like it or when he can.

Rhythm, or at least its spatial equivalent, is also present in many aspects of human relations. This spatial equivalent is symmetry. Rhythm is symmetry in time, just as symmetry is rhythm in space. The development of symmetrical systems of relationships has gone hand in hand with the development of rationalism. Where man organizes relationships on a rational basis, he organizes them in symmetrical forms, be it in the business world or in his dealing with social and political systems.

But rhythm and its opposite do not occur only as alternative forms in the life-series of man; they also appear at the same time as two fundamentally opposed principles of life, which may be indicated as the rhythmic-symmetrical and the spontaneous-individualistic. And in their simultaneous existence no reconciliation by alternation can be effected. This fundamental opposition is most clearly manifest in the relations between the individual and the social totality, be it an economic, political, religious, or family group. It is the fundamental principle of symmetry that each element of a totality obtains its position, its rights and significance, only through its relations to the other elements and to the common center. If each element obeys only itself and develops according to its own laws and desires, the totality must inevitably be asymmetrical. The individual desires to be a closed totality himself, a form with a center of its own, from which all the elements of his existence and activity receive their meaning and significance. But if the superindividual totality is to be a closed whole, if it is to objectify an idea with self-sufficient significance, it cannot allow the full rounding out of its elements. The totality of the whole is in eternal conflict with the totality of the individual.

Money seems at first to serve the realization of only one of these forms. It is formless itself. It conquers all distance and reduces all things to economic values, and thereby levels the fluctuations between distance and proximity and abolishes the regular alternation of movement and rest which formerly characterized life. Yet, on the other hand, this same lack of form makes it also an adequate means for the systematic and rhythmic tendency of life wherever the phase of social development or the needs of the individual tend in that direction.

In this respect money belongs to the category of forces which are characterized by the fact that, although in essence and origin they are above and beyond the contradictions and oppositions of life, they none the less also descend from their absolute position and take sides in the opposition of relative parts. To this category belongs, in the first place, religion, which man needs to reconcile the contrasts between his needs and his satisfaction, between his norms and his practice, and between his ideal of the world and its actuality. But, once created, it does not remain above the relativities of existence, but becomes one of them and takes sides in their opposition. It is a total organism and at the same time an element; it is a part of existence and at the same time the whole of existence on a higher plane. This holds also for the state. It stands above all parties and above all conflicts of interests, and yet it takes part in these conflicts and allies itself with some party. It places itself thereby in opposition to the party which, in a wider sense, it embraces and includes. Metaphysics creates the same double position for its highest concept if it declares the absolute to be mental substance. This absolute becomes then at the same time a relativity. As mind, it can find its meaning and significance only in contrast and opposition to matter, and, as absolute mind, it must then be distinguished from mental appearances of an inferior and evil nature which it yet embraces in its absoluteness. This double relationship is most clearly manifest in the concept of the ego. The ego stands above all of its contents, all of its inner oppositions and contradictions. But it descends from its lofty position and identifies itself closely with some of its contents and tendencies in their opposition to others.

This is also the form of the relation of money to the contents of life. In essence it stands above and beyond the oppositions and contradictions of life, above and beyond the particular tendencies and style forms. Yet, characterized by its indifference to all that is particular and one-sided, it nevertheless places itself at the disposal of every particular tendency and desire. But here it shows the fundamental difference between itself and those other forces referred to above. Religion, the state, the absolute mind, and the ego—all take one side as against the other if they descend to the plane of the particular interests. Money, however, serves both sides and all sides. It maintains its all-embracing character also on the plane of the particular interests. The objectivity of money is not something that really lies beyond the contradictions and is only illegitimately used by one of them. Its objectivity signifies from the start its willingness to serve both sides of the contradiction, and its significance for the style of life lies therein, that on account of its indifference to all one-sidedness it adapts itself to every one-sidedness.

The third item which is characteristic for the style of life is its tempo Persistence or change and the relative tempo of the latter are immediately characteristic for the style of life of a specific period.

The introduction of money and the growth of the money economy have meant a tremendous increase in the tempo of life. The quick circulation of money and goods, the fluctuations in individual wealth, the concentration and accumulation of money in centers and the resulting increase in individual contacts—all these phenomena which are the immediate outcome of the money economy have increased the changes in the contents of life so greatly that the preceding natural economy seems static by comparison. But the full significance of money as such for the tempo of life, apart from the technical results of its introduction, can be shown only by a further consideration.

An analysis of the concepts of persistence and change shows a double contradiction. If we view the world with regard to its substance, we are led to a concept of an unchangeable reality which, because it excludes all increase or decrease, gives to matter the character of absolute persistence. If, on the other hand, we regard the form of this substance, then the persistence is completely dissolved. One form changes incessantly into another, and the world seems a *perpetuum mobile*. This is the double aspect of cosmological existence, which is often given a metaphysical significance. On another empirical plane, however, the opposition between persistence and mobility is divided differently. There we see the persistence of forms during a certain period, while the real elements of which they are composed are in constant movement. The rainbow persists, although the water particles change; the organic and the social forms persist, although their elements come and go; and even in inorganic objects there persist only the relations and the reciprocities of their minute elements, while the latter are in constant movement. In this case reality itself is in constant flux, but, as the latter cannot be seen, the forms and constellations of its movements solidify in the phenomena of persistent objects.

Apart from these two contradictions which result from the application of the ideas of persistence and movement to the conceived world, there exists a third. Persistence

may mean infinite duration, existence beyond time, timeless existence. The simplest illustration of this is the concept of natural law. The content of the known natural causality may change in the course of time, but the meaning,
the conception, the idea of natural law remains unchanged.
It is the concept of absolute validity, of timeless uniformity beyond and above all partial and incomplete realiza-
tions. The opposite of this peculiar form of absolute persistence is the concept of absolute movement, of timeless
change. The concept of timeless persistence or absolute
duration finds its opposite in the concept of timeless change
or absolute non-duration.

For the absolute mobility of the world, money is the
most adequate symbol. Its significance and meaning lie in
the fact that it moves, that it changes hands, in its mobility. The moment it rests, it is no longer money in the specific sense of the term. And even the influence which it
then exerts consists only in the anticipation of its renewed
mobility. It is nothing but a bearer of movement from
which everything that is not movement has been excluded.

But money is also a symbol for the opposite way of
making the world intelligible. It is symbolic for persistence
as it is symbolic for movement. The single quantum of
money is in incessant movement because the value it repre-
sents is related to the valuable objects as the general law
to the concrete forms in which it is realized. The general
law, however, is above and beyond all the movements of
which it is the form and basis. In a similar fashion the abstract money value of which money is the bearer is the form
and the basis of all economic movements. Money value,
wealth, is the abstract general concept for objects in so
far as they are economic goods. They are not necessarily
economic goods, but they can only become economic goods

according to the law of evaluation which is condensed in money.

The fact that money is symbolic for both fundamental forms of expressing the actuality indicates their mutual relation. The meaning of each of these forms is only relative. Each finds its logical and psychological possibility of rendering the world intelligible only in the other. Only because reality is in absolute mobility is there any sense in placing opposite it an ideal system of valid timeless laws, and only because the latter exists can the former, which would otherwise remain an indefinable chaos, be grasped and made intelligible. The general relativity of the world, which seems at first to be manifest only in one aspect of this opposition, in reality also embraces the other and shows itself as ruler where at first it seemed only a party. In the same way money builds above its meaning as a single economic value a higher meaning, namely, that of expressing abstract economic value as such; and it intertwines these two functions in an indissoluble correlation in which neither is the first.

By symbolizing the factual relationships between objects, money as a historical structure creates a special bond between that factual world and historical life. Money is only the relativity of economic goods, which signifies their value, condensed in a special structure. Therefore, the more social life comes to be pervaded by the money economy, the more clearly and explicitly does the relativistic character of existence come to be expressed in conscious life. Just as the absolutistic viewpoint represented a phase of intellectual development which was intimately correlated with specific practical, economic, and emotional forms and constellations of cultural objects, so the relativistic viewpoint, which seems to express or rather to be the present form of intellectual adaptation, is also inti-

mately correlated with analogous counterparts in social
and subjective life. This relativistic viewpoint has found
in money both the real effective bearer and the reflecting
symbol of its forms and movements.[1]

Money is, therefore, more than a standard of value
and a means of exchange. It has a meaning and significance
over and above its purely economic function. Modern
society is a monetary society not merely because its economic transactions are based on money, or because its
manifold aspects are influenced by money, but because it
is in money that the modern spirit finds its most perfect
expression.

[1] *Phil. des Geldes*, pp. 534–85.

SUMMARY

THE two chapters of this book give a brief synopsis of Simmel's social metaphysics as given in his *Philosophy of Money*. They illustrate the function of a social metaphysics as contrasted with the function of an empirical social science and with the philosophic inquiry into the presuppositions of the social sciences. They also illustrate what his conception of metaphysics and his emphasis on function and thought form rather than on dogma and system lead to in practical application. They do not lead to a well-rounded, systematic social philosophy. But that, according to Simmel, is their strength, not their weakness.

Absolute and abstract philosophic systems are too far removed and remain too far distant from the single appearances of practical life to be capable of lifting them out of their isolation and relating them to all other appearances of life. They fulfil their function of seeing life whole and the manifoldness of the cosmos as a unitary totality only at the cost of neglecting large numbers of single phenomena. Simmel's functional relativism and subtle dialectic give the metaphysical thought form a sufficient mobility and flexibility to enable it to relate even the most fleeting historical appearance on the surface of life to the most fundamental aspects of existence.

The total inquiry pursued in this third book is a metaphysical inquiry. The unity of the single inquiries lies, therefore, not in the relation between their propositions or in their contribution to a special field of knowledge, but in the unitary thought movement which aimed through these inquiries to find in a single appearance of life the meaning of the whole. The appearance selected was money. It has been related to the outstanding phenomena of the social and cultural world, to liberty and rationalism, and to the most profound currents of individual life and of history. It has been shown to be the functional category of modern civilization and the symbol of the forms and movements of modern thought.

CONCLUSION

CONCLUSION

THIS study is an effort to give in a comprehensive and yet reasonably detailed form a synopsis of Simmel's social theory and the essentials of his formal sociology. An appreciation of his general philosophy would hardly be in place here, and the reader is therefore referred to the more competent scholars who have given a valuation of that aspect of his work.[1]

In the light of Simmel's own viewpoint that a complete understanding involves both a general and a historical understanding, this study is one-sided. It has aimed only at what might be called the general aspect of the factual understanding, and has dealt only with Simmel's work in and for itself. It is impossible within the scope of this study to trace the historical origins of his ideas, and we must therefore waive detailed questions regarding his indebtedness to his predecessors. But before we can summarize in a few words the significance of his specific contribution, we must briefly indicate the position of his sociology in the general development of the subject.

The foundations of nineteenth-century sociology were laid by Auguste Comte and Herbert Spencer. Spencer is usually referred to as the founder of the organic school, although with very little historical discrimination, and Comte as nothing less than the father of sociology. From Comte the nineteenth century inherited in a simple, easily assimilable synthetic form the whole range of philosophic

---

[1] A. Mamelet, *Le relativisme philosophique chez Georg Simmel;* Siegfried Kracauer, "Georg Simmel," *Logos,* IX (1920), 307–38; Hermann Smalenbach, "Simmel," *Sozialistische Monatshefte,* XXV (1918), 283–88; Max Frischeisen-Köhler, "Georg Simmel," in *Kantstudien,* No. 24.

concepts by means of which previous periods had organized their knowledge of society, together with the characteristic historical point of view of the romantic movement. It contained the time-worn analogy between society and the individual, the mixture of value and existential judgments known as the idea of progress together with the search for the law of that mixture, the interest in the historical dimension, the general rationalistic prejudice, and the interest in historical prediction. In other words, it contained all the basic presuppositions and fundamental categories that were necessary to reduce all social study inevitably to some form of social philosophy or philosophy of history.

The history of social theory in the nineteenth century is the history of a gradual methodological clarification and of the slow liberation of the study from restricting presuppositions and confusing aims. Comte may have thought of himself as the herald of the positive stage, but in reality he left his scientific descendants an estate which was still largely incumbered with metaphysics. However, even if he was the father of modern sociology, he must have had a few paternal ancestors himself, and so there are a few others to blame for the rather doubtful heritage. But among descendants of patriarchal Aryans it is not considered good form to criticize one's paternal ancestors too severely, so instead of merely referring to Comte's doubtful methodology, let us also admit that he has been the stimulus to a renewed study of social phenomena.

Comte has been the starting-point for a great many different trends of social theory. With the help of a little imagination, the most divergent types of thought could be easily traced back to his works. They contain in embryo so many ideas that have later been developed into distinct theories that it is just as easy to view them as the beginning of the biological as of the psychological school. Like the holy books of the Christian and the Marxian gospels, the holy books of the positivist gospel are catholic enough to offer the most divergent sects a storehouse of infallible dogma. Luckily, however, it is not necessary for an understanding of nineteenth-century social theory to trace all of it back to Comte, and so we can be satisfied with a brief sketch of its development.

The history of Continental social theory in the nineteenth century can be briefly summarized as the gradual change from a philosophy of society to a science of association. In that development certain well-defined steps can be traced without difficulty. During the first two phases, the old analogy between society and the individual continued to shape social theory. Its influence is manifest both in the biological school and in the school of the folk psychologists. This influence led to a pronounced sociological realism. The first school saw society as an individual organism in biological terms, as body; the second saw society as an individual organism in psychological terms, as mind.

During the second two phases, the influence of the old analogy was absent. One of these phases was expressed in a school of sociological nominalism which finally found shelter among social psychologists. The other found expression in a school of sociological relativism which laid the foundations for our modern science. The first tried to understand society in terms of processes in the individual minds. It was based on a point of view which avoided the pitfalls of its predecessors, but it did not lead to a science of society, as it neglected the essential sociological category. The latter school, although fully admitting that in the last instance social life rests on processes in individual minds, turned its attention, not toward these processes, but

toward the social aspect of their result. It was based on a
point of view which saw sociology as the study of association, sociation, socialization, reciprocal determination, or
whatever other term was used for indicating the unique
sociological subject-matter.

The actual historical development has not, of course,
followed this schematic simplicity. Certain theories can
just as easily be classified under one heading as under another. But the general trend has been more or less in this
direction. Our aim here, moreover, is not the careful tracing of exact historical sequences, but the understanding
of a period. For that reason we feel justified in using this
simplified schema, although we are fully conscious of the
distortion of historical reality which results from it.

The organic school of sociologists fulfilled two functions of considerable importance. It gave the concept of
social unity a concrete expression and imbedded it for all
time in social thought. Apart from this contribution, it
functioned as an antidote to one-sided romanticism. It
directed attention toward that which is timeless and universal in social life instead of toward that which is historical and unique, and thereby took the first step in the liberation of sociology from the philosophy-of-history tradition.

Within the organic school there occurred a gradual
change of emphasis from a biological to a psychological
viewpoint. Not even Spencer has ever pretended that
social processes are of a physical nature, but he was too
much interested in structural analysis to pay much attention to the nature of social functions. With Schäffle the
emphasis came to be placed on the functional aspect of
social life, and this resulted in a definite change toward a
psychological point of view. He suggested that the bond
of social unity consists of psychical processes of interaction

between individuals, and, conscious of the fact that with the change in emphasis to the functional aspect of social life the method of analogy had lost its usefulness, he advocated an actual first-hand study of the processes of interaction. He did not overindulge in his own medicine, however, and his work has many of the shortcomings of the organic school, but among much that is obsolete today there is much that has a very modern sound. In Germany, where he has been not only talked about but actually read, he exerted a great deal of influence and definitely prepared the way for the psychological point of view.

This change in viewpoint was largely determined by the important development in the field of psychology in the second half of the century. Out of the school of Herbart in Germany came the work of Waitz, Lazarus, and Steinthal in ethnological psychology, and indirectly the work of Bastian. Within this group the concept of the fundamental psychological nature of society found complete expression. It took in some cases the form of a conceptual realism, and the *Zeitgeist*, the social mind, the spirit of the people, was sometimes thought of as an entity with ontological existence; but this was a preliminary philosophical formulation which was later changed to a formulation in terms of functional relationships. The important contribution of this group was their rejection of analogy as a method of study. They did not free themselves completely from its influence, as their realistic conceptions show, but they undertook at least an actual investigation of group conduct and of group feeling on the basis of a comparison of historical appearances.

A similar change of emphasis appeared in France, also influenced by a renewed interest in psychological study. Folk psychology did not find the same amount of acceptance as it did in Germany. The work of Taine, which most closely resembles it, owes perhaps more to Comte directly than to the more recent German developments. But the work of Ribot, Poulhan, and others in the field of feeling and sentiment, and other studies in the field of suggestion, undoubtedly influenced the development of the social sciences.

With the eighties the psychological point of view had begun to be more or less accepted. In the German group it was expressed by Tonnies and Gumplowicz, and in the French group by de Roberty, de Greef, and Fouillée. In this group the doctrine of Fouillée is an interesting combination of biological and psychological concepts similar to that of Schäffle in Germany. While maintaining that society was an organism, he explicitly stated that it was of a psychological nature, and he combined these two notions in the more or less contradictory concept of a contractual organism.

With the nineties, the psychological point of view had become commonplace, not only in Europe, but also in America. France added Tarde and Durkheim, Germany Simmel, Ratzenhofer, Stein, and Barth to its adherents; and the group of American sociologists, such as Giddings, Small, Vincent, and Stuckenberg, had a definite leaning in that direction.

With the acceptance of the psychological point of view and the renunciation of the method of organic analogy, a great step had been taken in the right direction, but the whole road from a philosophy of society to a science of association had not yet been traversed. There was agreement regarding the fundamental nature of society, but that was all. There was neither a consensus of opinion regarding the task of sociology nor regarding its subject-matter. Some of the adherents of the psychological point of

view thought of sociology in terms of a general social psychology (Le Bon, Sighele), some in terms of a science of
social interactions (Gumplowicz, Giddings), some in terms
of a philosophy of history (Barth), some in terms of a social
philosophy (Stein), and some in terms of a philosophy of
the social sciences (Ratzenhofer, Small). Nor was there
any more agreement regarding the fundamental category
of this study of sociology; but here, at least, the fundamental differences were not quite so great as the discrepancies in terminology would seem to indicate. The essentially
social category was, for de Roberty, sociality; for de Greef
and Fouillée, contract; for Gumplowicz, conflict; for Tarde,
imitation; for Durkheim, coercion; for Giddings, consciousness of kind; for Ratzenhofer and Small, association;
and for Stuckenberg, sociation. These different terms con-
note very different concepts, but they indicate also the
gradual realization that the aim should be not so much a
philosophy of society as a whole as a study of the specific
phenomena of social interaction.

In this period of confusion appeared the work of Georg
Simmel. The fundamental points in his theory were formulated well before the end of the century, and he therefore definitely belongs to the nineties. His great contribution is a methodological foundation for a science of sociology distinct and separate from social psychology, the
social sciences, social philosophy, and the philosophy of
history. He defined the subject-matter of that science as
the forms of socialization, that is, as the purely social aspect of socialization or association as such. The value of
his work does not lie in its startling originality, but in the
careful methodological justification of its essential concepts. He owed a great deal to his predecessors, perhaps
more in particular to Gumplowicz, but his philosophic

training and his native ability gave him a critical attitude toward presuppositions that seems to be lacking in a great many social scientists.

The relativistic viewpoint has led Simmel to conceive of society as the sum of the interactions between the individuals. The group unity is for him a functional unity, not a substantial unity; society is a process, not a thing. This conception is in harmony with the modern tendency which places the emphasis on the functional rather than on the substantial and on the dynamic rather than on the static aspect. But Simmel has not only gone farther than most of his contemporaries; he has also taken more pains to define his basic concepts and to show their validity and usefulness.

This relativistic viewpoint which sees the group unity as a functional unity has naturally led to a strong emphasis on the individual elements, which are the actual bearers of the processes of socialization. The individual has once more become of importance in social theory. He is not, as for many sociologists, merely a social product, or merely a social factor. He is at the same time social product and social factor, the result of socialization and the producer of socialization; and it is this double capacity that determines him as a social being. This conception yields a better approach toward an understanding of the social actuality than can be obtained by viewing only one aspect and neglecting the other. The essence of social life and group unity is reciprocity, and that essential characteristic is ignored if the approach toward an understanding is based on a one-sided view.

If the individual is regarded solely as the social agent, the influence of the social environment is ignored. If the individual is regarded solely as a social product, the fact that individuals create that social environment is ignored, and the society which molds him comes to be viewed in a half-mystical light. The eighteenth century—mechanistic, rationalistic, and individualistic—has tended mainly toward the first view; the nineteenth century—biological, idealistic, and collectivistic—toward the latter.

The eighteenth-century view found expression in the different social-contract theories. The individual reigned supreme. Political society was his creation, the result of his conscious voluntary activity. It was a means to his end, be it liberty, justice, or the protection of property. The fact that the individual was the actual bearer and positive factor of the social structure was fully realized and led the social theorists to devote considerable attention to individual psychology. The approach was from the individual toward the group, and the social or political structure was valued in terms of its significance for the individual life.

The nineteenth-century view found expression in the organic theories of society on the one hand, and in the idealistic conceptions of the state on the other hand. The realization of the importance of environment in the biological studies reinforced this tendency to place the emphasis on society, the state, the group; in a word, on the social environment rather than on the individual. He was merely a product of the social environment, a cell in the social organism. The state was not a means to his ends; it was an end in itself. The approach was from the group toward the individual, and the individual was valued in terms of his significance for the social or political structure.

Simmel's conception may be regarded as a conciliation between the two. It leads to a viewpoint which brings the immediate realization of the necessity for reciprocity or at least constant alternation between the two modes of approach. Viewed in the light of the tendencies of the nineteenth century, his approach seems a return to the conceptions of the eighteenth. In reality he does not return completely, but takes up an intermediate position. This partial return is a distinct departure from the mysticism that has been rampant in social and political thought in the nineteenth century, and is a definite approach toward a more scientific view. The great importance of Simmel for all social theorists lies in the fact that his methodology explodes the last survivals of rationalism, mysticism, and anthropomorphism which still cling to our thinking about the socio-historical actuality.

Social philosophy as metaphysics has a great and definite function and significance for Simmel, but that function is wholly different from that of science. As a forerunner of science, it has a value and significance only in relation to science; but in neither case can it pretend to be science. The differentiation which leads from philosophy to science, the approach toward the immediate actuality, should be ruthlessly continued until the actual factors and the direct primary processes have been discovered. As long as the inquiry has not reached that stage, it cannot be called scientific, and the investigation which aims at scientific knowledge cannot rest.

Simmel's criticism of rationalism is most evident in his emphasis on the necessity for continuing the historical investigation until the non-scientific concept of historical law dissolves. It is also apparent in his stress on the need for abstaining from speculation about the "social process" and for investigating the minute processes of socialization.

His contention that the concept of a historical law resembles more closely metaphysical speculation than scientific thought is especially of interest in view of the fact that some of his critics have accused him of neglecting the historical dimension. This criticism seems hardly justified. In his discussions on method Simmel points out that an understanding of the factual contents of social life requires two modes of approach. Only through the reciprocity or the alternation between the historical method and the method aiming at general timeless laws can we reach an understanding of the social actuality. The task of sociology has been described by him as the determination, the psychological explanation, and the tracing of the historical development of the forms of socialization. It is true that he has given more attention to the first two than to the last, but there is usually a short treatment of historical development in his essays on social forms. This investigation of the historical development, however, is for the distinct purpose of reaching, in combination with the inquiry aiming at general timeless laws, a complete understanding of the actual sociological structure. If, therefore, the criticism of his neglect of the historical dimension implies that he has not conceived the investigation of the historical development as an end in itself, it contains a statement of fact. But, far from considering this fact a weakness, it would seem to us rather a valuable contribution, if only as a reaction against the one-sided emphasis on historical development in the social sciences in the nineteenth century.

During this period the social sciences, and especially sociology, have suffered from an overemphasis on the historical dimension. They were so much imbued with the spirit of social philosophy and the philosophy of history that Barth could consider sociology and the philosophy of history as identical. The historical investigation as an end in itself has a value and significance only as history. From the point of view of science, it has a value only as a means, not as an end. It is useful only in so far as it permits the discovery of the general timeless correlation which is the aim of science.

Science is pre-eminently practical. In the last instance, it is directed toward the external world. Its aim is to find that knowledge which will lead actions built on it to give desired results. Its purpose is to discover the means which will make it possible to obtain that which is not yet out of that which is. For that reason it has to aim at the general timeless law, because only on that type of knowledge can adequate action be built. From the point of view of science, the self-sufficient historical investigation, aiming at the discovery of the successive stages of development or at the discovery of the historical law, is a blind alley which leads nowhere. Or rather it leads to the present, to what is, but no farther. It leads to a fatalism in some form or other, whether optimistic or pessimistic, which is essentially contradictory to the scientific spirit.

This overemphasis on the historical dimension has been due largely to the fact that the interest in the social sciences was mainly philosophical and theoretical rather than practical. The specific philosophic concept which has done more than any other to retard the advancement of the social sciences is the concept of progress. This somewhat mystical concept is largely responsible for the emphasis on the historical dimension. Under the assumed name of evolution it tried to pass as a scientific concept, but the notion of social evolution has usually been more metaphysical than scientific. In this latter form it has acted as a tremendous stimulus to the investigation of social history, but it has not led to much practical information for the solution of social problems. The social scientists displayed a religious zeal in their endeavor to picture the historical development of social institutions, but paid very little consideration to the question of where it was going to lead them. The result was that the tracing of that evolution became an end in itself. The historical dimension in the social sciences seemed to monopolize all the energy. What should have been a means had become an end in itself, and the sociologists were hardly less satisfied with their institutional genealogies than the Greeks were with their personal genealogies.

It might therefore easily be maintained that from the point of view of science, the concept of social evolution has done more harm than good. The great advance of the natural sciences is perhaps to a large extent due to the fact that they were well under way before the evolutionary viewpoint invaded scientific thinking in those fields. Another element which has no doubt contributed is the fact that they have always been imbued with a spirit which was directed toward ultimate practical results and not toward the discovery of material for philosophic or historical speculation.

Modern chemistry would not be where it is today if most of its energy had been spent in trying to find out how the lead atom has developed out of the helium atom in the course of time. That problem indicates the existence of another legitimate field of inquiry, but it does not mean that the inquiry regarding the properties of elements is of no importance. It is because chemistry has been directed primarily toward the processes of function and not toward the process of growth that it has reached a stage where it is of practical value and can supply the answers to questions regarding the means to definite ends. In the medical sciences, the great advance is due in similar fashion to the study of functional processes as independent of species, and not primarily to evolutionary biology.

The evolutionary viewpoint, which in practice turned out to be merely a reversed teleological viewpoint, has led in the social sciences to an emphasis on the time series and a neglect of the timeless aspect. And even the study of the time series was far from scientific. As each change was regarded primarily in the light of a later change, the series of changes came to be regarded as one unitary immanent process of change. The series of changes in the institution came to be viewed as its evolution, as the mystical unfoldment of its immanent form. The result was that the actual primary processes of change, the effective factors and forces, were neglected. Not only did this type of investigation in the social fields not contribute to general scientific knowledge, but it was not even satisfactory from the point of view of history. The historical development can be understood only on the basis of a knowledge of the timeless laws, but the investigation required to find those timeless laws was omitted.

The knowledge that the organic form, man, developed from the organic form, amoeba, and the economic form, capitalism, from the economic form, tribal communism, through different intermediary stations is not of immediate practical value. Not the fact that capitalism developed out of tribal communism and the monogamic marriage out of general promiscuity is of importance, but the causes of change at each point of change. The social sciences draw their material, of course, from historical data. But they should use these data for the purpose of a general induction which will lead to a timeless law. They should use these data as Simmel uses them, without any consideration for their specific place in the time series. Historical data can also be used for an inquiry into the so-called historical law, but that is the function of history, not of science. Science can fulfil its function only if it turns once and for all, not only from all philosophic and historical speculation, but also from all such concepts as evolution and historical law.

The fact that the historical dimension as an end in itself has entirely disappeared out of Simmel's method, and that he makes a clear distinction between history and science, is perhaps his most valuable contribution. A study of his works will make possible an understanding of the function and method of the social sciences which ought to do much for real progress in these fields.

With regard to Simmel's conception of sociology, there have been critics who have objected to his differentiation between form and content. As all scientific investigation rests in the last instance upon an abstraction, there seems little justification for a condemnation of his sociology on that ground. The particular difficulty about the sociological abstraction is a problem of technique, not of method, and there is no reason for assuming that it will not be solved in time. It is due to the unfamiliarity with the new differentiation, not to any inherent obstacles. The differentiation between the form and the content of the social life is in essence not more unnatural than the similar differentiation between the form and the content of the psychological process in the individual mind. The differentiation of the content of the social life in the fields of different social sciences has also become an established fact during the last century. It has taken time, but it came about gradually and naturally like the similar differentiation in the ancient world. The early Greeks would probably have thought a differentiation of the social life in the fields of ethics, jurisprudence, and political science an impossibility. Yet that differentiation had been practically accomplished by the time of the Roman lawyers, and it was only with that differentiation that real progress began to be made. We may therefore expect that in time the differentiation between the content and the form of society will come just as naturally as that between the form and the content of a psychological process or between the logical form and the content of an argument.

Simmel's conception of sociology and its subject-matter

is not new, although his definition is original. The general tendency during the last twenty years has been in the same direction. But he has realized better than anybody else the implications of the new orientation and the necessity for a complete methodology. His theory of association is a science of association, not a philosophy of society, as it is for some American sociologists who define their inquiries in the same terms. The significance of a study of the forms of socialization may not be immediately apparent. When it is realized that the investigation aims at an understanding of the processes of socialization, its importance becomes evident. Not only is a knowledge of those processes necessary for an understanding of all social contents, but it is the only knowledge which will lead to a fundamental understanding of the social life itself.

The advantage of his conception of sociology is not only that it leads to investigation of processes which shape all kinds of content, but also that it includes in one study the investigation of instinctive and voluntary groupings, of communities and associations, of contract and coercion, in a word, of all forms of interaction. It would seem, then, that his conception of the science suggests a practically unlimited possibility of work. He has none the less been criticized for limiting the investigation to the study of the social forms. But this limitation is the result of the fact that he conceives of sociology as a science, and therefore as a limited science. Sociology has been taken down from the elevated position where it was enthroned as the synthesis of all sciences. But it has apparently not quite lost its former grandeur for a great many of its admirers who still like to think of it as at least a synthesis of the social sciences. It can maintain that position just as long as it is content to be a social philosophy. To become a science, it has to renounce all pretense of being the apotheosis of the social sciences and take its place among them. In the new order of things its position is far less assuming. A large part of its new function will be the modest task of searching for a knowledge of the social forms, so as to enable the social sciences to reach a full understanding of the social content. The myth of a science of society has been exploded. What remains is a series of social sciences, of which sociology is merely one, even if it finds its subject-matter through a different abstraction.

One may object to the term "sociology" or "formal sociology" which Simmel applies to the study of the forms of socialization, but that objection would involve only the necessity for searching for a new name. If one insists on applying the term "sociology" only to a synthesis of the social sciences or to the study of practical social problems involving a knowledge of all social sciences, there is no fundamental objection, provided one does not call it a science.

But apart from all questions of terminology, Simmel's contributions to social theory are of the utmost importance, not so much for the amount of new factual knowledge they contain as for the new orientation and clarification which they have brought to the intricate problems of the methodology of the social sciences. His ideas may be partially accepted or wholly rejected; they cannot be ignored.

It is for that reason that this study has been written, in the hope that it may serve as a starting-point for a renewed discussion of social methodology, and in the hope also that it may contribute in some way to the finding of the common method which the social sciences will have to adopt if they are ever to advance to a point where they can effectively help man in his liberation from the despotic leviathan.

BIBLIOGRAPHY

BIBLIOGRAPHY

I. BOOKS AND ARTICLES BY GEORG SIMMEL

1881 *Das Wesen der Materie nach Kants physischer Monadologie* (Thesis), Berlin. (1)

1882 "Psychologische und ethnologische Studien über Musik," *Zeitschrift für Völkerpsychologie*, XIII, 261–305. (2)

1887 "Über die Grundfrage des Pessimismus in methodischer Hinsicht," *Zeitschrift für Philosophie und Philosophische Kritik*, XC, 237–47. (3)

1888 "Einige Bemerkungen über Goethes Verhältniss zur Ethik," *ibid.*, XCII, 101–7. (4)

1888 "Bemerkungen zu sozial-ethischen Problemen," *Vierteljahresschrift für wissenschaftliche Philosophie*, XII, 1, 32–49. (5)

1889 "Psychologie des Geldes," *Jahrbücher für Gesetzgebung, Verwaltung und Volkswirtschaft*, XIII, 1251–64. (6)

1890 "Zur Psychologie der Frauen," *Zeitschrift für Völkerpsychologie und Sprachwissenschaft*, XX, 6–46. (7)

1890 "Über soziale Differenzierung," in *Staats- und Sozialwissenschaftliche Forschungen*, ed. Gustav Schmoller, Leipzig, X, 1–147. (8)
Inhalt

    K. 1. Zur Erkenntnisstheorie der Sozialwissenschaft

    K. 2. Über Kollectivverantwortlichkeit

    K. 3. Die Ausdehnung der Gruppe und die Ausbildung der Individualität (See No. 85)

    K. 4. Das soziale Niveau (See No. 128)

    K. 5. Über die Kreuzung sozialer Kreise (See No. 85)

    K. 6. Die Differenzierung und das Prinzip der Kraftersparnis

1892 *Die Probleme der Geschichtsphilosophie*, Leipzig. (9)
Inhalt

    K. 1. Von den inneren Bedingungen der Geschichtsforschung

    K. 2. Von den historischen Gesetzen (See No. 107)

    K. 3. Vom Sinn der Geschichte

278   THE SOCIAL THEORY OF GEORG SIMMEL

1892–93 *Einleitung in die Moralwissenschaft*, Berlin, 2 vol.   (10)
Inhalt
  B. I
    K. 1. Das Sollen
    K. 2. Egoismus und Altruismus
    K. 3. Sittlicher Verdienst und sittliche Schuld
    K. 4. Die Glückseligkeit
  B. II
    K. 5. Der kategorische Imperativ
    K. 6. Die Freiheit
    K. 7. Einheit und Widerstreit der Zwecke

1893 "Moral Deficiencies as Determining Intellectual Functions," *International Journal of Ethics*, III, 490–507.   (11)

1894 "Parerga zur Sozialphilosophie," *Jahrbücher für Gesetzgebung, Verwaltung und Volkswirtschaft*, XVIII, 257–65.   (12)

1894 "Das Problem der Soziologie," *ibid.*, pp. 1301–7. (See Nos. 14, 17, 85, 93, 128.)   (13)

1894 "Le problème de la sociologie," *Revue de Métaphysique et de Morale*, II, 497–504. (See Nos. 13, 17, 85, 93, 128.)   (14)

1894 "La différentiation sociale," *Revue Internationale de Sociologie*, II, 198–213. (Extract from No. 8, tr. M. Parazzoli.)   (15)

1894 "L'influence du nombre des unités sociales sur les caractères des sociétés," *Annales de l'Institut International de Sociologie*, I, 373–85. (See No. 51, 85.)   (16)

1895 "The Problem of Sociology," *Annals of the American Academy of Political and Social Science*, VI, 412–23. (See Nos. 13, 14, 85, 93, 128.)   (17)

1895 "Was ist uns Kant?" *Sonntagsbeilage der Vossischen Zeitung*, Nos. 31–33.   (18)

1895 "Über eine Beziehung der Selectionslehre zur Erkenntnisstheorie," *Archiv für Systematische Philosophie*, I, 34–45. (See Nos. 20, 25.)   (19)

1896 "Sur quelques relations de la pensée théorique avec les intérêts pratiques," *Revue de Métaphysique et de Morale*, IV, 160–78. (See Nos. 19, 25.)   (20)

1896 "Skizze einer Willenstheorie," *Zeitschrift für Psychologie*, IX, 206–20.   (21)

1896 "Friedrich Nietzsche: Eine moralphilosophische Silhouette," *Zeitschrift für Philosophie und Philosophische Kritik*, CVII, 202–5. (See No. 71.) (22)

1896–97 "Comment les formes sociales se maintiennent," *Année Sociologique*, I, 71–109. (See Nos. 26, 27, 85.) (23)

1896–97 "Superiority and Subordination as Subject-Matter for Sociology," *American Journal of Sociology*, II, 167–89, 392–415 (tr. Albion Small). (See Nos. 76, 85.) (24)

1897 "Über den Unterschied der Wahrnehmungs- und Erfahrungsurteile," in *Kantstudien*, I, 416–25. (See Nos. 19, 20.) (25)

1898 "Die Selbsterhaltung der sozialen Gruppe," *Jahrbücher für Gesetzgebung, Verwaltung und Volkswirtschaft*, XXII, 598–640. (See Nos. 23, 27, 85.) (26)

1897–99 "The Persistence of the Social Group," *American Journal of Sociology*, III, 662–98, 829–36; IV, 35–50 (tr. Albion Small). (See Nos. 23, 26, 85.) (27)

1898 "Georg Stefan: Eine kunstphilosophische Betrachtung," *Die Zukunft* (Berlin), pp. 386–96. (See No. 44.) (28)

1898 "Rom: Eine ästhetische Analyse," *Die Zeit* (Vienna), No. 191, pp. 137–39. (29)

1898 "Soziologie der Religion," *Neue Deutsche Rundschau* (Berlin), pp. 111–23. (See Nos. 42, 61, 63, 69, 90, 107.) (30)

1898 "Fragment aus einer Philosophie des Geldes: Das Geld und die individuelle Freiheit," *Zeitschrift für Immanente Philosophie*, pp. 395–428. (See No. 37.) (31)

1898 "Die Rolle des Geldes in den Beziehungen der Geschlechter," *Die Zeit* (Vienna), No. 172, pp. 38–40; No. 173, pp. 53–54; No. 174, pp. 69–71. (32)

1898–99 "A Chapter in the Philosophy of Value," *American Journal of Sociology*, V, 577–603 (tr. Albion Small). (See Nos. 37, 107.) (33)

1899 "Fragment aus einer Philosophie des Geldes: Substanzwert," *Jahrbücher für Gesetzgebung, Verwaltung und Volkswirtschaft*, XXIII, 813–54. (See No. 37.) (34)

1899 "Kant und Goethe," *Beilage zur Allgemeine Zeitung* (Munich), Nos. 125–27. (See Nos. 58, 112.) (35)

1899 "Philosophie der Arbeit," *Neue Deutsche Rundschau* (Berlin), pp. 449–63. (36)

1900 *Philosophie des Geldes*, Leipzig.   (37)
    Inhalt
        Analytischer Teil
            K. 1. Wert und Geld (See No. 33)
            K. 2. Der Substanzwert des Geldes (See No. 34)
            K. 3. Das Geld in den Zweckreihen
        Synthetischer Teil
            K. 4. Die individuelle Freiheit (See No. 31)
            K. 5. Das Geldequivalent personaler Werte
            K. 6. Der Stil des Lebens

1900 "Einige Bemerkungen zu Schmollers Grundriss der allgemeinen
    Volkswirtschaftslehre," *Beilage zur Allgemeine Zeitung* (Munich),
    No. 222, pp. 1–3.   (38)

1900 "Zu einer Theorie des Pessimismus," *Die Zeit* (Vienna), No. 277,
    pp. 38–40.   (39)

1900 "Sozialismus und Pessimismus," *ibid.*, No. 279, pp. 70–71.   (40)

1901 "Die beiden Formen des Individualismus," *Das Freie Wort* (Frank-
    fort), pp. 397–403.   (41)

1901 "Beiträge zur Erkenntnisstheorie der Religion," *Zeitschrift für
    Philosophie und Philosophische Kritik*, CXIX, 11–22. (See Nos.
    30, 61, 63, 69, 90, 107.)   (42)

1901 "Zur Psychologie der Scham," *Die Zeit* (Vienna), No. 371, p.
    84.   (43)

1901 "Georg Stefan," *Neue Deutsche Rundschau* (Berlin), pp. 207–15.
    (See No. 23.)   (44)

1901 "Die ästhetische Bedeutung des Gesichts," *Der Lotse* (Hamburg),
    I, No. 35, 280–84.   (45)

1902 "Tendencies in German Life and Thought since 1870," *Inter-
    national Quarterly* (New York), V, 93–111, 166–84 (tr. W. D.
    Briggs).   (46)

1902 "Zum Verständniss Nietzsches," *Das Freie Wort* (Frankfort), II,
    6–11. (See No. 75.)   (47)

1902 "Vom Pantheismus," *ibid.*, pp. 306–12.   (48)

1902 "Weibliche Kultur," *Neue Deutsche Rundschau* (Berlin), pp. 504–
    16. (See Nos. 101, 104.)   (49)

1902 "Vom Heil der Seele," *Das Freie Wort* (Frankfort), II, 533–38.
                                                                         (50)

1902–3 "The Number of Members as Determining the Sociological Form of the Group," *American Journal of Sociology*, VIII, 1–46, 158–96 (tr. Albion Small). (See Nos. 16, 85.) (51)

1903 "Soziologie des Raumes," *Jahrbücher für Gesetzgebung, Verwaltung und Volkswirtschaft*, XXVII, 27–71. (See No. 53.) (52)

1903 "Über räumliche Projectionen sozialer Formen," *Zeitschrift für Sozialwissenschaft*, VI, 287–302. (See Nos. 52, 85.) (53)

1903 "Soziologie der Konkurrenz," *Neue Deutsche Rundschau* (Berlin), pp. 1009–23. (See No. 85.) (54)

1903 "Die Lehre Kants vom Pflicht und Glück," *Das Freie Wort* (Frankfort), III, 548–53. (See No. 58.) (55)

1903 "Grosstädte und Geistesleben," in *Die Grosstadt: Vorträge und Aufsätze*, ed. v. Zahn und Jaensch, Dresden, pp. 185–206. (56)

1903 "Die ästhetischen Quantitäten," *Der Zeitgeist: Beilage zum Berliner Tageblatt*, No. 13, March 30, pp. 1–2. (57)

1903 *Kant: Sechzehn Vorlesungen gehalten an der Berliner Universität*, Leipzig. (58)

1903–4 "The Sociology of Conflict," *American Journal of Psychology*, IX, 490–525, 672–89, 798–811. (See No. 85.) (59)

1904 *Einleitung in die Moralwissenschaft*, Stuttgart (2d ed.). (See No. 10.)

1904 "Fashion," *International Quarterly* (New York), X, 130–55. (See Nos. 66, 104.) (60)

1904 "Die Gegensätze des Lebens und der Religion," *Das Freie Wort* (Frankfort), IV, 305–12. (See Nos. 30, 42, 63, 69, 90, 107.) (61)

1904 "Über Geschichte der Philosophie," *Die Zeit* (Vienna), No. 504, p. 99. (62)

1905 *Über soziale Differenzierung*, Leipzig (2d ed.). (See No. 8.)

1905 *Die Probleme der Geschichtsphilosophie*, Leipzig (2d ed., completely revised). (See No. 9.)

1905 "A Contribution to the Sociology of Religion," *American Journal of Sociology*, XI, 359–76 (tr. Albion Small). (See Nos. 30, 42, 61, 90, 107.) (63)

1905 "Ende des Streits," *Neue Rundschau* (Berlin), XVI, 746–53. (See No. 85.) (64)

1905 *Kant: Sechzehn Vorlesungen gehalten an der Berliner Universität*, Leipzig (2d ed.). (See No. 58.)

1905 "Ästhetik des Porträts," *Neue Freie Presse* (Vienna), April 22, p. 22.   (65)

1905 "Philosophie der Mode," in *Moderne Zeitfragen*, No. 11, Berlin Pan-Verlag. (See Nos. 60, 104.)   (66)

1906 "Kant und Goethe," *Die Zukunft* (Berlin), LVII, 315–19. (See Nos. 68, 112.)   (67)

1906 *Kant und Goethe*, in *Die Kultur*, No. 10, Berlin.   (68)

1906 *Die Religion*, in *Die Gesellschaft*, No. 2: *Sammlung sozialpsychologischer Monographien*, Frankfort.   (69)

1906 "Über die dritte Dimension in der Kunst," *Zeitschrift für Ästhetik und Allgemeine Kunstwissenschaft*, I, 65–69.   (70)

1906 "Soziologie der Armut," *Archiv für Sozialwissenschaft und Sozialpolitik*, XXII, 1–30. (See No. 85.)   (71)

1906 "The Sociology of Secrecy and of the Secret Society," *American Journal of Sociology*, XI, 441–98 (tr. Albion Small). (See No. 85.)   (72)

1907 *Die Probleme der Geschichtsphilosophie*, Leipzig (3d ed.). (See No. 9.)

1907 *Philosophie des Geldes*, Leipzig (2d ed.). (See No. 37.)

1907 "Soziologie der Sinne," *Neue Rundschau* (Berlin), XVIII, 1025–36. (See No. 85.)   (73)

1907 *Kant und Goethe*, Leipzig (2d ed.). (See No. 68.)

1907 "Philosophie der Herrschaft," *Jahrbücher für Gesetzgebung, Verwaltung und Volkswirtschaft*, XXXI, 439–71.   (74)

1907 *Schopenhauer und Nietzsche: Ein Vortragszyklus*, Leipzig.   (75)
Inhalt

 K. 1. Schopenhauer und Nietzsche in ihrer geistesgeschichtlichen Stellung

 K. 2. Schopenhauer. Der Mensch und sein Wille

 K. 3. Schopenhauer. Die Metaphysik des Willens

 K. 4. Schopenhauer. Der Pessimismus

 K. 5. Die Metaphysik der Kunst

 K. 6. Schopenhauer. Die Moral und die Selbsterlösung des Willens

 K. 7. Nietzsche. Die Menschheitswerte und die Dekadenz

 K. 8. Nietzsche. Die Moral der Vornehmheit

1907 "Soziologie der Über- und Unterordnung," *Archiv für Sozialwissenschaft und Sozialpolitik*, XXII, 477–546. (See Nos. 24, 85.) (76)

1907 "Venedig," *Der Kunstwart* (Munich), XX, pp. 299–303. (See No. 107.) (77)

1907 "Christentum und Kunst," *Morgen* (Berlin), No. 8, pp. 235–43. (78)

1907 "Dankbarkeit," *ibid.*, No. 19, pp. 593–99. (See No. 85.) (79)

1907 "Bemerkungen über Goethe," *ibid.*, No. 13, pp. 393–95. (80)

1908 "Der Mensch als Feind," *ibid.*, No. 2, pp. 55–60. (81)

1908 "Über das Wesen der Sozialpsychologie," *Archiv für Sozialwissenschaft und Sozialpolitik*, XXVI, 285–91. (See No. 85.) (82)

1908 "Psychologie des Schmucks," *Morgen* (Berlin), II, No. 15, 454–59. (See No. 85.) (83)

1908 "Der Brief," *Die Rundschau* (Vienna), XV, 334. (See No. 85.) (84)

1908 *Soziologie: Untersuchungen über die Formen der Vergesellschaftung*, Leipzig. (85)
Inhalt
K. 1. Das Problem der Soziologie (See Nos. 13, 14, 17, 93, 128)
Exkurs über das Problem: Wie ist Gesellschaft möglich? (See No. 94)
K. 2. Quantitative Bestimmtheit der Gruppe (See Nos. 16, 51)
K. 3. Über- und Unterordnung. (See Nos. 24, 76)
Exkurs über die Überstimmung
K. 4. Der Streit (See Nos. 54, 59, 64)
K. 5. Das Geheimnis und die geheime Gesellschaft (See No. 72)
Exkurs über den Schmuck (See No. 83)
Exkurs über den schriftlichen Verkehr (See No. 84)
K. 6. Die Kreuzung sozialer Kreise (See Nos. 8, 15)
K. 7. Der Arme (See No. 71)
Exkurs über die Negativität kollectiver Verhaltungsweise
K. 8. Die Selbsterhaltung der Gruppe (See Nos. 23, 26, 27)
Exkurs über das Erbamt
Exkurs über Sozialpsychologie (See No. 82)
Exkurs über Treue und Dankbarkeit (See No. 79)

K. 9. Der Raum und die räumlichen Ordnungen der Gesell-
schaft (See Nos. 52, 53)
Exkurs über die soziale Begrenzung
Exkurs über die Soziologie der Sinne (See Nos. 73, 107)
Exkurs über den Fremden

K. 10. Die Erweiterung der Gruppe und die Ausbildung der
Individualität (See No. 8)
Exkurs über den Adel
Exkurs über die Analogie der individual-psychologischen
und soziologischen Verhältnisse

1908 "Vom Wesen der Kultur,"*Die Rundschau* (Vienna), XV, 36–42. (86)

1908 "Realismus in der Kunst," *Morgen* (Berlin), II, No. 31, 992–98.
(See No. 107.)   (87)

1908 "Zur Philosophie des Schauspielers," *ibid.*, Nos. 51–52, 1685–89.
(88)

1908 "Das Problem des Stils," *Decorative Kunst* (Munich), I, 307–16.
(89)

1909 "Religion," *Nord und Süd* (Berlin), CXXVIII, 366–69. (See Nos.
30, 42, 61, 63, 69, 90, 107.)   (90)

1909 "Kant und Goethe," *Altpreussische Monatsschrift*, No. 118. (91)

1909 "Die Kunst Rodins und das Bewegungsmotiv in der Plastik,"
Nord und Süd (Berlin), CXXIX, 189–96. (See Nos. 104, 107.) (92)

1909 "The Problem of Sociology," *American Journal of Sociology*, XV,
289–320 (tr. Albion Small). (See Nos. 13, 14, 17, 85.)   (93)

1910 "How Is Society Possible?" *ibid.*, XVI, 372–91 (tr. Albion Small).
(See No. 85.)   (94)

1910 "Soziologie der Gesellschaft," *Berliner Tageblatt*, October 10. (See
Nos. 100, 128.)   (95)

1910 "Zur Metaphysik des Todes," *Logos*, I, 57–70. (See Nos. 107,
130.)   (96)

1910 "Michelangelo: Ein Kapitel zur Metaphysik der Kultur," *ibid.*,
pp. 207–27. (See No. 104.)   (97)

1910 *Hauptprobleme der Philosophie*, in Göschen, No. 500, Leipzig. (98)
Inhalt
Einleitung
K. 1. Vom Wesen der Philosophie (See No. 107)
K. 2. Vom Sein und vom Werden
K. 3. Vom Subjekt und Objekt
K. 4. Von den idealen Forderungen

1911 *Einleitung in die Moralwissenschaft*, Stuttgart (3d ed.). (See No. 10.)

1911 "Das Problem der religiösen Lage," in *Weltanschauung: Philosophie und Religion in Darstellungen*, ed. Max Frischeisen-Köhler, Berlin, XXII, 527–40. (See No. 104.)   (99)

1911 *Hauptprobleme der Philosophie*, Leipzig (2d ed.). (See No. 98.)

1911 "Soziologie der Geselligkeit," in *Schriften der Deutschen Gesellschaft für Soziologie: Verhandlungen des Ersten Deutschen Soziologen Tages*, Tübingen, XII, 1–16. (See Nos. 95, 128.)   (100)

1911 "Weibliche Kultur," *Archiv für Sozialwissenschaft und Sozialpolitik*, XXXIII, 1–36. (See Nos. 49, 104.)   (101)

1911 "Der Begriff und die Tragedie der Kultur," *Logos*, II, 1–25. (See No. 104.)   (102)

1911 "Relatives und Absolutes im Geschlechterproblem," *Frauen-Zukunft* (Munich), pp. 157–72, 253–65. (See No. 104.)   (103)

1911 *Philosophische Kultur: Gesammelte Essais*, in Philosophische-Soziologische Bücherei, Leipzig, Vol. XXVII.   (104)
Inhalt
Einleitung
Zur philosophischen Psychologie
Das Abenteuer (See No. 107)
Die Mode (See Nos. 60, 66)
Zur Philosophie der Geschlechter
Das Relative und Absolute im Geschlechter-Problem (See No. 103)
Die Koketterie
Zur Ästhetik
Der Henkel
Die Ruine (See No. 107)
Die Alpen
Über künstlerische Persönlichkeiten
Michelangelo (See No. 97)
Rodin (See No. 92)
Zur Religionsphilosophie
Die Persönlichkeit Gottes
Das Problem der religiösen Lage (See No. 99)
Zur Philosophie der Kultur
Der Begriff und die Tragedie der Kultur (See No. 102)
Weibliche Kultur (See Nos. 49, 101)

1912 *Die Religion*, Frankfort (2d ed., revised). (See No. 69.)

1912 "Die Wahrheit und das Individuum: Aus einem Goethebuch," *Logos*, III, 15–28. (See No. 112.)   (105)

1912 "Goethes Individualismus," *ibid.*, pp. 251–74. (See No. 112.) (106)

1912 *Mélanges de philosophie relativiste: Contributions à la culture philo-sophique*, tr. A. Guillaume, Paris.   (107)

    Table des matières

      Préface

      Le but de la vie dans les philosophies de Schopenhauer et de Nietzsche (See No. 75)

      Essai sur la sociologie des sens (See Nos. 73, 85)

      Sur la notion de valeur et les relations entre le sujet et l'objet (See Nos. 33, 37)

      Le Christianisme et l'art (See No. 78)

      Du réalisme en art (See No. 87)

      Étude sur Venise (See No. 77)

      Réflexions suggérées par l'aspect des ruines (See No. 104)

      L'œuvre de Rodin comme expression de l'esprit moderne (See No. 104)

      La philosophie de l'aventure (See No. 104)

      La religion et les contrastes de la vie (See Nos. 42, 61, etc.)

      Métaphysique de la mort (See No. 96)

      De la responsabilité juridique et de la liberté

      Essai sur le matérialisme historique (See No. 9)

      Les formes de l'individualisme et la philosophie de Kant (See No. 106)

      De l'essence de la philosophie (See No. 98)

1913 *Kant: Sechzehn Vorlesungen gehalten an der Berliner Universität*, Leipzig (3d ed.). (See No. 58.)

1913 "An Professor Lamprecht," *Die Zukunft* (Berlin), LXXXIII, No. 33, 230–34.   (108)

1913 *Hauptprobleme der Philosophie*, Leipzig (3d ed.). (See No. 98.)

1913 "Das Problem des Schicksals," *Geisteswissenschaften*, I, 112–15. (109)

1913 "Die Philosophie der Landschaft," *Die Guldenkammer*, III, No. 11, 635–44.   (110)

1913 "Das individuelle Gesetz: Ein Versuch über das Prinzip der Ethik," *Logos*, IV, 117–60. (See No. 130.)   (111)

1913 *Goethe*, Leipzig. (112)
Inhalt
    K. 1. Leben und Schaffen
    K. 2. Wahrheit
    K. 3. Einheit der Weltelemente
    K. 4. Getrenntheit der Weltelemente
    K. 5. Individualismus
    K. 6. Rechenschaft und Überwindung
    K. 7. Liebe
    K. 8. Entwicklung

1914 "Bergson und der deutsche Zynismus," *Internationale Monatsschrift für Wissenschaft* (Berlin), IX, 197. (113)

1914 "Der Fall Jastrows," *Die Zukunft* (Berlin), LXXXIX, 33–36. (114)

1914 *Deutschlands innere Wandlung: Rede gehalten in Strassburg,* Strassburg. (See No. 127.) (115)

1914 "Rembrandtstudie," *Logos,* V, 1–32. (See Nos. 117, 121.) (116)

1914 "Studien zur Philosophie der Kunst, besonders der Rembrandtschen," *ibid.,* pp. 221–38. (See Nos. 116, 121.) (117)

1915 "Europa," *Berliner Tageblatt,* March 7. (See No. 127.) (118)

1915 "Vom Tode in der Kunst," *Frankfurter Zeitung,* No. 92, April 2. (119)

1915 "Europa und Amerika," *Berliner Tageblatt,* July 4. (120)

1916 *Kant und Goethe,* Leipzig (3d ed., revised). (See No. 68.)

1916 *Rembrandt: Ein kunstphilosophischer Versuch,* Leipzig. (121)
Inhalt
    Vorwort
    K. 1. Der Ausdruck des Seelischen
    K. 2. Die Individualisierung und das Allgemeine
    K. 3. Religiöse Kunst
    Zum Abschluss

1916 "Die Dialektik des deutschen Geistes," *Der Tag,* September 28. (See No. 127.) (122)

1916 "Fragmentcharakter des Lebens," *Logos,* VI, 29–40. (123)

1916 "Vorformen der Idee: Aus den Studien zu einer Metaphysik," *ibid.,* p. 103. (See No. 130.) (124)

1916 "Das Problem der historischen Zeit," in *Philosophische Vorträge,* No. 12, veröffentlicht von der Kantgesellschaft, Berlin. (125)

1917 *Hauptprobleme der Philosophie*, Leipzig (4th ed.). (See No. 98.)

1917 "Über die Karikatur," *Der Tag*, February 27.   (126)

1917 *Der Krieg und die geistigen Entscheidungen*, Leipzig.   (127)
Inhalt

   K. 1. Deutschlands innere Wandlung (See No. 115)
   K. 2. Die Dialektik des deutschen Geistes (See No. 122)
   K. 3. Die Krisis der Kultur
   K. 4. Die Idee Europa (See No. 118)

1917 *Grundfragen der Soziologie*, in Göschen, No. 101, Leipzig.   (128)
Inhalt

   K. 1. Das Gebiet der Soziologie (See No. 85, etc.)
   K. 2. Das soziale und das individuelle Niveau (Beispiel der allgemeinen Soziologie) (See No. 8)
   K. 3. Die Geselligkeit (Beispiel der reinen oder formalen Soziologie) (See Nos. 95, 100)
   K. 4. Individuum und Gesellschaft in Lebensanschauungen des 18. und 19. Jahrhunderts (Beispiel der philosophischen Soziologie)

1918 *Kant: Sechzehn Vorlesungen gehalten an der Berliner Universität*, Leipzig (4th ed.). (See No. 58.)

1918 "Vom Wesen des historischen Verstehens," in *Geschichtliche Abende im Zentralinstitut für Erziehung und Unterricht*, No. 5, Berlin.   (129)

1918 *Lebensanschauung: Vier metaphysische Kapitel*, Leipzig.   (130)
Inhalt

   K. 1. Die Transcendenz des Lebens
   K. 2. Die Wendung zur Idee (See No. 124)
   K. 3. Tod und Unsterblichkeit (See No. 96)
   K. 4. Das individuelle Gesetz (See No. 111)

1918 "Die historische Formung," *Logos*, VII, 113–52.   (131)

1918 "Gesetzmässigkeit im Kunstwerk," *ibid.*, pp. 213–23.   (132)

1918 *Der Konflict der modernen Kultur*, Leipzig.   (133)

1919 *Kant und Goethe*, Leipzig (4th ed.). (See No. 68.)

1919 "Aus Georg Simmels nachgelassenem Tagebuch," *Logos*, VIII, 121–51.   (134)

1919 *Rembrandt: Ein kunstphilosophischer Versuch*, Leipzig (2d ed.). (See No. 121.)

1919 *Philosophische Kultur: Gesammelte Essais*, Leipzig (2d ed., enlarged). (See No. 104.)

1920 "Zur Philosophie des Schauspielers," *Logos*, IX, 339–62. (135)

1920 *Philosophie des Geldes*, Leipzig (3d ed.). (See No. 37.)

1920 *Schopenhauer und Nietzsche: Ein Vortragszyklus*, Leipzig (2d ed.). (See No. 75.)

1920 *Der Krieg und die geistigen Entscheidungen*, Leipzig (2d ed.). (See No. 127.)

1920 *Hauptprobleme der Philosophie*, Leipzig (5th ed.). (See No. 98.)

1921 *Goethe*, Leipzig (4th ed.). (See No. 112.)

1922 *Zur Philosophie der Kunst: Philosophische und kunstphilosophische Aufsätze* (ed. Gertrud Simmel), Potsdam. (136)

1922 *Schulpädagogik* (ed. Hauter), Osterwieck Harz. (137)

II. BOOKS AND ARTICLES ON GEORG SIMMEL

BOUGLÉ, C., "Les sciences sociales en Allemagne," *Revue de Métaphysique et de Morale*, II (1894), 329–55.

BERNHARD, E., "Simmel als Soziologe und Sozialphilosoph," *Die Tat*, V (1913–14), No. 10, 1080–86.

LUDWIG, E., "Simmel auf dem Katheder," *Schaubühne*, X (1914), No. 15.

MAMELET, ALBERT, *Le relativisme philosophique chez Georg Simmel*, Paris, 1914.

FISCHER, A., "Simmel," *Der Kunstwart*, XXXI (1918), 43–47.

HOEBER, FRITZ, "Simmel," *Neue Jahrbücher für das klassische Altertum*, 1918, pp. 475–77.

FRISCHEISEN-KÖHLER, MAX, "Simmel," in *Kantstudien*, Vol. XXIV (1919).

HOEBER, FRITZ, "Der deutsche Kulturphilosoph unserer Zeit," *Die Hochschule* (Berlin), III (1919), 25–27.

HURWICZ, E., "Simmel als jüdischer Denker," *Neue Jüdische Monatshefte*, 1919.

JOEL, H., "Simmel," *Neue Rundschau* (Berlin), 1919, pp. 241–47.

SCHMALENBACH, H., "Simmel," *Sozialistische Monatshefte*, 1919, pp. 283–88.

KRACAUER, SIEGFRIED, "Georg Simmel," *Logos*, IX (1920), 307–38.

III. HISTORY OF SOCIAL THEORY

BARNES, HARRY E., "Sociology before Comte," *American Journal of Sociology*, XXIII, 174.

BARTH, PAUL, *Die Philosophie der Geschichte als Soziologie*, Leipzig, 1922 (3d and 4th ed.).

BOGARDUS, E. S., *A History of Social Thought*, Los Angeles, 1922.

BOUGLÉ, C., *Les sciences sociales en Allemagne: Les méthodes actuelles*, Paris, 1896, p. 172.

BRANFORD, VICTOR, "The Founders of Sociology," *American Journal of Sociology*, X, 94–120.

BRISTOL, L. M., *Social Adaptation*, Cambridge, 1915.

COKER, F. W., *Organismic Theories of the State*, New York, 1910.

DAVIS, M. M., *Psychological Interpretations of Society*, New York, 1909.

DUNNING, W. A., *A History of Political Theories*, Vol. III: *From Rousseau to Spencer*, New York, 1920.

FANELLES, A., *Les études récentes de sociologie*, Paris, 1897.

FIAMINGO, GIUSEPPE, "Sociology in Italy," *American Journal of Sociology*, I, 41.

GIDDINGS, F. H., "Modern Sociology," *International Monthly*, November, 1900.

GIDE, CHARLES, and RIST, CHARLES, *A History of Economic Doctrines*, New York, 1913 (English tr. of 2d ed. [1913] by R. Richards).

HECKER, JULIUS, *Russian Sociology*, New York, 1915.

JACOBS, P. P., *German Sociology*, New York, 1909.

LICHTENBERGER, JAMES P., *Development of Social Theory*, New York and London, 1923.

MACKINTOSH, ROBERT, *From Comte to Benjamin Kidd*, New York and London, 1899.

MERZ, J. T., *History of European Thought in the Nineteenth Century*, Edinburgh and London, 1896–1914.

MEYER, B. H., "Four synthesists: Cross-Sections from Comte, Spencer, Lilienfeld and Schaeffle," *American Journal of Sociology*, VI, 20.

MING, J. J., "Modern Theories of Society," *American Catholic Quarterly*, January, 1896.

SMALL, ALBION W., "Fifty Years of Sociology in the United States," *American Journal of Sociology*, XXI, 744.

————, *General Sociology*, Chicago, 1905.

SOMBART, WERNER, *Soziologie*, Berlin, 1923.

SQUILLACE, FAUSTO, *Die soziologischen Theorien*, Leipzig, 1911 (tr. from the Italian by Dr. Rudolf Eisler).

STEIN, DR. LUDWIG, *Die soziale Frage im Lichte der Philosophie*, Stuttgart, 1923 (3d and 4th ed.).

TENNEY, ALVAN A., "Some Recent Advances in Sociology," *Political Science Quarterly*, XXV, 500–522.

THON, O., "The Present Status of Sociology in Germany," *American Journal of Sociology*, II, 567–88, 718–36, 792–800.

TOWNE, EZRA T., *Die Auffassung der Gesellschaft als Organismus, ihre Entwickelung und ihre Modifikationen*, Halle, 1903.

TUFTS, JAMES H., "Recent Sociological Tendencies in France," *American Journal of Sociology*, XVIII, 446–56.

VINCENT, GEORGE E., "Development of Sociology," *ibid.*, X, 145.

————, "Varieties of Sociology," *ibid.*, XII, 1.

WARD, LESTER F., "Contemporary Sociology," *ibid.*, VII, 476, 749.

IV. MISCELLANEOUS

COMTE, AUGUSTE, *Cours de philosophie positive*, Paris, 1830-42 (1st ed.).

SPENCER, HERBERT, *Social Statics*, London, 1850 (1st ed.).

————, *The Study of Sociology*, London, 1873.

LILIENFELD, PAUL VON, *Gedanken über die Sozialwissenschaft der Zukunft*, Mittau, 1873–81 (5 vols.).

SPENCER, HERBERT, *The Principles of Sociology*, London, 1876–96.

GUMPLOWICZ, LUDWIG, *Rechtstaat und Sozialismus*, Insbruck, 1881.

ROBERTY, EUGÈNE DE, *La sociologie*, Paris, 1881.

SCHÄFFLE, ALBERT, *Bau und Leben des sozialen Körpers*, Tübingen, 1881.

GUMPLOWICZ, LUDWIG, *Der Rassenkampf*, Insbruck, 1883.

FOUILLÉE, ALFRED, *La science sociale contemporaine*, Paris, 1885.

GUMPLOWICZ, LUDWIG, *Grundriss der Soziologie*, Insbruck, 1885.

GREEF, GUILLAUME DE, *Introduction à la sociologie*, Paris, 1886–89.

Tonnies, F., *Gemeinschaft und Gesellschaft*, Leipzig, 1887.

Giddings, F. H., *The Province of Sociology*, New York, 1890.

Tarde, Gabriel, *Les lois de l'imitation*, Paris, 1890.

Durkheim, E., *De la division du travail social, étude sur l'organisation des sociétés supérieures*, Paris, 1893.

Ratzenhofer, Gustav, *Wesen und Zweck der Politik, als Theil der Soziologie und Grundlage der Staatswissenschaften*, Leipzig, 1893.

Giddings, F. H., *The Theory of Sociology*, New York, 1894.

Small, Albion, and Vincent, George E., *The Study of Sociology*, New York, 1894.

Tarde, Gabriel, *La logique sociale*, Paris, 1895.

Giddings, F. H., *Principles of Sociology*, New York, 1896.

Tarde, Gabriel, *L'opposition universelle*, Paris, 1897.

Ratzenhofer, Gustav, *Die soziologische Erkenntniss: Positive Philosophie des sozialen Lebens*, Leipzig, 1898.

Stuckenberg, J. H. W., *Introduction to the Study of Society*, London, 1898.

Tarde, Gabriel, *Les lois sociales*, Paris, 1898.

INDEXES

INDEX OF SUBJECTS

INDEX OF NAMES

PRINTED IN THE U.S.A.